THE ULTIMATE STEP-BY-STEP
kid's first gardening book

THE ULTIMATE STEP-BY-STEP
kid's first gardening book

More than 120 fabulous projects for kids to do, complete with clear stage-by-stage instructions and over 1200 stunning photographs

Fantastic gardening ideas for 5–12 year olds, from growing fruit and vegetables and fun with flowers to wildlife gardening and craft projects

Jenny Hendy

LORENZ BOOKS

To Mum and Dad for that first pansy seed packet.

This edition is published by Lorenz Books,
an imprint of Anness Publishing Ltd, Hermes House,
88–89 Blackfriars Road, London SE1 8HA
tel. 020 7401 2077; fax 020 7633 9499
www.lorenzbooks.com; www.annesspublishing.com

If you like the images in this book and would like
to investigate using them for publishing, promotions
or advertising, please visit our website
www.practicalpictures.com for more information.

UK agent: The Manning Partnership Ltd;
tel. 01225 478444; fax 01225 478440;
sales@manning-partnership.co.uk

UK distributor: Book Trade Services; tel. 0116 2759086;
fax 0116 2759090; uksales@booktradeservices.com;
exportsales@booktradeservices.com

North American agent/distributor: National Book Network;
tel. 301 459 3366; fax 301 429 5746; www.nbnbooks.com

Australian agent/distributor: Pan Macmillan Australia;
tel. 1300 135 113;fax 1300 135 103;
customer.service@macmillan.com.au

New Zealand agent/distributor: David Bateman Ltd;
tel. (09) 415 7664; fax (09) 415 8892

Publisher: Joanna Lorenz
Senior Editor: Lucy Doncaster
Designer: Lisa Tai
Photographer: Howard Rice
Models: Ashley, Holly, Lucy I., Jenny, Imogen, Lucy P., Michael,
Alyson, Jessica, Christian, Viv, Siani, Anna, Juliet, Lucy D., Eleanor,
Grace, Lorna, Matthew, Kirsty, Matthew, Rhys, Aidan
Production Controller: Wendy Lawson

© Anness Publishing Ltd 2010

Ethical trading policy

At Anness Publishing we believe that business should be
conducted in an ethical and ecologically sustainable way,
with respect for the environment and a proper regard to the
replacement of the natural resources we employ.

As a publisher, we use a lot of wood pulp to make high-quality
paper for printing, and that wood commonly comes from spruce
trees. We are therefore currently growing more than 750,000 trees
in three Scottish forest plantations: Berrymoss (130 hectares/
320 acres), West Touxhill (125 hectares/305 acres) and Deveron
Forest (75 hectares/185 acres). The forests we manage contain
more than 3.5 times the number of trees employed each year in
making paper for the books we manufacture.

Because of this ongoing ecological investment programme,
you, as our customer, can have the pleasure and reassurance of
knowing that a tree is being cultivated on your behalf to naturally
replace the materials used to make the book you are holding.

Our forestry programme is run in accordance with the UK
Woodland Assurance Scheme (UKWAS) and will be certified by
the internationally recognized Forest Stewardship Council (FSC).
The FSC is a non-government organization dedicated to
promoting responsible management of the world's forests.

Certification ensures forests are managed in an
environmentally sustainable and socially responsible way.
For further information about this scheme, go to
www.annesspublishing.com/trees

Publisher's note

Although the advice and information in this book are believed
to be accurate and true at the time of going to press, neither the
authors nor the publisher can accept any legal responsibility or
liability for any errors or omissions that may be made nor for any
inaccuracies nor for any harm or injury that comes about from
following instructions or advice in this book. All children need
to work with adult guidance and supervision and it is the parent's
or carer's responsibility to ensure the child is working safely.

Contents

Having fun in the garden

Even without trees to climb there are more possibilities for adventure in a garden than indoors and, with a little guidance, some basic equipment and a few plants, kids can transform even the smallest outdoor space into a blooming oasis they can be proud of.

▶ *It's really satisfying picking bright flowers that you have grown in the garden.*

The great outdoors

Green spaces represent freedom – the chance to let off steam, to play more physical and rambunctious games and to simply become carefree. Games created in open air tend to be different to those played indoors, partly because the fluctuating environment stimulates imaginations. The seasons, weather and daily pattern of light and dark affect plants and creatures in many tangible ways and help us to mark the passage of time naturally.

It is a sad fact, however, that kids can be more or less oblivious to such things without direction from adults. Many are reluctant to leave the comfort of the sofa, or to break away from their favourite TV programme or computer game to venture outdoors, especially in cold or damp weather. Entice them out with one of the many projects in this book and be prepared to join in and offer plenty of help and encouragement! Consider giving children their own plot or pots too. Not only does this feel like a special treat, it also helps to teach responsibility. With very young ones, however, you'll need to act as backup, doing extra watering and pest control so that the results of their efforts don't disappoint.

▲ *You can help with all kinds of gardening jobs and maybe even have a patch of your own to tend.*

▲ *Flowers attract a host of insects for nature study.*

▲ *Make your garden a home for nesting birds.*

Designing a children's garden

Having access to a garden can be something of a luxury in urban areas, although a tiny flower- or vegetable-filled balcony can fulfil our basic need to grow food and nurture nature, even in the middle of a city. There are many kinds of garden, large and small, formal and informal, wild or manicured, and some styles and layouts are undoubtedly better suited to the needs of children. Don't worry if your garden is not specifically designed for little ones, however, because any open space where plants are grown has the potential to encourage an interest in gardening and the wild world.

Why should children garden?

Modern living keeps us all indoors for longer than is healthy in terms of body, mind and spirit. Being able to see the sky and experience daylight directly, to breathe in fresh air and to smell flower perfumes or the damp earth after rain, and to become aware of the natural world, all help us to reconnect with nature on a primal level. Modern technology has done nothing to help foster the connection and mobile phones, personal hi-fis and computer game units should be banned from the garden!

Research has shown that children who are able to play in and explore gardens and green spaces in an unstructured way are better able to remain grounded and in tune with nature as adults. Not surprisingly, this ability helps us to cope better with stress. And children who have positive experiences of gardening and outdoor play and who are encouraged to observe nature often return to these pastimes as adults even after a break of several years.

◀ *Plants are fascinating and very beautiful to look at. To get a really close-up view and see all the details, and perhaps even spot tiny insects, you just need a small magnifying glass and a little patience!*

▼ *There's a whole other world to discover outdoors in your garden and further afield. Why not keep a record of the plants and animals you find so you can see how the seasons affect them.*

ADAPTING A GARDEN FOR CHILDREN

There are plenty of steps you can take to make a garden more child-friendly and stimulating. Try the following where space allows:

✔ Create lots of hidden or secret corners using evergreen shrubs, rigid screens or brushwood or bamboo roll attached to posts or canes.

✔ Consider making a raised platform or build a boardwalk or walkway to wind through plantings.

✔ Introduce a see-through division using trellis or robust plants, such as bamboo, to protect delicate plantings from an area used for ball games.

✔ Have as large a lawn or open grassy area as you can manage. Sow or turf with a hard-wearing grass or grass/clover mix. Any lawn areas, but especially weedy ones, are good for wildlife too!

✔ If you have room, plant a mini woodland or copse. Set the saplings relatively close together for more instant results and greater potential for play. Silver birch (*Betula pendula*) is ideal.

✔ Leave wild margins or relatively uncultivated areas with long grass, weeds and wild flowers to encourage insects, butterflies and birds.

✔ Grow fruit and vegetables – you don't need a vegetable plot as such, just a few tubs on the patio will suffice. Include fruits that can be picked and eaten straight from the plant, such as tomatoes, raspberries and strawberries.

✔ Grow big, bright colourful blooms – don't worry about colour schemes, especially when the kids are little – as well as larger-than-life foliage plants to tower over children.

✔ Buy a few child-size tools and a small wheelbarrow so that young children can garden alongside you and help move around plants, pots, material for the compost heap etc.

▲ *Create wild areas.*

▲ *Grow fruit and vegetables.*

How to use this book

This book is intended to be used as an inspirational sourcebook by parents and children alike. It is hoped that the projects will act as catalysts, promoting further adventures in gardening and wildlife spotting as kids grow in confidence with their new-found knowledge.

▶ *You will get a kick out of raising plants from seed.*

How to garden

The introductory parts of this book look at how to approach gardening, how to understand some of the common terms and jargon, and how to stay safe, as well as what tools and equipment you will need. This is followed by fascinating facts about plants and soil, with lots of easy mini projects for the junior plant scientist to carry out. We look at how plants grow and what they need to thrive; the seasonal variations; how to control pests and diseases through natural, organic methods, and how to be a 'green' gardener. Gardening really is one of the best ways for children to learn about the cycle of life, to find out where food comes from, and to become aware of the importance of nurturing and supporting the environment.

A wealth of ideas

There then follow seven practical, hands-on chapters including Hands-on Gardening, which is devoted to developing good skills, such as taking cuttings, pruning and weeding; Flower Power, which is all about growing beautiful blooms; Fork to Fork, an introduction to growing fruits, vegetables and herbs; and Wildlife Gardening, which examines ways to encourage and observe all kinds of exciting creatures. Many of the Garden Craft projects can be done

▲ *Have fun experimenting with plants.*

▲ *Children can help with most garden tasks.*

Gardening safely

Children develop at different rates and only parents or guardians will know when their kids are ready to be introduced to using specific tools or are able to help with certain jobs. Working alongside a grown-up and having a go at something (under close supervision at first) is a great way for children to learn safe practices and to gain the skills needed for greater independence, although continuing adult guidance will be required.

Some of the projects in this book use knives, scissors or garden cutting tools, such as secateurs and pruners, or a saw, hammer and nails. Adult supervision is always required when using these, no matter how old or experienced the child, and more help will be required for younger children. Pictures showing how to do something dangerous, which will require adult help or supervision, have been highlighted with icons, shown below:

$(!)$ = the task being shown uses sharp or dangerous implements, such as secateurs, scissors, hammers or spades. Adult help may be required to do the step or, at the very least, supervise children very carefully.

$(\clubsuit)$ = the task being shown involves moving or lifting something heavy, using heat or a dangerous substance, or doing something difficult. Adult help may be required to do the step or, at the very least, supervise children very carefully.

indoors on rainy days and there is also a whole chapter of Indoor Projects, ranging from making miniature gardens to growing windowsill crops and funky houseplants. In addition, you'll find a section called Plant Profiles and a calender of what to do when, which provide really useful information that will help you garden your way to green-fingered glory!

Choosing a project

When selecting a project, first check the coloured strip across the top of the page to see if it's the right time of year to start the project and how long it might take to make or grow. In order to help you see how easy or difficult a project is, we've also added a star rating system, which works as follows:

★ = the project is 'easy peasy'. All children from 5 to 12 should be able to tackle these, and there isn't any cutting or specialist tool use involved so it's nice and safe for younger kids. Adult supervision may still be required.

★★ = you should 'have a go'! There might be some cutting or more manual dexterity involved and children might have to keep tending to the project over a longer period of time. With parental supervision and occasional help, most children will be able to enjoy them.

★★★ = the project is 'nice and challenging'. These are designed for older children and perhaps kids who already have some gardening experience and are ready to try some more advanced techniques. Adult supervision will still always be required for any steps involving dangerous implements.

▲ *Gardening and exploring alongside an adult is the best way to teach children safety in the garden and further afield.*

Getting organized

It's worth reading the brief introduction to the projects, which shows you what you can achieve. So that you know you have everything to hand, use the 'you will need' list to draw all the materials together. There is also a separate 'plant list' with common and Latin names, making it easier to shop for plants or seeds.

You may already have most things needed for the projects and, if not, the materials specified are often inexpensive and easy to obtain. Many can be sourced from recycled items. You might also consider substituting bits and pieces of equipment with similar elements already in your supplies. And, rather than buying all the plants for a scheme, why not work with the children to see what seedlings, cuttings and divisions might be grown to prepare for planting later in the season or next year? It is both fun and economical.

Preparing to garden!

After ensuring that the garden is as risk-free as it can reasonably be, children should have as much freedom within its boundaries as possible. Dig out plenty of old clothes so that they can run around and get as mucky as they like. The following pages cover the essentials of preparing your young gardeners or wildlife explorers for outdoor fun and helping them stay safe and secure.

▲ *Choose a project suitable for the age of your child.*

▲ *Try propagating plants yourself to save money.*

Playing safe

Compared to the great outdoors, gardens represent a relatively safe haven for children. There are a few things that you can do to lessen the risk of accidents. Make preparing to garden or play outdoors a simple routine with easy-to-follow rules and boundaries.

▶ It is important to wear sensible clothes when you are gardening.

Safety first
reducing risk in the garden

Before you allow children to roam free in a garden, you need to carry out a basic risk assessment, especially when moving to a new house:

✗ Never leave young children unattended in the garden.

✔ Look for open or poorly secured manhole or cellar covers and make sure they are secure before letting children out.

✔ Check that all boundaries are impenetrable and gates are locked.

✔ Where young children, including friends of your own kids, are likely to use the garden, securely fence off or drain ponds.

✔ Look out for sharp objects, including barbed wire, around the garden boundary and consider removing or relocating plants with sword-like leaves (e.g. yucca, agave) as well as prickly or thorny plants, such as roses and barberry (*Berberis* spp.).

✔ Make sure your family is up to date with their tetanus immunizations as even a small cut or thorn prick can introduce the disease.

✔ Put cane tops on canes to protect eyes.

✔ Children love to climb so secure steep drops, such as those next to decks, retaining walls and steps, with guardrails.

✔ Lock away tools as well as chemicals, including outdoor paints and preservatives, lawnmower fuel, oils, lubricants and fertilizers.

✔ If there are pets around, check the garden for any faeces and pick it up and dispose of it on a regular basis. Stress to children that they must not touch it, and always ensure they wash their hands as soon as they come in.

Local knowledge

Talk to your children about any specific local hazards that may come into the garden from the outside. These might include aggressive ant species, wasp or hornet nests, snakes and other poisonous or biting creatures as well as wild and cultivated plants that can sting or potentially cause allergic reactions. If these could be a problem, adults should be extra vigilant with their supervision.

Summer sun

Children are particularly vulnerable to damage from the sun, especially those with fair or freckly skin, or with blonde or red hair. The results of sunburn are not only painful but can also potentially store up health problems for later life.

1 Apply specially formulated children's sunscreens with a high UVA and UVB protection. Reapply often and limit the amount of time spent in midday sun.

2 Provide shaded rest areas under trees, in tents or under temporary canopies. Offer drinks to keep kids hydrated.

3 Put on a brimmed hat. Boys will often be reluctant but could be persuaded with a cowboy stetson, Indiana Jones-style explorer's hat or pirate's tricorn.

4 Cover up with a T-shirt or long-sleeved shirt.

▲ Long-sleeved T-shirts help protect skin from the sun.

▲ Make sure you apply high factor sun cream frequently.

Safety first
poisonous and irritant plants

Most plants used in this book are safe to handle, unless consumed. If you suspect your child has eaten something poisonous, take them straight to the hospital emergency department with a sample of the plant. Don't try to make them vomit. Never grow *Ricinus communis* (castor oil plant) in a garden used by children as it is highly toxic. Some plants have potentially irritant hairs, or sap that may react with sunlight, and may irritate skin. *Ruta graveolens* (rue) is one of the worst examples of the latter type and contact can require emergency medical treatment.

The list below doesn't include wild plants or mushrooms/toadstools, whose dangers children should also be made aware of. Neither is it comprehensive, so if you are unsure, check first.

- ✳ **Angel's trumpets**
  Brugmansia spp. and cvs.
- ✳ **Castor oil plant**
  Ricinus communis
- ✳ **Cherry laurel**
  Prunus laurocerasus
- ✳ **Daffodil** (may irritate skin)
  Narcissus
- ✳ **Delphinium**
- ✳ **Foxglove**
  Digitalis
- ✳ **Ivy**
  Hedera spp.
- ✳ **Laburnum**
  Laburnum anagyroides
- ✳ **Lily of the valley**
  Convallaria majalis
- ✳ **Mezereon**
  Daphne mezereum
- ✳ **Monkshood**
  Aconitum
- ✳ **Portugal laurel**
  Prunus lusitanica
- ✳ **Rhubarb**
  (toxic leaves)
  Rheum raponticum
- ✳ **Rue** (may irritate skin)
  Ruta graveolens
- ✳ **Spurge** (may irritate skin)
  Euphorbia
- ✳ **Tobacco plant**
  Nicotiana
- ✳ **Yew**
  Taxus baccata

▲ *Rue can irritate skin.*

▲ *Castor oil plant is toxic.*

Hands and feet

Where possible children should be encouraged to garden without gloves as this increases their sensory experience. However, when using digging or cutting tools or handling prickly or irritant plants, they should put on a pair of children's gardening gloves. Ask your children to wash their hands when they come in from the garden, especially before eating, and discourage nail biting or finger licking when outdoors.

Wellington boots or stout shoes protect toes from accidents with tools or sharp objects in the soil, so should always be worn when gardening.

Safety first
using tools and equipment

Showing children how to use tools properly helps prevent accidents and makes gardening more rewarding. Encourage them to clean, tidy away or hang up their garden tools and equipment after use, so they are out of the way and will last longer.

- ✔ Wear thick gardening gloves when using digging or cutting tools. Adult supervision is always required when using these tools.
- ✔ Distribute the load in a wheelbarrow evenly.
- ✘ Don't overload wheelbarrows or garden trolleys, and use one that is a suitable size.
- ✘ Don't try to lift too much soil on a fork or spade when digging. Adult supervision is required, and help should be given.
- ✘ Don't use secateurs or pruners unsupervised and always leave them closed with the safety catch on. Younger children should not use them.
- ✘ Never leave rakes, hoes or other long-handled tools lying on the ground.

▲ *Put away tools.*

▲ *Take care when digging.*

Dictionary of gardening terms

When you first start gardening some of the words and phrases you'll hear may sound rather confusing. Don't be put off though. We've explained some of the more commonly used terms for you here, and any that aren't listed will be in the dictionary or on the internet.

▶ *You will already know some gardening terms, but not others.*

Annual This is a plant that grows from seed, flowers, makes more seed and then dies, all in one year. 'Hardy annuals' are easy to grow from seed sown straight in the ground and 'half-hardy' annuals, which need extra warmth to germinate and grow in spring, can't be planted outdoors until the risk of frosty weather has passed. Usually this is early summer.

Bulb This is an underground swelling at the base of a plant's stem that stores food as well as a tiny flowering plant, ready to bloom in the following year.

Chitting In order to encourage seed potatoes to start growing, you place them in a light place with their 'eyes' or buds uppermost and allow them to sprout. This is called chitting.

Compost Used frequently in the garden, compost is the dark brown, crumbly rotted-down remains of plant material that is worked into the ground to improve the soil and help grow bigger, better flowers, fruits and vegetables. Compost also describes the bags of potting soil bought to fill pots and baskets.

Crock This is a piece of broken clay pot or tile put into the bottom of a planting container to cover the drainage hole(s) so that soil doesn't block them. You can also use stones or broken-up Styrofoam plant trays.

Cutting A shoot tip, piece of stem or sometimes the root of a plant, cuttings are put into pots or trays of compost, or, for easy plants, jars of water. With luck, these pieces make new roots and eventually a whole new plant develops.

Deadheading This is the action of removing old or fading flowers by cutting or pinching them off with thumb and forefinger, to prevent the plant from making seeds. Annual plants may stop flowering altogether if allowed to form seed-heads and most plants look better with old flowers removed.

Deciduous This term describes shrubs, trees and climbers that lose their leaves in autumn and grow fresh leaves in spring.

Evergreen Trees, shrubs, climbers and perennial plants that keep their leaves even through the colder winter months are called evergreens.

Fertilizer Another word for plant food, fertilizer comes in different forms, ranging from well-rotted manure to granular or liquid feeds.

Germination When a seed swells with water and starts to grow into a baby plant, unfolding its seed leaves and pushing out its root, this is called

▲ *Sweet peas are beautiful, scented annual plants.*

▲ *Bulbs are little time capsules containing sleeping plants.*

▲ *Compost is made from rotted-down plant waste.*

▲ *Deadheading flowers keeps them looking fresh.*

▲ *Use a cold frame as part of the hardening off process.*

▲ *Prick out seedlings when large enough to handle.*

▲ *Perennial plants, such as red crocosmia, come up every year.*

▲ *Pollination is carried out by insects, such as bumble-bees.*

germination. You can see germination in action when you put bean seeds or sprinklings of cress seed on damp blotting paper (*see* page 28).

Hardening off The shoots or leaves of young plants grown from seeds or cuttings indoors or in the greenhouse are too soft at first to be planted straight out in the garden. They must be gradually introduced to cooler outdoor temperatures, stronger light levels and breezier conditions in order to toughen them up. This process is called hardening off and takes two to three weeks. A glass or plastic **cold frame** is often used as a halfway house. Lightly shaded at first, the lid or vents are raised by increasing amounts in the day but are closed at night.

Manure Usually cow or horse dung mixed with straw bedding, this is left to rot down to make garden fertilizer. It's also a great soil improver and mulch. The heap takes about three to four years to break down.

Mulch A thick layer of material, such as chipped tree bark, put on to the soil around plants to help smother weeds. Mulches, such as well-rotted manure or garden compost, also help to keep soils, such as sandy loams, from drying out in summer and these types also provide plant fertilizers.

Naturalize Particularly important for the wild garden look, naturalizing is where certain bulbs or perennials that spread and multiply easily are planted to form large, natural-looking patches in lawns, long grass or the ground under trees.

Perennial This term describes non-woody flowering or foliage plants that are evergreen or more usually **herbaceous**, i.e. they die down in winter and regrow from ground level in spring. The hardy herbaceous perennials as a group contain most of the common border flowers.

Pinching out Carefully nipping off the shoot tip or growing point of a plant, often a seedling or young plant, is called pinching out. It encourages the plant to produce side shoots and become more bushy.

Plunging This is an easy way of thoroughly wetting the roots of a potted specimen before planting. Fill a bucket of water and hold the plant pot under the water surface until the air bubbles stop.

Pollination Bees and other insects transfer male pollen to the female part of the flower – a process called pollination. This allows seed to be produced and fruits to ripen.

Pricking out When a tray of seedlings starts to grow their first set of true leaves and are large enough to handle, each baby plant is moved to another container to give them more room to grow. This is called pricking out. The seedlings are very delicate and the tiny roots should be lifted out of the compost or cuttings mix with the end of a pencil or stick while holding a leaf for support.

Propagation This technique makes more plants and includes several methods, such as sowing seed, taking cuttings, divisions or rooting offshoots or runners. Seeds and cuttings may be put in a **propagator**, which keeps the compost or seed and cuttings compost warm and moist to encourage germination or rooting.

Pruning Cutting off parts of a woody plant, such as a shrub or climber, to improve its shape, get rid of diseased or damaged stems and branches, or to encourage flowering and fruiting, is called pruning.

Staking This involves using a stick or bamboo cane to prop up a plant and prevent it being damaged by wind or rain or falling over because it is top-heavy.

Tools and equipment

You can now find quite a wide range of gardening tools especially designed to suit the height and body size of younger gardeners. They aren't as heavy as tools for grown-ups and some have adjustable handles so that you can keep using them as you grow.

▶ *Pick tools that are just the right size for you to use.*

Trowel

One of the most important pieces of kit in any garden, a trowel is a mini hand-held spade that is used for making small holes and digging up weeds. They come in various sizes, so make sure you choose one that fits comfortably in your hand and is not too heavy for you to use. They need to be sturdy enough to handle a bit of digging. Take care when using.

▲ *Trowel*

Hand fork

There are two main types of hand fork: angled ones and flat ones. The angled type is best for loosening the soil between plants in small flower-beds and in window boxes. This makes it easier to sow seeds or plant seedlings, and to pull up any smaller annual weeds that grow between established plants. The flat fork is best for lifting up bigger weeds, complete with their roots, once you have loosened the ground. Take care when using.

▲ *Flat and angled hand fork*

Gardening scissors

Like normal scissors, gardening scissors can be used for all manner of tasks in the garden, from cutting string and twine to length and opening seed packets to snipping off dead flower-heads and tidying up straggly plants. They are safer than secateurs, although they will not cut through thicker twigs or branches in the same way, so you may need to use secateurs sometimes with adult supervision. Take care when using them and never leave them lying open on a surface or the ground. Adult supervision is required.

▲ *Gardening scissors*

Dibber

Used for making a deep hole in which to plant a seedling, or to make drills (long, shallow grooves) for sowing rows of seeds, a dibber is a useful, but not essential, piece of kit. If you don't have one, you can use a thick stick instead. Take care when using.

▶ *Dibber*

Plant labels

It is useful to mark where you've sown seeds or planted bulbs in the border, and sowings in pots and trays should always be labelled with the plant name and date. On bigger labels you could also add notes to yourself saying how often plants need feeding or when to harvest. There are many fun labels to buy, or make your own from old lolly sticks or strips of plastic cut from washed-out yogurt pots.

▲ *Plant labels*

Garden twine

Thicker and softer than normal string, garden twine is used for tying canes together, for fixing plants to supports or for marking straight lines for sowing.

▲ *Garden twine*

Gloves

Use these to protect your hands from thorns, wood splinters and stinging nettles and to keep them clean when doing a really mucky garden job. Try to find a pair that fits properly – if they are too big they can be difficult to work in. Some types are thicker for thorn protection and others have rubber grips on the palms.

▲ *Gloves*

Bucket

Having a bucket to hand is very useful. They are great for plunging plants to wet the roots before planting, collecting clippings, carrying soil and compost and even for transporting hand tools. There are many sizes, but do not overfill a larger one or it may be too heavy to carry.

▲ *Bucket*

Hoe

A long-handled piece of equipment, a hoe or cultivator is useful for weeding and breaking up the soil surface ready for sowing. It slices like a knife under the roots of weeds, which then shrivel up and die in dry weather and can easily be pulled up. Because the hoe has a long handle, you don't have to bend down to weed, so no backache! Like spades, hoes have a sharp cutting edge, so you must always ask an adult to supervise and take great care when using.

◀ *Standard rake*　　　▶ *Hoe*

Watering can

An essential piece of equipment for watering and feeding, try to get a can with a handle at the side and the top, since this will help you handle it and put water where it is needed. Ones with a 'rose' or sprinkler fitting on the end are best for watering delicate seedlings and young plants. Take it off to water the base of a plant, under the leaves. Do not overfill or it may be too heavy to carry.

▲ *Watering can*

Rakes

There are two types of rakes: standard soil rakes and spider or spring tine rakes. Soil rakes have rigid prongs set at a right angle to the handle. They are used for loosening and levelling out soil. Spider or spring tine rakes have much thinner prongs that fan out from the end of the handle. These are used for gathering leaves or small bits of twig from lawns. Never leave rakes or other long-handled tools lying on the ground. Adult supervision is required.

▶ *Spade*

Spade

Used for digging big holes or for turning over the soil to mix in compost or manure, spades are one of the most useful pieces of equipment. Try to get one that is not too tall for you, or you will find it hard to use. Since the edge of the blade is sharp, you must always wear stout shoes or boots. Adult supervision is required and great care should be taken when using one.

Wheelbarrow

Extremely useful for transporting tools, compost and plants around the garden, wheelbarrows are available in several sizes. Use one that is the correct size for you, and never overload it. They can be heavy, so adult supervision is required and you may need to ask for help.

▲ *Spider rake*

Warning!

Adult supervision is always required when children are using sharp or potentially dangerous implements, such as garden forks. Adult help may also be required for any lifting or moving anything heavy. Children should not use saws, hammers, drills or other electrical garden equipment. It is up to the parent or carer to ensure the child is working safely.

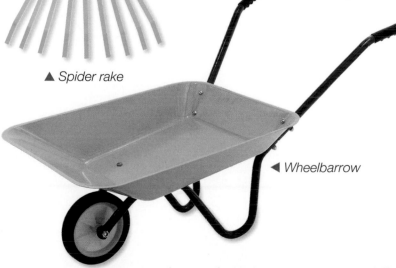
◀ *Wheelbarrow*

How does your garden grow?

In this chapter you'll find out how plants work, what they need to thrive and why they are so useful to us. You'll be introduced to the way plants are named and what plant parts are called. Budding scientists will enjoy looking at soil and investigating minibeasts and there are fascinating facts about nature's cycles, the weather and seasons.

Why we need plants

If it wasn't for the green stuff all around us, we simply wouldn't exist. Plants create the air we breathe (oxygen) as a by-product when they use the sun's energy to convert carbon dioxide into sugars. These sugars form the building blocks right at the start of the food chain.

▶ You can grow many plants in all kinds of different containers.

Nature's favourite colour

The leaves and stems of plants contain a green colouring or pigment called chlorophyll. Sometimes it is masked by other colours, such as reds and purples, but it is always there. It allows plants to trap the sun's energy (photons) and use it to split water absorbed from the soil into hydrogen and oxygen. The hydrogen is combined with carbon dioxide, which the plant takes in through special holes in the leaves, and the end result is sugar and oxygen. The sugar is used as the plant's energy source, while the oxygen is released into the atmosphere through the same little holes and we, and other animals, can breathe it in.

Although you can tell from looking at a beautiful green forest or a meadow that there's masses of chlorophyll in plants, you may not realize that seas, lakes and rivers are also full of tiny plants, called algae and phytoplankton. These are some of the most important in the earth's defences, helping to mop up excess carbon dioxide – a potentially harmful greenhouse gas – and stopping the earth from becoming too hot.

Food for all

Plants, like us, need food to survive. Theirs is created in the leaves during an amazing chemical reaction called photosynthesis, when the sugars made from trapped sunlight join together to make other materials including cellulose, a major plant building block, and starch. Starch is a way for plants to store excess sugars for future use. Potato tubers contain a lot of starch.

Everybody can benefit from plants, whether they are eaten directly or by the animals that are then eaten. Cows, for instance, which provide us with meat or milk, eat grass or are fed with grains or seeds that are produced by crops growing in fields. In addition, little water creatures eat algae and phytoplankton and eventually are themselves eaten by fish, which end up on the dinner table.

As well as leafy vegetables, such as lettuce, 'flower' vegetables, such as cauliflower and broccoli, and root vegetables, like carrots, there are all kinds of fruits, seeds, grains and nuts that we can eat. And, for a touch of sweetness, there's sugar from sugar cane or sugar beet; honey, made by bees from the plant nectar they collect, and maple syrup.

▲ Algae produces oxygen and can be eaten by water creatures.

▲ The green colour of leaves is due to chlorophyll.

▲ Cows eat grass and use this food to grow and to make milk, which we can drink.

Plants are cool!

In our gardens we use trees and climbers to provide shade, but plants in general help to keep our surroundings cool, especially in towns and cities where concrete, tarmac and brick buildings store and give out a lot of heat. Parks, gardens and tree-lined roads help to make life in urban places more enjoyable, provide shade and do not store heat in the same way as man-made materials. You may also see some buildings being fitted with 'green' roofs planted with grass or drought-resistant plants. Plants act like sponges, absorbing harmful air pollution, soaking up rainfall and helping to prevent flooding. The protective covering of greenery also slows down the wearing away of soil by wind and rain.

Brightening our world

Plants, both indoors and outside, make our world more beautiful and colourful. In addition, when they do take root, all kinds of creatures can move in too. By gardening you can turn a 'desert' balcony, roof terrace or concrete-covered yard into an oasis, lush with aromatic leaves and fragrant flowers and buzzing with insects. Although green is usually the background colour and comes in a great many shades, there's a dazzling array of flower colours and forms to marvel over, as well as two-tone and textured foliage. All the effort you put into a garden or green space is paid back by the wheelbarrow load! You get such a great feeling of achievement from the plants you have nurtured, the pots and beds you have planted, and the fruits, vegetables and herbs you have grown, picked and eaten – and you are also helping the environment.

▲ *A green roof such as this creates another habitat for insects and helps keep buildings cool.*

Useful plants

While not all plants are edible (some are poisonous!), man has discovered, often by trial and error, that certain types can help us feel better if we become ill. Many of the medicines we use today are based on chemicals made originally by plants. Some of the common kitchen herbs, such as sage, mint and thyme, now mainly used for flavouring food, have also been used as medicines in the past. Today, you can buy herbal remedies from high street chemists and supermarkets, as well as teas and infusions, such as chamomile and peppermint.

Plants are also grown to provide materials for a huge range of things, including dry vegetation, such as straw, sedge and rushes, for building thatched roofs or for weaving. We make clothes from spun cotton, hemp and flax (used for linen). Trees are cut for timber used to build houses and other structures, and wood pulp makes cardboard and paper. Plants that died millions of years ago and that have turned into coal are burnt as fuel to keep us warm or to generate electricity. In the future, plants may be grown to produce biofuels, a renewable energy source used to power cars and machines.

▲ *Everyone enjoys the fragrance and aroma of plants.*

▲ *Many herbs and plants have medicinal benefits.*

Parts of a plant

There are lots of types of plants. Many have flowers, some have hairy leaves, some are tall and woody, and others creep along the ground. However different they look, they mostly work in a similar way and garden plants usually have a common basic structure.

► If you look closely at plants you will be able to see the different parts.

The structure of plants

Plants come in a huge range of shapes and sizes. Ones pollinated by insects tend to have similarly structured and quite colourful and showy blooms. Those pollinated by wind are mostly plain without petals as they don't need to do any advertising.

The blanket flower shown below is a typical example of one of the largest plant families, the daisy family. Like most plants it has a **root system**, which supplies the plant with water and nutrients from the soil. These are drawn up the **main stem**, along branches to **leaves** and **flowers**. This species has open-centred blooms but the actual flowers are tiny, without **petals** and are tightly clustered in the central disc. Botanists call these **disc florets**, and the petals **ray florets**. Notice the protective covering of green, leaf-like bracts that encase the flower-buds. These are called **sepals**.

The structure of flowers

Most flowers have male and female parts. Some are able to pollinate themselves, while others need wind or insects to carry the pollen from one flower to another. In order to attract insects, they often have brightly coloured **petals**, which make up the majority of the flower. The centre may be marked with a contrasting 'target' that helps insects home in on the nectar and pollen. The lines are called **nectar guides**.

The reproductive parts of the flower are clustered together. The female part, or **stigma**, which sticks out to receive the male pollen, is usually surrounded by a number of male **stamens**. These stamens are each made up of a stalk (called a **filament**) and the pollen-bearing **anther**. The stigma, its stalk (called a **style**) and the seed-bearing **ovary** at its base make up the female reproductive organs. Together these are called the **carpel**. When the pollen grains land on the sticky stigma, they grow down the style into the ovary. When this happens, pollination takes place and seeds are produced.

PARTS OF A PLANT

disc florets
sepals
flower stem
seed-head
flower
petal (ray floret)
main stem
flower-bud
leaf
root system

PARTS OF A FLOWER

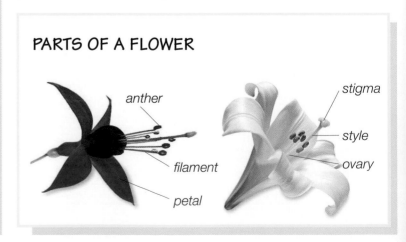

anther
filament
petal
stigma
style
ovary

How plants are named

One of the hardest things about gardening is learning scientific names. Buttercup and daisy are easy to remember, so why bother? Well, the same plant can have many common names but these don't usually tell you much.

▶ All plants have a unique scientific name, and most have a common one.

Unlocking the secret code!

All living things, not just plants, are given a scientific name that helps us to understand the relationships between them. It also means that whoever is talking about the plant or animal, in whatever country, everyone is using the same name and there's no confusion.

The system of naming was invented by the Swedish botanist, Carl Linnaeus in the 18th century. It's mostly based on Latin but Greek is also used. The code can incorporate things such as the name of the person who discovered the particular plant or animal, its country of origin, flower colour, leaf shape and so on. In fact you'll discover there's a lot of useful information in the scientific name once you start decoding!

Genus and species

The first word of the two-part name is the **genus**. This describes a group of plants that are more closely related to each other than to anything else. This can contain a wide range of plants, from trees, shrubs and climbers to herbaceous perennials or annuals. Some of the plants might only be found high up in mountains, while others might live in boggy ground next to a low-lying lake or river.

The second word refers to the **species**. This word identifies all the different plant types that belong in the genus. With some plants, there is only one plant or species in the genus, but in many cases there is more than one. For example, *Prunus persica* is a peach, while *Prunus avium* is a cherry. The first word, *Prunus*, tells you that they belong to the same genus, while the second words, *persica* and *avium*, tell you what species the plant is.

Variations

Subtle differences within a species that occur in nature are described by a third word, which tells you what variety, subspecies or form the particular plant is. If man has artificially created the plant, the variation is called a **cultivar**. The variations are written

ALL IN A NAME

The first word in a name tells you what 'genus' the plant belongs to. This can be a big group of plants, or just one.

The second word shows you what 'species' the plant is. This helps you tell the difference between plants in the same genus.

Prunus | *persica* | 'Peregrine'

The word in single quotes and different writing is the 'variety'. This identifies different plants within the same species.

◀ *Prunus persica* 'Peregrine'

in single quotation marks, so they are easy to spot. For example, a variety of *Prunus persica* is *Prunus persica* 'Bonanza'. Lots of species, such as apples, peaches, potatoes and many others, have many varieties, including names you will recognize, such as 'Granny Smith' or 'Golden Delicious'.

Common names

As well as their scientific names, many plants also have common names, which you may be more familiar with. Some well-known names are 'daisy', 'poppy' or 'lily'. While these are fine for talking about plants in general, you do need to know the scientific names if you want to be more precise. Some plants do not have common names, or if they do then they can also vary from country to country, and there is often more than one name for the same thing, so they can be confusing! For this reason we have given the scientific names as well as the common names (where there is one) in the plant lists and the Plant Profiles section. This means you can buy exactly the right thing, and learn the proper names at the same time. It will also impress your parents!

What is soil?

When you're digging in the dirt or making mud pies, you might not realize how valuable the crumbly brown stuff is. If it wasn't for soil, the earth would be a pretty barren place. Most plants need it to grow into, as few, apart from mosses and lichens, can survive on bare rock.

▶ *Knowing your soil type lets you look after it better.*

Raw materials

Soil is a mixture of finely ground-up rocks, sand and rotted-down plant and animal remains. There are many different soil types named according to how they were formed and where they come from. Basic types include sand, loam or clay, each of which has different properties.

Acid or alkaline?

As well as the different soil types, soil can have a different pH. The pH scale runs from 1 to 14, where 1 is extremely acidic and 14 extremely alkaline. The number 7 is the midway or neutral point. Most garden soils have a pH ranging from slightly above or slightly below neutral. On the vegetable patch

WHAT'S YOUR SOIL TYPE?

To work out your soil type, go into the garden and see what it looks like and how it feels.

Sandy soils These types are pale and very free-draining because of the high sand content in them. They are easy to weed and warm up quickly in spring, but can dry out easily.

Loam soils These types of soil are dark and crumbly and usually quite fertile. They contain a mixture of clay and sand as well as lots of rotted plant and animal matter.

Clay soils These types of soil are slow to warm up in spring and in winter are often waterlogged. In summer they can sometimes dry hard like concrete, and crack.

TESTING THE pH OF SOIL

A simple pH testing kit will quickly show you if you have acid, neutral or alkaline soil.

1 Use the end of an old teaspoon to scoop a moist soil sample into the test tube provided with the kit. Carefully break the capsule containing the chemical and pour it on to the soil.

2 Add water to the test tube, following the instructions . Put the stopper in the test tube and, holding firmly between thumb and forefinger, give it a really good shake.

3 Leave the contents to settle, then hold the test tube up to the chart provided with the kit and compare the liquid with the chart. Read off the pH value.

MAKE A MINI WORMERY

If you want to study the activities of earthworms for a few days, make this mini wormery. You will be able to see how they pull substances from the surface of the soil down, mixing in beneficial nutrients.

1 Cut the top section off a plastic bottle and ask an adult to make some holes in the base using a skewer. Fill the bottle with alternating layers of washed sand and garden soil enriched with compost.

2 Very carefully dig up three or four worms from the garden using a trowel, then add them to the top of the soil layer in the mini wormery. They will quickly burrow down out of sight.

3 Add food in the form of broken-up pieces of potato peelings to the top of the bottle. Don't add too many at once or they will start to rot before the worms can deal with them.

4 Water the mixture with a watering can. Don't make it too soggy. Replace the top section of the bottle but leave the lid off for ventilation, or the peelings will rot and the worms will suffocate.

5 Stand the wormery in a cool, sheltered place outside, such as in a shady border or under a tree, and loosely cover the whole bottle with black plastic to completely keep out light.

6 After a few days you will see that the worms have pulled the peelings down into the soil. Can you spot any worms? You have to be quick as they don't like light! Release back into the wild when you have finished.

you may need to add lime before sowing or planting brassicas, for example. Always pH test your soil before trying to adjust the acidity or alkalinity and never apply lime at the same time as fertilizer or manure.

Some plants can only grow on acidic or lime-free soils. These are known as ericaceous plants and include rhododendrons, azaleas, pieris, camellia and many heathers. Others prefer alkaline or neutral soil, so it is important to work out which type you have.

Teeming with life

Healthy, fertile soil is crammed full of tiny creatures – if you could shrink yourself down to the size of a grain of sand it would seem full of terrifying monsters! As well as these organisms, which are mostly harmless vegetarians living on decaying vegetable matter, there are fungi and bacteria. These last two groups break down plant and animal remains and produce materials that help bind microscopic particles together and convert hard-to-break-down substances into useful plant foodstuffs. Fungi often have a special relationship with particular plants too, helping their seeds to germinate and their roots to grow properly.

At the next size up, there are the invertebrates, meaning animals that don't have a backbone. These include worms, slugs, ants, fly and beetle larvae, mites, centipedes, woodlice, springtails and fungus gnats. Worms are especially important as they are like mobile factories moving through the soil, pulling dead plant material below and mixing plant foods deeper. As they tunnel, they create channels that allow air and water to get down to where the roots need them. The channels also help soils drain and open up the structure so that plant roots can grow more easily.

What plants need

Light, water and food are essential for survival and growth, but different plants need more or less of them. Fitting the right plant to the right spot in the house or garden is part of the skill you will develop as a gardener. You can find helpful information in Plant Profiles.

▶ *Potted plants need plenty of water and sunshine to thrive.*

Light of life
Wherever they are located, whether in a shady corner of the garden, on a windowsill or on a sunny patio, plants need and use light from the sun to make energy for life (*see 'Nature's favourite colour' on page 18*). Different plants require different amounts of light, however, and if they get too little or too much they can become very unhappy. There are two types of plants: those that love sun and those that like shade.

Sun-loving plants
You can often spot plants that thrive in hot, dry places just by looking at them. The leaves may be thick and fleshy with a waxy coating, storing water inside them. Sometimes though, the leaves are very small and covered in a mealy or flour-like coating, hairs or wool that makes them appear grey or white. This reflects the light, keeping the plant cool and reducing evaporation. Other plants need more moisture and may have large colourful leaves and flowers. In general, plants with purple- or red-tinged leaves and gold variegated kinds need more light than plain green ones.

TURNING HEADS
You may not realize it, but plant stems, leaves and flowers move during the day. You can observe this with pansies, which all turn to face the same direction to get the maximum amount of light. This has an added benefit, as the display attracts passing insects.

1 Fill a pot with potting compost and plant with a tray of pansies. Arrange them so that the flowers are all facing in different directions.

2 Water the plants and stand in a spot in good light. After about a week you will see that the flowers have all turned to face the sun.

Shade-loving plants
These often come from woodland areas and tend to be quieter in colouring than sun lovers, with dark green leaves (maximum chlorophyll) and white, blue, yellow or soft pink flowers more common than red or orange blooms. Leaves may be large, to try to capture as much light as possible and, in the case of ferns, the blades are often finely cut and lacy. Woodland plants thrive in soils full of decayed leaf and plant material that acts like a sponge, keeping water available. The roots may be quite fine and fibrous, so they are not designed for storing water and withstanding drought. If you put a shade-loving plant in full sun, the thin leaves tend to scorch or turn yellow.

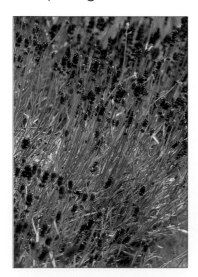

▲ *Sun-loving plants, such as lavender, prefer hot, dry spots.*

▲ *Shade plants tend to need more moisture than others.*

Why plants need water

If you have ever seen brown grass or shrivelled flowers during hot weather then you will know that plants become ill-looking and can die if they don't get enough water. This is because it is water that moves minerals and stored food around the plant, as well as keeping the cells, the building blocks of life, the right shape so that they can work properly. Evaporation of water from the leaves also helps to keep the plant cool, in much the same way as sweating cools us down. Water is required right at the start of a plant's life too, to trigger germination, which is when a seed starts to grow a baby plant.

Overwatered plants, on the other hand, are drowning. When the roots are too wet and haven't got enough air, they begin to die and may have trouble taking up nutrients. Very wet weather can cause this problem outside, and it is common in plants in containers that have been given too much water.

It is important, then, that you keep an eye on your plants and feel the soil to see if it is too dry or wet. Wilting leaves are often a sign of thirst and if the soil is dry it's safe to give it a thorough soaking. However, if the soil is damp, it could mean that something has attacked or blocked the roots under the soil surface and the plant simply can't drink the water that's there. If you don't tackle a thirsty plant quickly, it may not recover fully. *See* page 26 for watering techniques.

Signs of overwatering include dropping or drooping leaves and soggy compost. You may need to carefully take the plant out of its pot and pat the root-ball with kitchen paper to draw out some of the excess water. If it is very wet, stand the plant on kitchen paper overnight. Repot the plant, adding extra compost if needed, and keep an eye on it.

How plants drink

The way plants draw up water from the soil is very clever. The action starts in the leaves, which release moisture into the air. The loss of water (**transpiration**) creates a suction through the fine water channels that connect the roots to the leaves and water is drawn up through the stems, rather like the way a drink is pulled up a straw when you suck on it. This process is called **capillarity**. Wind and heat makes plants transpire (lose moisture through the leaves) faster, which means that more water is drawn up and the soil or compost dries out more quickly. In cool or still weather, plants transpire at a slower rate, so plants need less water at their roots.

PLOTTING THE ROUTE OF WATER

Using food dyes and a couple of white flowers (which will show the result most clearly), you can see the movement of water through the stems to the leaves and flowers (capillarity). It may take a day or two, so be patient!

1 Take three tall drinks glasses and three-quarters fill them with water. Divide a sachet of cut flower food between the glasses. This gives the blooms the energy they need to survive without their roots.

2 Add a few drops of coloured food dye so that you end up with one yellow, one red and one blue. Later you can experiment by mixing the colours to make green, purple and orange.

3 Take some white cut flowers, in this case chrysanthemums, and cut the stems at an angle to increase the surface area over which water can be absorbed and ensure they don't have an airlock. Put a flower stem in each glass.

4 Stand the flowers out of direct sunlight, but not in the dark. The flowers should show traces of colour in the petals within two days, showing how the water moved up the stem to the petals.

WAYS TO WATER

There are several ways of watering plants. Potted outdoor ones may need watering at any time of the year.

Misting The air indoors is too dry for some plants. Spray regularly with a hand mister or stand plants on a tray of moist gravel. Don't spray plants with felted leaves, succulents or cacti.

Watering from below Plants with hairy leaves can rot if watered from above. Soak the roots from below by standing in a bowl of tepid water. Water trays of newly sown seed in the same way.

Plunging Always plunge plants in a bucket of water before planting to give them a drenching. Hold the surface of the potting compost under the water and wait for the bubbles to stop.

Directing water Take the rose off a watering can to direct the flow under the leaves, straight where it's needed. Avoid watering overhead as droplets bounce off leaves and are wasted.

Watering with a rose Use a fine rose to water cuttings and seedlings that could be damaged by a strong jet of water. Use a slow sweeping motion, starting away from the pot or tray.

Feed me!

Plants, like us, require food to survive. Rather than cooking and eating things, plants draw up nutrients from the soil through their roots and circulate them via their stems to leaves, buds and, in particular, any new growth, such as buds, shoots or baby leaves. Because they can only get nutrients from the soil, it is important that the earth plants stand in is well fertilized before they are sown or planted to give them a good start in life. They will eventually use up the food, however, which is why you need to add extra fertilizer, especially during the growing season. Plants that are in pots or containers need most attention as they have access to only the compost in the pots, and will use up their supplies more quickly than those in the ground.

Lack of the right foods or nutrients can cause all kinds of visible changes in plants. Leaves may turn red, purple or, most often, yellow and look sickly when starved, although some fungal diseases or stresses, such as too much light and heat or overwatering, can make that happen too. Another sign of starvation is that leaves and flowers get smaller and overall growth looks stunted. Correct the problem by applying diluted liquid feed to moistened soil or compost, following packet instructions. Keeping a close eye on your plants will help you spot problems early on.

Feeding techniques

Food is available as soluble fertilizer, a powder which needs to be mixed with water before applying; liquid feed, which also needs diluting; granular fertilizer, which can be mixed with compost or sprinkled on the surface; and compost or manure, which is either dug into soil or used as a mulch.

Feed plants during or just before the growing season. Always follow manufacturer's instructions when applying fertilizers and ask a parent to help if you aren't sure. Giving more than the recommended dose can damage plants. Wear gloves and/or wash your hands after handling fertilizers.

Each packet of fertilizer will have an NPK ratio, which tells you relatively speaking how the three main nutrients (nitrogen, phosphorous and potassium) are balanced. Different plants need an appropriate fertilizer, so always check. For example, tomato food is high in potassium (K) because more potassium is needed for fruits, such as tomatoes, to grow. As well as these main nutrients you will also often see trace elements, such as iron, magnesium and copper, listed in the ingredients. Plants use these in minute amounts.

These are the main nutrients in fertilizer:

Nitrogen This has the chemical symbol N. It is used for new shoots and leaves. Yellowing older leaves may indicate nitrogen deficiency.

Phosphorous This has the chemical symbol P. It is involved in the healthy growth of a plant's roots.

Potassium This has the chemical symbol K. It is essential for flower and fruit production.

FOOLPROOF FERTILIZERS

It is important to use the correct technique for applying different fertilizers. Always wash your hands afterwards.

Soluble fertilizer This is usually powder or crystals. Use the scoop provided to measure the right amount of feed. Mix thoroughly with water. Follow packet instructions. Wash your hands.

Liquid fertilizers These must be diluted. Use the measuring cap and stir the correct amount into the water using a bamboo cane or stick. Follow packet instructions. Wash your hands.

Granular fertilizers These are often slow-release types. Work into the compost or soil or mix with potting compost before planting. Follow packet instructions. Wash your hands.

Compost and manure Home-made compost or well-rotted manure feeds plants and improves the condition of the soil. Fork in during late winter/early spring or spread on the surface as a mulch.

▲ *The tomato plant on the left is starving. Its leaves are yellow and it hasn't produced any fruits. The plant on the right has strong, healthy growth with green leaves and plenty of fruits ready to ripen.*

Be a weather monitor

It's fun to keep track of the weather and to record temperatures and rainfall just like meteorologists (people who study weather and climate) do. You can use the information to work out when you might need to carry out gardening activities, such as sowing, harvesting, protecting tender plants or watering pots and containers. If it is going to be very hot, move shade-loving house plants to a spot away from windows, and make sure they get enough water.

To measure the amount of water falling in a day you can use a specially calibrated rainwater gauge, which is pushed into the ground and gives the measurement in millimetres or inches. Hold the gauge perfectly level, with your eye on the water line, to read it accurately. Empty the gauge each day after rain or you will get a false reading.

A garden thermometer measures the temperature in degrees centigrade or fahrenheit. Attach to a wall or post in a sheltered, shaded part of the garden, as direct sun or wind can affect the accuracy of your readings. Some thermometers record both the minimum and maximum daily temperatures.

▲ *Read the rainwater gauge at eye level.*

▲ *Use a garden thermometer to check daily temperatures.*

Nature's natural cycle

A garden is a wonderful place to observe the cycle of life. Whether you like watching the magic of a seed germinating and growing into a plant, or enjoying the changes in the seasons in the garden, there is always something going on outside!

▶ It is fun to germinate seeds and watch them grow into little plantlets.

The story of seeds

The cycle of growth for plants starts with a seed. This may be as small as a poppy seed or as large as a coconut, but the process is exactly the same. Some seeds lie dormant until there are exactly the right conditions – enough moisture and warmth – to trigger germination. This is when the seed swells and a shoot starts to grow. This will keep on growing up towards the light until it pops up above the earth. The plant should then mature and, in time, will produce its own seeds. Many of these may be lost to wind or eaten by animals (incuding us!), but some find their way into the soil and the process begins all over again.

Nature's recycling

Nothing is wasted in the natural world. After plants have died down and leaves have fallen from the trees, their remains rot down and return to the soil. Here they feed and nurture the next round of growth.

A rotten apple is a good example of nature's recycling. When it ripens and falls to the ground it might be fed upon by birds and wasps. Soon, microscopic fungi get to work, breaking down the fruit and releasing substances that butterflies can feed on too. Finally, the fungus itself starts to reproduce. Meanwhile, if the seeds inside the apple survive they may germinate and grow into another apple tree, starting off a new cycle.

FROM SEED TO SHOOT

Seeds must absorb moisture to trigger germination. You can watch this in action when you take a dry, dormant broad bean and wedge it next to damp blotting paper. It soon activates and bursts into life!

1 Cut a piece of blotting paper to fit inside a large glass jar. Press it against the sides and overlap the edges. Blotting paper is ideal because it is thick enough not to collapse when wet.

3 Take three or four dried broad beans and push them down between the glass and the damp blotting paper, spaced evenly around the jar. The paper should hold the beans in position.

2 Fill the space inside with cotton wool balls, then pour in water to a depth of 2cm/¾in. Keep this water topped up but below the bean seeds. Seeds need water plus air to germinate as otherwise they would drown.

4 Replace the lid to keep humidity high and stand in a light, warm spot. After 5–7 days you will see roots and a green shoot appear. The roots will grow downwards and the shoot will grow upwards and develop leaves.

FROM FLOWER-BUD TO SEED-HEAD

Here you can see how a flower, in this case a viola, transforms from a tightly folded bud to an open bloom ready to be pollinated. After the bee has visited, the flower begins to fade and the seed-head swells. Finally the ripe head bursts, releasing the seed.

THE LIFE CYCLE OF A LEAF

This shows the development of a leaf. It starts with a leaf that has just unfurled from a bud. It continues to grow to full size, then, in autumn, it turns yellow and the shrub reabsorbs all useful substances. The brown remains are then broken down by fungi on the ground.

THE CYCLE OF THE SEASONS

In many countries away from the Equator, each season is different, bringing assorted weather, shorter or longer days and varying temperatures. These all affect the plants in your garden, as well as the rhythm of life.

Winter Short days and long nights along with cold temperatures slow most plant growth down to a full stop. Rain turns to hail, sleet or snow. Evergreen plants, some hardy flowering shrubs, heathers, climbers and a few early flowering bulbs provide scatterings of blossom. Birdbaths need thawing and birds need feeding regularly.

SPRING

Spring Bulbs are some of the first flowers to appear in early spring, followed by fruit tree blossoms. The newly opened leaves of deciduous trees are bright green. Perennial plants push up and weeds also start to grow. Insects and other creatures slowly come out of hibernation. Birds start to sing again and build nests.

WINTER

SUMMER

Autumn Days start to get shorter and noticeably chilly. Many plants produce fruits, berries or seed-heads. Birds, mammals and other creatures feast on the bounty, fattening up ready for hibernation or to help them survive the winter. The leaves of deciduous trees and shrubs begin to change colour. Leaves drop and herbaceous perennials die down.

AUTUMN

Summer Early summer flowers burst into bloom and the vegetable garden produces its first crops. The days get longer and the temperatures increase. Baskets and patio pots must be watered regularly and birdbaths topped up daily as rainfall decreases. Insects multiply and you can hear the buzz of bees at work as they pollinate your plants.

Growing with nature

Gardeners can worry a lot about bugs and other creatures nibbling at their prize flowers or vegetables. Though we might be tempted to think a garden belongs solely to us, many insects and animals also make it their home, so we should respect their rights too.

▶ Creepy-crawlies are fascinating to watch and many are beneficial.

Getting a balance
You don't need to use chemicals for every type of pest. For every sort of bad guy there is a predator that feeds on it. Sometimes there will be so many pests that you will notice them on your plants. This is because it can take a little while for the good guys to move in and eat them! But, rather than reaching for the bug killer and risk harming beneficial insects too, it is better to wait a while. With some chemical-free techniques you can grow healthy plants without harming vulnerable creatures such as bumble-bees.

Encouraging the good guys
Although you might be scared of spiders or bees, they are actually extremely helpful and important, so should be encouraged. Here are some of the most beneficial insects and animals for the garden:

Bees Almost all types of bee are under threat. They are vital pollinators. Don't use insecticides or weedkillers. Leave untidy corners with weeds and long grass, and provide nectar plants.

Birds Feeding birds year round and creating habitats (shelters and places to nest) encourages them to stay and forage for insects. Even seed-eating birds feed their young on insects.

Centipedes These are brown, fast-moving hunters with lots of legs that skulk in similar places to ground beetles. Build them a log pile home.

Frogs and toads These amphibians eat flies and slugs. They like the cover of long grass and log piles as well as damp places, such as bog gardens or mini ponds.

Ground beetles These fast-moving predators scurry unseen beneath leaf litter, bark mulch and ground cover plants, where they attack insect pests and slugs at night.

Hoverflies These flies look like small wasps. Their larvae gobble up aphids, and adults are excellent pollinators, so they are a welcome addition to the garden. Provide nectar-rich flowers, especially in white, yellow or orange colours to tempt them.

Lacewings Larvae of these boggle-eyed beauties with green or brown bodies and lacy wings love aphids. *See* 'Lacewing Lodge' on page 183.

Ladybirds Both the larvae and adults of these spotted beetles munch aphids. An evergreen climber-covered wall will shelter adults over winter.

Spiders Web builders and species that pounce on prey are useful for controlling mosquitoes and gnats.

MAKING A GROUND BEETLE TRAP
If you want a closer look at these beneficial beetles, check this trap each morning, then release them.

1 Dig a hole with a trowel just large enough to hold a clean tin can.

2 Put the can in the hole so that the rim is just below the soil surface.

3 Push four pebbles into the soil around the submerged can.

4 Place a flat tile over the trap. Camouflage with twigs.

MAKING A SLUG OR SNAIL TRAP

Slugs and snails can munch through your plants, so trap them and release away from your garden.

1 Eat half a grapefruit. Turn the skin upside down and place on the ground by target plants.

2 Leave the trap overnight, then next morning see who's taken the bait!

MAKING AN EARWIG TRAP

If you see earwigs on your crysanthemums, dahlias or artichokes, trap them and put on the compost heap.

1 Fill a clay plant pot with hay or straw. Push a stout cane into the ground between plants.

2 Upturn the pot and balance it on the end of the cane. Earwigs will be drawn to the pot.

Controlling the bad guys

Most of the time you can ignore the following creatures, but occasionally they cause problems in particular areas of the garden, such as the vegetable plot. Picking the culprits off by hand is a quick and environmentally friendly way of tackling many garden pests, but you may need to take more action. Here are some of the common culprits:

Aphids Also known as greenfly, aphids can be white, pink or black. These tiny sap-sucking insects collect around shoot tips and flower-buds, causing leaves and blooms to shrivel. They also spread viruses. Rub off colonies between your thumb and forefinger or blast them off plants with a strong jet of water from a hosepipe. Encourage natural predators, such as lacewings, ladybirds and insect-eating birds.

Caterpillars Many caterpillers grow into beautiful butterflies and moths, but some species have huge appetites for certain plants, such as cabbages and other brassicas. You'll need keen eyesight as they can be very well camouflaged. Pick off even the tiny ones as soon as you spot them and relocate in a wild patch, long grass or hedgerow. Stop adult butterflies from laying eggs on crops by covering plants with a fine garden mesh or horticultural fleece.
CAUTION Some caterpillars have poisonous or irritant hairs or bristles. Don't touch them if you aren't sure, or you can wear gloves.
Earwigs These minibeasts are not usually a problem in the garden, despite their fearsome-looking pincers. However, if you grow globe artichokes, dahlias or chrysanthemums, they can hide in the flowers and munch away unnoticed. Trap (see box above) and transfer to the compost heap.
Slugs and snails These molluscs love to eat big ragged holes in delicate flowers, young leaves and seedlings. They hide away during the daytime, so the best way to catch them in the act is to wait until nightfall. Ask your parents to go on a torch-lit hunt with you after dark. Wear thin gloves if you don't like the slime! You could also put out grapefruit traps (see box above). Take collected molluscs to a wild patch well away from vulnerable plants. You can also try barriers of grit (which they don't like to crawl over) around targeted plants or position copper tape around pot rims.

▲ Blast off aphids with a strong jet of water.

▲ Wearing gloves, hand-pick and relocate caterpillars.

Recycling

Everyone can be involved in recycling, whether it is sorting rubbish into the right piles or collecting peelings for the compost heap. There are plenty of projects in this book that use recycled materials and not only is it good for the environment, but it saves money too.

▶ *It is easy to make your own compost using apple cores and other kitchen scraps.*

Making things last

Gardeners often pride themselves on looking after their clay pots, plant labels, bamboo canes and tools well. Some have spades, forks and rakes that go back generations because they have been cared for. As long as you clean them out, you can use plant pots and seed trays over and over again. Before there were garden centres and home improvement stores, gardeners would make do and mend, repairing anything that got broken, and they were inventive. Try to follow that example and keep an eye open for things such as food containers and packaging that could be put to good use in the garden.

What to recycle

Reduce the amount of rubbish you throw away and benefit the garden at the same time by recycling the following items:

Jam jars Use jam jars for sprouting seedlings, rooting cuttings in water or for airtight seed storage. Decorate with glass paints to make pretty nightlight holders for summer evenings on the patio.

▲ *Jam jar*

Newspaper Use newspaper to line the base of runner bean or sweet pea trenches, to supply moisture to the roots. Water well. You can also roll pieces to make long, tube-like containers for starting off the sweet pea seeds. The long taproot can grow in the tube. You can also use layers of black and white newsprint to mulch fruit and vegetables to suppress weeds and hold in moisture. Weigh down with bricks. Scrunch up newspaper and mix into the compost heap to add air and soak up excess moisture.

▲ *Newspaper*

Cardboard Shred cardboard and add it to the compost heap in alternating layers with grass clippings, soft hedge clippings and kitchen vegetable scraps. Use kitchen paper roll inners and cardboard egg boxes for sowing seeds and potting plants.

▲ *Cardboard*

Plastic Cut up clear plastic bottles to make mini windowsill propagators (*see* page 41), mini cloches and slug guards (*see* page 41). Plastic yogurt pots, milk bottles and soup cartons can be used as plant pots of varying sizes. Cut white plastic down to make plant labels (*see* page 124) and use coloured bottle lids for decorating the heads of cane toppers (*see* page 125).

▲ *Plastic*

▲ *Look for objects around the house or at car boot sales or junk shops to recycle as pots or garden decorations.*

From kitchen to garden

Fruit and vegetable scraps, peelings, apple cores and so on can all be collected and kept in a covered container for a few days before being transferred to the compost heap. *See pages 36–7 for how to build your own quick and easy heap* or, alternatively, put this kind of kitchen waste into a wormery where a special kind of worm processes the mix and converts it to a fine quality compost and liquid fertilizer. Kits are available or ask your parent to help you build your own wormery.

Other indoor materials that you can add to the compost heap include tea bags and coffee grounds, egg boxes and toilet roll centres. Don't use cooked materials or any animal products.

▶ *Collect fruit and vegetables scraps for composting in a container.*

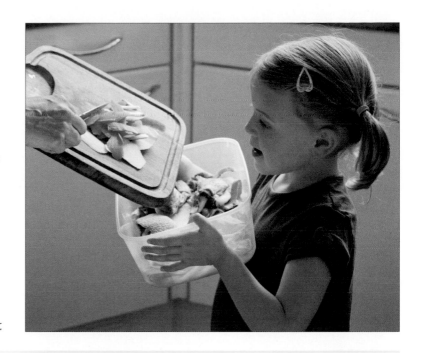

MAKING RECYCLED PLANT POTS

Materials ranging from cardboard egg cartons to yogurt pots can be used for growing seeds, cuttings and young plants. The advantage of cardboard containers is that they gradually disintegrate and plantlets can be put straight into the ground still in their pots, avoiding disturbing the roots. Egg cartons not only make perfect holders for chitting seed potatoes on the windowsill, but they can also be filled with compost for seed sowing or for growing on seedlings. Yogurt cartons only need a few drainage holes to be turned into mini plant pots.

1 With adult help, cut the top off a 1.2 litre/2 pint or 2.4 litre/4 pint milk container using a pair of scissors. Lay the bottle flat and puncture down into the plastic with the point of one blade. Take great care when using scissors.

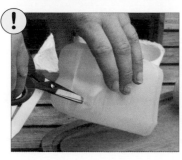

2 To create drainage holes, puncture the plastic in a few places with adult help. The top section can be used as a funnel, or for sinking, pointed-end down, into the ground to direct water to the roots.

3 With adult help, cut the cardboard inner from a finished roll of kitchen paper in half widthways. These are ideal as they will biodegrade when planted out and provide nice deep pots for seedlings.

4 With adult help, make four or five cuts in one end of the tube and fold the pieces inwards to form the base of the pot. Turn it up the right way and fill with compost. Ideal for pea and bean seeds.

Hands-on gardening

In the following pages you will discover many of the skills you need as a gardener, from making compost out of recycled materials to collecting and saving water, pruning, weeding and deadheading. Soon you will be growing your own plants from seed (collected from your own garden) and learning how to take different kinds of cuttings.

Clever compost

Compost is made up of rotted down scraps, prunings, grass cuttings and cardboard. Not only will your garden benefit from the rich mix of plant foods and other helpful ingredients, but you'll also be able to do more recycling and throw away a lot less, which is good for the environment. This handy compost technique is easy to carry out in a spare corner of the garden, provided you follow a few simple rules.

you will need

- **border fork**
- **stiff plastic clematis mesh**, 1m/3ft width
- **1.2m/4ft bamboo canes**, 4–5
- **rubber mallet**
- **Cane Heads** (see page 125)
- **garden twine** or **plastic-coated wire plant ties**
- **plastic refuse sack**
- **clothes pegs**
- **scissors**
- **non-woody prunings**
- **annual weeds**, seed-heads removed
- **secateurs**
- **kitchen waste**, such as raw fruit and vegetable
- **teabags**
- **coffee grounds** and **paper filters**
- **cardboard**, ripped up into small pieces
- **cardboard kitchen roll inners**
- **compostable food packaging**
- **fibre** or **recycled pulp egg boxes** or **cartons**
- **grass cuttings**

plastic refuse sack

fibre egg box

banana skins

1 Fork over the ground to loosen the soil and improve drainage. Arrange the plastic clematis mesh to form a circle, and knock in bamboo canes with a mallet to keep the mesh upright. Adult supervision is required.

2 To protect your eyes while you work, push on polystyrene cane tops. Tie the mesh securely to the canes at several points along their length using garden twine or plastic-coated wire plant ties.

3 Line the mesh with a refuse sack, attaching it with pegs. Make a few holes in the bottom of the sack with scissors and ensure that it is touching the ground to allow worms to enter.

4 Put some non-woody prunings and annual weeds in the bottom to provide drainage. Ask an adult to help you cut them up with secateurs if they are too hard to break up by hand.

5 Over a period of several weeks, continue adding alternating layers of wetter and drier materials to the refuse sack. For example, follow wet or damp material, such as vegetable scraps, teabags and coffee grounds or used filters from the kitchen with dry material, such as torn-up cardboard, egg boxes and compostable food packaging, then add grass cuttings on top.

6 When the bag is full, but not too heavy, unclip the pegs and lift it out of the mesh surround. It's easier to do this with two people. Tie off the top of the bag with garden twine.

 = Watch out! Sharp or dangerous tool in use.   = Watch out! Adult help is needed.

7 Position a new plastic sack in the mesh and begin filling it with garden and kitchen waste as described. Meanwhile, put the filled, sealed bags in a shady corner of the garden, standing on bare earth.

8 After a year or more, the contents of the bags will have turned into compost. Coarse, twiggy material will take longer to break down. Dig the compost into borders to improve your soil.

TOP TIPS

▶ Mix kitchen scraps or lawn clippings with absorbent materials, such as shredded cardboard and egg cartons, to avoid the compost becoming too wet and airless, which would make it slimy.

▶ Water the contents of the bag occasionally during hot weather if necessary.

Be water wise!

During hot weather there is less rain and plants get thirsty more quickly, so you need to give them a drink more often. It is important, though, that we all try and save water in the house and the garden, especially in the summer. So, here are some simple ideas for collecting and reusing water for the garden, as well as ways to help plants stay moist for longer.

you will need

- watering can
- spade
- chipped bark, garden compost, manure, coir or cocoa shells, for mulching
- plastic bag or sheet
- scissors
- crocks
- gravel
- moisture-retentive potting compost with added water-retaining gel crystals

- plant
- bucket of water
- glass or acrylic chippings

bark

cocoa shells

TOP TIPS

► Create a shallow, circular groove around newly planted specimens and bank the soil up to stop water from the can running away. It then pools and sinks in round the roots right where it's needed.

► Another trick is to cut the bottom out of a large plastic bottle and bury it, top end down, next to the plant. Water into the bottle to reach the roots directly.

1 Mulching is an excellent way of sealing moisture into the ground round plant roots but it needs to be at least 8cm/3in deep to work, and the ground must be damp beforehand. Check the area and water if necessary.

2 Apply mulch from early to late spring when the ground is naturally moist. Shovel on bark, garden compost, manure, coir or cocoa shells. Keep it clear of the neck of plants. Adult supervision is required.

3 Plants in porous clay or terracotta pots lose moisture more quickly than those in wood, glazed ceramic or plastic pots. Lining clay pots with thin plastic before planting them reduces moisture-loss.

4 You can recycle thin plastic bags. To avoid drainage problems, pull the bag through the hole at the bottom of the pot and cut the end off with scissors. Adult supervision is required.

5 Add crocks and gravel for drainage, then pour in some moisture-retentive compost with added water-retaining gel crystals. Some mixtures have this in already. Try the plant for size.

6 Plunge a plant in a bucket of water and wait for the bubbles to stop. Plant, adding compost, leaving a gap at the top. Trim the plastic to be level with the top of the pot.

7 Mulches can also be decorative and made from materials that don't rot down, such as glass or acrylic chips. They can still help to conserve moisture. Water the newly positioned plant thoroughly.

8 Water in the kitchen used for peeling and preparing fruit and vegetables might contain soil or dirt but it's perfectly fine for watering plants. Instead of pouring it down the sink, hold the peelings back with your hand, pour the water on the garden, then compost the peelings.

TOP TIP

▶ Water in the cool of morning or evening, not in the heat of the day. Concentrate on new plantings and give vulnerable plants a good long drink at ground level under their leaves rather than lots of little overhead sprinklings.

Rainwater collector

Collecting rainwater in a special butt is good for the environment and many plants prefer it to tap water.

you will need

- **water butt connection kit**
- **hacksaw** (for adult use only)
- **water butt**
- **water butt extension kit** (optional)
- **water butt stand** or **bricks**
- **childproof lid**
- **watering can**

watering can

TOP TIP

▶ Rainwater is perfect for most houseplants, especially if the tap water is hard. Some plants dislike the shock of cold water so top up indoor watering cans with water from the butt and let it warm up.

1 You can fit a water butt to any drainpipe on the house or garage and, if you fit guttering and drainpipes to sheds and greenhouses, you can collect rainwater from them too if you have more than one butt.

2 Ask an adult to help you set up one or more water butts in your selected position. Buy a connection kit that diverts water from a drainpipe to the butt, but which prevents the water butt from overflowing.

3 Ask an adult to cut the drainpipe with a hacksaw so that you can fit the water diverter, following packet instructions. Push the flexible pipe into the top of the butt. A water butt stand or bricks raises the butt to allow for watering cans.

4 When it rains, average-size water butts quickly fill up, but they also empty quickly too! Make the most of the work you've already done, if you like, by connecting another butt using an extension kit, which collects any overflow.

5 To prevent accidents and to stop debris falling into the water, it is essential that you fit a childproof lid on to the butt. Keeping out sunlight also stops green algae forming. Use a space-saving butt for tight corners.

  = Watch out! Sharp or dangerous tool in use. = Watch out! Adult help is needed.

Mini cloches and slug guards

Don't throw away plastic bottles. You can use them to make a mini cloche, a slug barrier or a mini propagator.

you will need
- large, clear plastic bottles
- scissors

TOP TIP

▶ It is easy to make a mini propagator at home from plastic bottles. Ask an adult to help you cut the middle section out of a bottle so that the top and bottom segments fit neatly together. Make some holes in the base for drainage and you have a propagator.

Step 1

Step 2

4 If you leave the lid screwed on the bottle cloche, the air inside will become warm and moist, which is ideal for plant growth. As the plantlet gets stronger you can remove the lid to increase the airflow and finally remove the cloche altogether.

plastic bottle

1 Ask an adult to help you cut the bottom off the plastic bottle using a pair of scissors. Cut as near to the bottom as you can so you have more bottle to work with. Cut off the top to make a mini cloche. Save the middle section.

2 Protect seedlings and young plantlets by covering them with the bottle cloche. Push it into the ground to stop it blowing over. The plastic keeps the plant warm and helps to protect it from slug attack.

3 The middle part of the bottle can be used to make a barrier for seedlings against slugs, especially in the vegetable patch where there are lots of tasty temptations! Simply push the base into the soil so it doesn't blow over.

Plant makeovers!

Two jobs that really tidy up the garden are weeding and deadheading. When you remove faded blooms you also encourage more to follow, especially with annuals, which can stop flowering if they are allowed to create seeds. Pruning also allows you to control a plant's shape and size and to remove damaged, diseased or weak growth. Note, not all plants require pruning and you should only use secateurs with an adult's help and supervision.

you will need
- **flower scissors**
- **secateurs** or **hand pruners**
- **gardening gloves (optional)**
- **hand shears**
- **hand** or **border fork**
- **bark chips**, **pine needles**, **coir** or **cocoa shells**

TOP TIP
▶ Prune deciduous shrubs and climbers (those that lose their leaves in winter) according to when they flower. For spring- and early summer-flowering kinds, such as forsythia, mock orange, weigela and large-flowering clematis, prune immediately after flowering. For late summer- and autumn-flowering kinds, such as *Clematis viticella* varieties, butterfly bush, and patio and bush roses, prune in spring.

1 Most single, wiry-stemmed flowers are easier to deadhead with flower scissors. Cut the faded bloom off at the base of the stem rather than just behind the head. Adult supervision is required.

2 Some soft or fleshy-stemmed flowers, such as those on this day lily, can be pinched out with your thumb and forefinger, leaving the freshly opened blooms and buds in the head to develop further.

3 With flower spires, cut the whole stem off at the base, rather than picking off individual blooms. Do this with plants such as hosta (shown here), penstemon, campanula and hollyhock.

4 Deadhead flowering shrubs, like roses, with secateurs or hand pruners. Ask an adult for help, and wear gloves if necessary. Cut away dead, diseased or weak growth at the same time.

5 Trimming with hand shears removes faded flowers on plants such as lavender and marguerite daisy and means you can shape the plant. Adult supervision is required.

6 Annual weeds are usually easy to pull out by hand, especially when still young and with a small root system. Add to the compost heap, having first removed any seed-heads.

(!) = Watch out! Sharp or dangerous tool in use.   = Watch out! Adult help is needed.

7 Perennial weeds living one year to the next usually have a big, tough taproot or creeping root network. Dig out as much of the root as you can with a hand or border fork as remaining pieces make more weeds.

8 Mulch the area with a thick bark, pine needle, coir or cocoa shell mulch (at least 8cm/3in deep) to prevent more weeds coming up in the flower border. Weeds compete with flowers for food, water and light, so need to be controlled.

cocoa shells

secateurs

bucket of weeding tools

Seed harvest

Collecting your own seed is satisfying and so easy! Fresh seed germinates more quickly than old stored seed, and harvesting flower and even vegetable seed from the garden saves money too. The main thing to bear in mind is to keep everything dry when harvesting, processing or cleaning and storing the seed. Don't gather seed from dead or diseased plants. Seal envelopes in an airtight container and keep in a cool place for up to two years.

you will need
- **scissors**
- **sheet** of **paper**
- **white envelopes**
- **coloured pens**, **pencils** or **crayons**
- **paper bag**

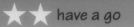

coloured pencils

plant list
- **Annual poppy**
  Papaver spp.
- **Bellflower**
  Campanula persicifolia
- **Big quaking grass**
  Briza maxima
- **Cosmos**
  Cosmos bipinnatus
- **Dusty miller or rose campion**
  Lychnis coronaria
- **English lavender**
  Lavandula angustifolia
- **Everlasting sweet pea**
  Lathyrus latifolius
- **French and African marigold**
  Tagetes

- **Granny's bonnet**
  Aquilegia vulgaris
- **Love-in-a-mist**
  Nigella damascena
- **Pot marigold**
  Calendula officinalis
- **Purple top verbena**
  Verbena bonariensis
- **Sunflower**
  Helianthus annuus

sunflower seeds

1 When a flower-head has faded, dried off and produced seed, as shown here with this lavender, cut the stems using scissors and take them inside. Gather one species at a time. Adult supervision is required.

2 Some seed drops easily when it is ripe, but for others you will need to keep the mature flower-heads for about a week in a warm, dry place. When you are ready to collect, fold a piece of paper in half.

3 Holding the lavender heads over the paper, gently rub the old flowers between your fingers to release the shiny black seeds. Use the same method for purple top verbena.

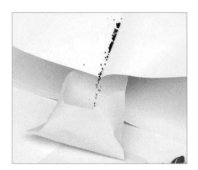

4 Carefully lift the two halves of the paper to form a scoop so that you can direct the seed into an envelope. Write the plant name and date on the envelope, then seal.

5 Hand-decorated packets of seed make lovely presents. Use pens or crayons to draw pictures of the plant in flower on the envelope so you know at a glance what it is.

6 For seed that scatters easily, such as quaking grass, dusty miller, poppy and bellflower, put a paper bag over the heads, cut the stems and, holding the bag securely, tip upside-down.

7 After a week in a warm place, much of this *Aquilegia* seed will have dropped into the bag. Empty the seed on to a sheet of paper. Hold the pods upside down and tap to shake out the remainder.

8 Try to separate as much debris or chaff (remains of the pod or flower) from the seed as possible. With lightweight debris and larger, heavier seed, gently blow the chaff away.

FACT FILE

SEEDS OF CHANGE

Not all plants sown from collected seed will end up looking the same as the original plant you collected it from.

Jam jar cuttings

It's fun to try rooting all kinds of cuttings in water, including houseplants, patio plants, herbs and shrubs. Some, such as African violets, root from a single leaf!

you will need
- **scissors**
- **clean glass jars**
- **small pots**
- **potting compost**
- **kitchen foil** or **waxed paper** (optional)
- **elastic band** (optional)

plant list
- ✳ **African violet**
  Saintpaulia ionantha
- ✳ **Busy Lizzie**
  Impatiens spp. and varieties
- ✳ **Coleus**
  Solenostemon scutellarioides
- ✳ **Geranium**
  Pelargonium spp.
- ✳ **Giant inch plant**,
  Tradescantia fluminensis
- ✳ **Mint**
  Mentha spp.

busy Lizzie

1 Cut off healthy young shoots with scissors (adult supervision is required) or break off with your hands. Have a jar of water ready.

2 Prepare the cuttings, in this case mint, by nipping off the lower leaves. You just need a few at the top of the cutting. Trim just below the bottom leaf joint.

3 Put a handful of cuttings into the glass jar so that the stems are covered with water. Place on a warm, light window ledge.

4 After a while you will see tiny roots starting to appear from the leaf joints along the submerged stems. Allow these to grow a little more.

5 When a good root system has developed, pot the cuttings up.

6 Plants with hairy or felted leaves, such as African violet, or ones that dislike wet conditions, such as geraniums, must be rooted with their leaves held above the surface of the water.

7 Fit a piece of foil or waxed paper over a glass jar and hold it in place with an elastic band.

8 Make holes in the foil or paper with scissors (adult supervision is required). Slot the cuttings or African violet leaves through the holes and pour enough water to cover the base of the stems through one of the holes.

African violet

Baby plants

It's possible to make more plants from semi-ripe cuttings in summer. You'll be amazed at how many plants you can raise from just one little piece!

you will need

- **knife**
- **chopping board**
- **small pots** or a **plastic bottle**, cut in half
- **cuttings compost**
- **pencil**
- **plant labels**
- **pen**
- **bowl** of **water**
- **plastic bag**
- **elastic band**
- **slender garden canes**, 3–4
- **medium pots**, filled with cuttings compost
- **scissors**

plant list

- ✳ **Beard tongue**
  Penstemon cvs.
- ✳ **Butterfly bush**
  Buddleja davidii
- ✳ **Geranium**
  Pelargonium
- ✳ **Hydrangea (mop head and lacecap)**
  Hydrangea macrophylla cvs.
- ✳ **Lavender**
  Lavandula spp. and cvs.
- ✳ **Sage**
  Salvia officinalis and cvs.
- ✳ **Thyme**
  Thymus spp.

1 In late summer you can take semi-ripe or heel cuttings from plants such as sage, shown here. Pull off side shoots with a piece of the main stem (heel) attached.

2 Trim off lower leaves with a knife on a chopping board. Ask an adult to help you. Trim away any long strips of bark.

3 Put some grit in the bottom of the pots or bottle. Make planting holes with a pencil. Put a cutting in each and firm in. Label.

4 Water the compost. Fit a clear plastic bag over the pot, support with canes and hold in place with an elastic band, or fit the top of the bottle over the bottom.

5 Place the pot or bottle in a light position, such as a windowsill, and leave for 2–8 weeks to root. When the plants have grown about 2cm/¾in they can be very carefully transplanted into slightly bigger individual pots. Take care not to damage the fragile roots when you move the plants.

6 Softwood or tip cuttings of plants such as courgette, tomato and fuchsia are taken earlier in the year using the top of a non-flowering shoot. Pinch off a cutting (*see Step 1*), trim the base under a leaf joint (as shown) with scissors (adult supervision is required), take off lower leaves and pot up in the same way.

Dividing plants

When planning a new border it can be costly to buy all the plants you need to fill the space. Dividing newly purchased plants or digging up and dividing perennials already in the garden can be a great solution. Adult supervision is required for cutting the root-ball.

you will need

- **slightly potbound plant** with **lots of young shoots** (*see Plant List*), 1
- **bucket** of **water**
- **old kitchen knife**
- **chopping board**
- **15–20cm/6–8in plastic plant pots**, 5
- **peat-free potting compost**
- **slow-release fertilizer granules**
- **watering can**
- **plant labels**, 5
- **pencil**

plant list

- **Aster**
  Aster
- **Bee balm**
  Monarda
- **Bellflower**
  Campanula
- **Black-eyed Susan**
  Rudbeckia
- **Border phlox**
  Phlox
- **Crane's bill**
  Geranium
- **Day lily**
  Hemerocallis
- **Funkia, plantain lily**
  Hosta
- **Ice plant**
  Sedum spectabile
- **Michaelmas daisy**
  Aster
- **Ornamental sage**
  Salvia
- **Peruvian lily**
  Alstroemeria

- **Purple coneflower**
  Echinacea
- **Shasta daisy**
  Leucanthemum x *superbum*
- **Sneezeweed**
  Helenium
- **Turtle's head**
  Chelone
- **Yarrow, milfoil**
  Achillea

purple coneflower

day lily

1 In spring, look for potted plants that are sprouting lots of new shoots, either in the garden or at a garden centre. When you gently ease the root-ball out of its pot you should see strong root growth.

2 It doesn't matter if it is slightly potbound – you will be giving room to grow when you divide it. Plunge the plant in a bucket of water and wait for the bubbles to stop. Try pulling the roots apart with your hands.

3 Sometimes it is easier to cut the root-ball with an old kitchen knife rather than pulling it. It doesn't need to be very sharp but take care when cutting and ask an adult to help.

4 Depending on the size of the plant and how many pieces of shoot (each with a reasonable-size chunk of root) you can separate off, you could end up with 3–7 divisions.

5 Plant or pot each small division into a plastic plant pot three-quarters filled with potting compost mixed with some slow-release fertilizer. Follow the packet instructions.

6 The pot should be large enough to give the plant plenty of room to grow, but not too huge. Firm the soil around the roots with your hands, water and label.

 = Watch out! Sharp or dangerous tool in use.   = Watch out! Adult help is needed.

7 Stand the young plants in a sheltered spot to grow on. Don't allow the compost to dry out. When the pots are filled with roots, and the shoots are growing strongly, plant out in the garden.

TOP TIP

▶ Divide herbaceous perennial plants every 2–3 years in spring or autumn. Ask an adult to help you dig the plant out, and, using two garden forks back to back as levers, prise the roots apart. Chop out dead bits and replant the younger sections in improved soil.

dividing plants   **49**

Hardwood cuttings

Though slow, this is one of the easiest ways to propagate shrubs and roses as well as several kinds of fruit.

you will need
- trowel
- digging spade (optional)
- washed horticultural sand
- secateurs
- watering can

plant list
- **Blackcurrant**
  Ribes nigrum
- **Butterfly bush**
  Buddleja davidii
- **Bush, patio and shrub roses**
  Rosa
- **Coloured-stemmed dogwoods**
  Cornus spp.
- **Common aspen**
  Populus tremula
- **Forsythia**
  Forsythia
- **Gooseberry**
  Ribes uva-crispa
- **Mock orange**
  Philadelphus
- **Ornamental elder**
  Sambucus
- **Privet**
  Ligustrum
- **Shrubby honeysuckle**
  Lonicera nitida
- **Weigela**
  Weigela cvs.
- **Willow**
  Salix

rose

privet

1 Prepare a narrow trench in a sheltered part of a border where you won't need to dig for a year. Use a trowel or ask an adult to help you open up a slit in the ground with a digging spade. The trench or slit should be about 5cm/2in wide and 20cm/8in deep when you have finished. Reserve the soil.

2 To help the cuttings roots and to improve poor drainage, add some sand to the trench.

3 With adult help, take some hardwood cuttings from one of the plants in the Plant List. Cut stems about the thickness of a pencil and 15–30cm/ 6–12in long with secateurs.

4 To help you remember which way up the cuttings grow, cut the top off at an angle. Cut off any soft shoot tips.

5 Put the cuttings upright into the trench so that about two-thirds of the stem is below ground. The angled cut should be at the top!

6 Move the soil back into the trench and firm the cuttings in well with your hands. Water as necessary during dry spells.

7 When you gently lift the cuttings the following autumn, they will have roots and new shoots and be ready for planting directly into a border.

 = Watch out! Sharp or dangerous tool in use. = Watch out! Adult help is needed.

Rooting runners

This propagation method takes advantage of the way some plants grow, sending out stems with baby plants on the end that are ready to root.

you will need
- **plants** with **offshoots/runners** (*see* Plant List)
- **plastic pots**
- **cuttings compost**, such as John Innes No.1
- **trowel**
- **plastic-coated training wire**, cut into short lengths

plant list
✳ **Bugle**
Ajuga reptans
✳ **Ivy**
Hedera helix
✳ **Lesser periwinkle**
Vinca minor
✳ **Pick-a-back plant**
Tolmiea menziesii
✳ **Spider plant**
Chlorophytum comosum
✳ **Strawberry**
Fragaria

spider plant

1 Some houseplants, including the familiar spider plant and pick-a-back plant, are fun and easy to root from runners. Fill a pot with compost using a trowel.

2 Pin the individual babies with lengths of wire bent over so that the base of each is in contact with the soil.

3 In summer, strawberry plants make lots of runners and you can increase your strawberry bed very quickly and easily by rooting the babies. Either pin down the runners in contact with soil using wire pins (as in Step 2) in the border or bury a pot of cuttings compost next to the plant and pin into that.

4 Once the babies have made their own roots you can cut the stem attaching them to the mother plant and pot up the plantlets individually.

5 Many plants, such as ivy and periwinkle, root where they touch the ground at each leaf cluster. Pin down shoots to speed rooting.

TOP TIP
▶ You can get many shrubs (such as cotoneaster), climbers, (such as honeysuckle), and fruits (such as blackberry) to root, by bending a stem to lie on, or loop down into, the ground and out again. Hold in place with a stone so that the stem is in contact with soil. This is called layering.

Fork to fork

You'll be amazed at how many different kinds of tasty herbs, sweet and juicy fruits and fresh vegetables you can grow even if you don't have any beds or borders. Lots of crops can be raised in pots, troughs and hanging baskets. This chapter is all about using your garden fork to make food for your table fork!

A basket of courgettes

Courgettes or zucchini (that's their Italian name) are very rewarding because they start to crop early and keep producing until autumn. Grow in large containers, such as this log basket, or in well-manured ground, from seed or bought plants. You'll only need one or two. Try a round, striped or coloured variety for something different. Crop when fruits are small and tender. If you leave them for too long then courgettes turn into marrows! Wear gloves if your skin is sensitive to the bristles.

you will need

- **courgette seeds** (*see* Plant List), 1–3
- **small plant pots**, 1–3
- **peat-free seed** and **cuttings compost**
- **windowsill propagator**
- **wicker log basket**
- **heavy-duty bin liner**
- **scissors**
- **gravel**
- **trowel**
- **peat-free potting compost** with **added loam (John Innes)**, 1 x 80-litre/21-gallon bag
- **watering can**
- **liquid plant food**, for edible plants

plant list

✹ **Green types of courgette (*Cucurbita pepo*):**
'Bambino' F1 (patio type)
'Black Forest' F1 (climber)
'Defender' F1 (virus-resistant)
'Jaguar' (no bristles)
'Tosca' (compact, mildew resistant)
'Tristan' F1 (no bristles)
'Venus' F1 (compact)

✹ **Yellow types of *Cucurbita pepo*:**
'Gold Rush' F1
'Jemmer' F1 (round fruits)
'Parador' F1
'Soleil' F1

courgette plant

1 Sow the seeds 1cm/½in deep in mid spring in pots of seed and cuttings compost. Stand in a propagator on a warm windowsill. After the seeds have germinated, remove the seedlings from the propagator.

2 When the young plants are growing well, begin to harden them off using a lightly shaded cold frame or by standing the plants out during the day for increasing amounts of time (*see* page 13).

3 After 10–15 days the seedlings can be planted outside. Line a log basket with a bin liner. Make holes in the bottom with scissors and add a layer of gravel using a trowel.

4 Cut open one end of a large bag of peat-free potting compost and turn it upside down into the basket. This is a two-person job so ask an adult to help. Shake out the contents.

5 Break up any lumps in the compost with your hands. Water the compost with a watering can if it is dry. The top layer should be thoroughly moist and ready for planting.

6 Plant one or two courgette plants in the compost, depending on the variety. Some patio varieties, such as 'Bambino' are dwarf and compact, so you could fit two in.

 = Watch out! Sharp or dangerous tool in use. = Watch out! Adult help is needed.

7 Water in the courgettes and keep them well watered as they are thirsty plants. Feed with liquid plant food, such as tomato food, every 14 days. Avoid overhead watering, which promotes powdery mildew.

FACT FILE

ALL SHAPES, SIZES AND SHADES

Courgettes come in a surprising range of types. There are green- or yellow-skinned varieties, ones with striped skins, and as well as the usual cylindrical courgettes, you can grow ones with fruits shaped like tennis balls!

yellow courgettes

Grow bag garden

Even if you don't have any beds or borders you can still grow many vegetables and herbs in grow bags. For this project, you'll need a sunny wall. Although you could grow your own plants from seed in early spring, it is much easier to buy plants.

you will need
- **range** of **edible plants**, (*see* Plant List)
- **felt-tipped pen**
- **grow bags**, 3
- **scissors**
- **bucket** of **water**
- **bamboo canes**, 9
- **corks** or **cane protectors**, 9
- **garden twine**
- **watering can**
- **liquid plant food**, for edible plants

plant list
- ✳ **3 cherry tomato plants**
  Lycopersicon esculentum 'Gardener's Delight' or 'Super Sweet 100'
- ✳ **3 aubergine plants (patio variety)**
  Solanum melongena 'Baby Belle', 'Bonica', 'Baby Rosanna' or 'Mohican'
- ✳ **3 basil plants**
  Ocimum basilicum 'Genovese'
- ✳ **3 bell pepper plants (patio variety)**
  Capsicum annuum var. *annuum* (Grossum Group) 'Redskin' or 'Mohawk'
- ✳ **1 tray of French marigolds**
  Tagetes patula

TOP TIP
► Plants that have already been hardened off are widely available from most garden centres in early summer. If you buy them from a protected glasshouse area, however, you'll need to do the hardening off yourself (*see* page 13). It takes about two to three weeks. Don't plant outside until after the risk of late frosts has passed.

TOP TIP
► The compost in grow bags is usually compacted. Ask an adult to help you shake the bags and fluff up the compost to make it easier for the plants to root into it.

1 Using one of the larger plants as a template, centre it on a grow bag and draw around the base of the pot with a felt-tipped pen. Repeat to make three evenly spaced circles down the middle of each grow bag.

2 With adult supervision, cut out the circles with a pair of scissors. Prepare a planting hole with your hands. Soak the plants by plunging in a bucket of water until the bubbles stop.

3 Plant the tomatoes in one of the grow bags and lightly firm with your fingers. Tomatoes can be prone to whitefly and traditionally marigolds are used to repel these pests.

4 Make a series of small holes along the front of the grow bag with scissors or simply snip 'X' shapes and peel back the plastic. Plant French marigolds in the holes.

5 Plant the aubergines in a different grow bag and lightly firm with your fingers. If you need to make the holes slightly bigger, snip the circle in four places to ease the root-ball in.

6 Like the pungent French marigolds, aromatic basil is another 'companion plant', helping to naturally protect plants from pests. Plant the basil in holes around the edge of one of the grow bags.

7 Plant the peppers in the final grow bag. Insert tall canes propped against the wall for the tomatoes and stick short canes into the compost for the other plants. Top with corks.

8 Loosely tie in the plants to the canes with garden twine as they grow. Water the grow bags daily. Once flowers appear, feed the plants regularly with liquid plant food, following instructions on the bottle.

twine and scissors

Patio veggie garden

Quick-growing summer vegetables can be grown in all kinds of containers on the patio. For instance, early potatoes are easy to grow in plastic crates (with drainage holes punched through the base). It feels great to be able to pick and eat fresh produce grown just by the back door and there are so many things to try. As well as growing from seed, you can buy potted seedlings.

you will need
- **assorted pots** and **containers**
- **utility knife** (for adult use only)
- **crocks** and **gravel**
- **peat-free potting compost** with **added loam (John Innes)**
- **slow-release fertilizer granules**
- **bamboo canes**
- **wire**
- **garden twine**
- **watering can**
- **liquid plant food**, for edible plants

FACT FILE
SMALL IS BEAUTIFUL
Look out for special dwarf or patio varieties designed for growing in pots. Also use quick-to-mature salads and vegetables that can be picked when still young and tender, such as baby carrots and beetroot. The tomato variety 'Totem' with medium-size fruits and aubergine 'Baby Rosanna' crop in just 20–25cm/8–10in pots, so are ideal for a small space.

tomato 'Totem'

plant list
❋ **Baby beetroot**
  Beta vulgaris 'Boltardy'
❋ **Dwarf French bean**
  Phaseolus vulgaris var. *nanus* 'Maxi'
❋ **Dwarf runner bean**
  Phaseolus coccineus 'Hestia'
❋ **Lettuce**
  Lactuca sativa 'Red Salad Bowl'
❋ **Patio courgette**
  Cucurbita pepo 'Bambino' F1
❋ **Radicchio/Italian chicory**
  Cichorium intybus var. *sativum*
❋ **Radish**
  Raphanus sativus 'Cherry Belle'
❋ **Round carrot**
  Daucus carota 'Parmex'
❋ **Salad onion**
  Allium cepa 'White Lisbon'

1 Any containers you use, whether plant pots and troughs or recycled containers, need to have good drainage. Ask an adult to make holes. Cover these with crocks and gravel.

2 Fill the containers with peat-free compost mixed with some slow-release fertilizer granules. Take a strip of radicchio plantlets, pull the roots apart and plant, firming in gently.

3 For other mild-tasting salad leaves, sow lettuce, such as 'Red Salad Bowl', a wavy edged oak leaf type (shown here). The small, hearting lettuce 'Little Gem' is also a good choice.

4 Some vegetables are quick to grow from seed and you can get several crops in one year. Sow radishes, salad leaves, round carrots and salad onions every two weeks.

 = Watch out! Sharp or dangerous tool in use.   = Watch out! Adult help is needed.

5 Raise or buy baby courgette plants of 'Bambino' and plant three in a large tub. Give them a warm, sheltered place to begin with and ensure the plants are hardened off.

6 Plant dwarf patio varieties of runner and French beans. These will need support, so make a wigwam of canes, coil round some wire and tie in the stems with garden twine.

7 Water all the seedlings. Leafy vegetables and plants with developing fruits need regular watering. Group the containers together to make watering easier.

8 There's only a small amount of compost in each container, so use a slow-release fertilizer at planting time and supplement with regular liquid plant food.

Colourful veg

Some vegetables are too attractive to be kept hidden away in the vegetable plot. Runner beans (main picture) make beautiful flowering climbers and some squash and pumpkin plants can be trained over trellises and archways. Red- or purple-leaved lettuce, curly kale, beetroot and ruby Swiss chard add colour to containers. Try mixing in some edible blooms, pots of purple-podded French beans and tomato-filled baskets.

you will need
- **small pots** and **seed trays**
- **peat-free seed** and **cuttings compost**
- **assorted plants** (*see* Plant List)
- **containers, window boxes** and **hanging baskets**
- **loam-based potting compost**
- **twiggy sticks**
- **sharp knife**
- **barrel**

plant list
- ✳ **Aubergine/eggplant**
  Solanum melongena 'Baby Rosanna'; 'Bonica'; 'Mohican'
- ✳ **Beetroot**
  Beta vulgaris 'Bull's Blood'
- ✳ **Courgette (yellow)**
  Cucurbita pepo 'One Ball', 'Gold Rush' F1
- ✳ **Curly kale (borecole)**
  Brassica oleracea 'Redbor' F1
- ✳ **Dwarf bush tomatoes**
  Lycopersicon esculentum 'Tumbler' F1, 'Totem'
- ✳ **Dwarf French bean**
  Phaseolus vulgaris 'Purple Queen', 'Purple Teepee'
- ✳ **Pumpkin**
  Cucurbita pepo 'Baby Bear', 'Jack Be Little'
- ✳ **Radicchio/Italian chicory**
  Cichorium intybus var. *sativum*
- ✳ **Red cabbage**
  Brassica oleracea var. *capitata* 'Red Jewel'
- ✳ **Red lettuce**
  Lactuca sativa 'Delicato', 'Red Salad Bowl'
- ✳ **Runner bean**
  Phaseolus coccineus
- ✳ **Squash (patty pan type)**
  Cucurbita pepo 'Sunburst' F1
- ✳ **Swiss chard**
  Beta vulgaris var. *flavescens* subsp. *cicla* 'Bright Lights'

1 Fill small pots and seed trays with compost and plant whichever seeds you like. Curly kale is good for autumn and winter cropping. Sow in mid spring and transplant seedlings in early summer to their final spot.

2 Dwarf aubergines, such as 'Baby Rosanna', with its silvery green leaves and dark purple, glossy fruits, make attractive patio plants. Pot on in containers that complement the colour of the flowers and fruits.

3 Aubergine blooms can be as attractive as that of any patio plant. Place the plants in a warm, sheltered spot and team up with tomato 'Totem' and baskets of cascading cherry tomatoes.

4 Dwarf purple French beans are grown in a similar way to runner beans (*see* page 81) but they only need a few twiggy sticks for support. The beans must be cooked before being eaten.

5 Many loose-leaf lettuce varieties (ones that don't make a solid heart) are quick to grow. Choose frilly red leaved types, such as 'Red Salad Bowl' and 'Delicato', for pretty edibles.

6 Radicchio, like lettuce, is easy to grow in pots and troughs. The red-tinged, mild outer leaves cover the dark red and white, strongly flavoured heart – the bit that's often added to salads.

(**!**) = Watch out! Sharp or dangerous tool in use.   ( ) = Watch out! Adult help is needed.

7 The Swiss chard 'Bright Lights' has rainbow coloured stems. Add baby leaves to a plain green salad or ask an adult to help you cut larger leaves, which can be shredded, then steamed or stir-fried.

8 With their large blooms, big leaves and attractive fruits, cucurbits, such as courgettes, squashes and pumpkins, will put on a show when planted in a barrel.

TOP TIP

▶ Swiss chard can survive the winter if the crowns are covered with a mulch of straw or a cloche in winter. Remove protection in spring and mulch soil with manure.

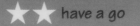
Spud bin

A dustbin might seem like a bizarre planter, but the black plastic heats up quickly and makes for speedy spud growth – just what you want when growing delicious 'new' potatoes at the beginning of the season. Potatoes are actually swollen underground stems that the plant grows to store food in. By partially burying the plant, you force more potato tubers to form and a dustbin has plenty of depth. Put the lid back on overnight if frost is forecast.

you will need

- **seed potato tubers** (see Plant List)
- **egg boxes**
- **plastic dustbin**, 1
- **drill** with a **large drill bit** (for adult use only)
- **gravel**
- **peat-free potting compost** with **added loam** (John Innes)
- **slow-release fertilizer granules** (suitable for fruit and vegetables)
- **watering can**
- **soluble** or **liquid general fertilizer** (suitable for fruit and vegetables)
- **plastic sheet**

TOP TIP

► Provided your potatoes were disease-free, you can reuse the potting compost. Remove any roots and fill the new containers with the soil. Grow quick-maturing salads, such as radish, lettuce and round carrots. Or, keep it until autumn and use for bulb planting. Alternatively, refill the bin, add fertilizer and plant a trailing squash.

potatoes

plant list

✳ **Early and salad varieties of potato (*Solanum tuberosum*):**
'Anya'
'Charlotte'
'Lady Christi'
'Maris Bard'
'Rocket'
'Swift'
'Winston'

WARNING – All green parts of the potato plant are poisonous. Covering developing tubers with compost keeps them in the dark and stops them turning green.

1 Place seed potato tubers in egg boxes, with the end that has the most 'eyes' or buds uppermost. Place on a cool windowsill two weeks before you intend to plant out, and watch the shoots grow.

2 Once the tubers have sprouted, or 'chitted', prepare the dustbin by making drainage holes in the base. Ask an adult to drill these with a drill bit. Plastic potato-growing sacks are a patio garden alternative.

3 Ask an adult to help you pour 13cm/5in of gravel into the base of the dustbin. Add about 15cm/6in of potting compost mixed with some slow-release fertilizer.

4 Taking care not to damage the shoot grown from each potato (these are quite brittle), plant five tubers so that the shoot tips are just showing above the soil surface.

5 As the shoots grow, keep earthing-up the stems. That means adding more potting compost (5cm/2in at a time) to bury the lower stems. Water to keep the soil just moist.

 = Watch out! Sharp or dangerous tool in use. = Watch out! Adult help is needed.

6 Continue adding compost mixed with a little slow-release fertilizer until the soil level is almost at the top. Use additional fertilizer to boost growth when plants are growing well.

7 You'll know it is time to harvest when the flowers appear. These can be quite attractive. You may be able to harvest some potatoes from down the sides of the bin.

8 For the main harvest, spread out a plastic sheet and, with help, tip over the bin and shake the plants and soil out on to it. Delve into the soil and pull out all the tubers you find.

TOP TIP
▶ New potatoes are delicious boiled or steamed, cooled and mixed with mayonnaise and chopped chives or salad onions for home-made potato salad.

Tumbling tomatoes

Trailing bush tomatoes make attractive basket plants and don't look out of place on the patio. You won't be able to resist eating the sweet, cherry-like fruits!

you will need

- **plastic-lined 35cm/14in hanging basket**
- **heavy pot**
- **scissors**
- **peat-free potting compost** (designed for flowering hanging baskets)
- **trowel**
- **water-retaining gel crystals** (see Top Tip)
- **dwarf bush tomato plants** (see Plant List), 3–4
- **bucket** of **water**
- **watering can**
- **liquid tomato food**

plant list
❋ **Trailing bush varieties of tomato (*Lycopersicon esculentum*):**
'Garden Pearl'
'Tumbler'
'Tumbling Tom Red'
'Tumbling Tom Yellow'
'Yellow Pygmy'

cherry tomatoes

TOP TIP
▶ To keep compost evenly moist between waterings, try using water-retaining gel crystals. Add water as per instructions. Mix into the compost before planting.

3 Soak the tomato plants (this variety is 'Tumbler') by plunging them in a bucket of water until the bubbles stop.

1 Stand the basket in a pot to stop it rolling around. Snip two or three holes in the liner about one-third of the way up using scissors. Adult supervision is required.

2 Part-fill with compost using a trowel. Add pre-soaked water-retaining gel crystals, if you like.

4 Put the first tomato plant in the prepared basket, angling it so that it hangs over the edge of the basket slightly.

5 Plant the remaining tomatoes and begin filling in between the root-balls with more potting compost. Firm lightly with your fingers. Water well.

6 Leave a gap of about 2.5cm/1in from the rim of the basket to allow the water to pool and soak in.

7 When the plants are hardened off (see page 13), ask an adult to hang up the basket in a sunny position.

8 Start feeding with tomato food once the first tiny fruits appear.

 = Watch out! Sharp or dangerous tool in use. = Watch out! Adult help is needed.

Swinging strawberries

With pretty flowers and cascades of ripe fruit, this is a must-have project for the productive patio garden! What's more, slugs and snails won't reach the fruits first.

you will need

- **plastic-lined 35cm/14in hanging basket**
- **heavy pot**
- **scissors**
- **peat-free potting compost** with **added loam (John Innes)**
- **trowel**
- **slow-releaser fertilizer granules**
- **water-retaining gel crystals** (*see Top Tip on opposite page*)
- **2-year-old strawberry plants** for **containers** (*see Plant List*), 3–4
- **bucket** of **water**
- **watering can**
- **liquid tomato food**

plant list
✹ **Container varieties of strawberry** (*Fragaria* X *ananassa*):
'Cambridge Favourite'
'Honeoye'
'Flamenco'

Also see page 242

strawberry plant

1 Stand the basket in a pot to stop it rolling around. Snip two or three holes in the liner about one-third of the way up using scissors. Adult supervision is required.

2 Part-fill the basket with compost that has had some slow-release fertilizer granules added, using a trowel. Add some pre-soaked water-retaining gel crystals, if you like.

3 Soak the strawberry plants by plunging them in a bucket of water until the bubbles stop.

4 Put the first plants in the basket, angling them so that they hang over the edge. Fill round the roots with compost as you go.

5 Continue, using up to five plants in total (put one in the middle). Don't forget you can mix varieties to extend fruiting.

6 Firm in the strawberry plants lightly with your fingers, checking that there aren't any gaps between the root-balls.

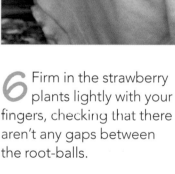

7 Water and ask an adult to hang in a sunny spot. Start feeding with tomato fertilizer once the fruits have started to form.

TOP TIP
▶ Avoid getting leaves, flowers and fruit wet after the initial watering, as this encourages fungal disease. Use a narrow-spouted watering can without a rose to reach under the leaves.

Fabulous figs

Figs can grow really big when planted in the ground, but are easier to manage and to get to fruit when grown in pots. They must have warmth and sunshine.

you will **need**

- **large terracotta pot**, 45–50cm/18–20in in diameter
- **crock** or **tile**
- **gravel**
- **trowel**
- **loam-based potting compost**, such as John Innes No. 3
- *Ficus carica* 'Brown Turkey', 1 plant
- **bucket** of **water**
- **watering can**
- **general-purpose liquid fertilizer**
- **liquid plant food**, such as tomato food

terracotta pot and compost

fig fruit and leaf

1 Cover the hole in the base of a pot with a crock or tile and ask an adult to help pour in about 2.5–5cm/1–2in gravel, or use a trowel.

2 Pour in a small quantity of potting compost. Meanwhile, soak the plant by plunging in a bucket of water until the bubbles stop.

3 Remove the fig from its pot and plant, adding more compost to fill in around the root-ball. Finish about 2½cm/1in below the rim of the pot. Water thoroughly with a watering can.

4 Feed weekly during spring and summer, alternating general-purpose fertilizer with tomato food.

5 Fruits ripen in autumn, turning golden or brown. They have very thin skins that sometimes start to split. The drooping figs pull off easily and should be eaten fresh.

6 After harvesting, pick off any fruits larger than marbles. Protect the plants from frost by putting them under cover.

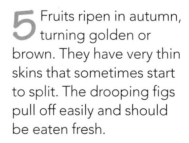

bucket

TOP TIPS

▶ Ask an adult to help you prune the fig plant lightly in late winter using secateurs to make an open bush shape. Remove dead wood in spring.

▶ Pinch summer-grown shoots back to 5–6 leaves in autumn.

▶ Wear gloves to keep the plant's sap off skin, as this may be an irritant when exposed to sunlight.

(!) = Watch out! Sharp or dangerous tool in use.   (🖐) = Watch out! Adult help is needed.

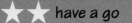
Blueberry bounty

A delicious treat, blueberries are irresistible to both humans and birds, so you need to be quick to pick them unless you cover the crop with netting!

you will need

- **blueberry bushes** (*see* Plant List), 2, different varieties
- **bucket** of **rainwater**
- **ceramic pots**, 2
- **crocks**
- **gravel**
- **ericaceous (lime-free) potting compost**
- **trowel**
- **rainwater**
- **watering can**
- **ericaceous fertilizer**, such as rhododendron and azalea feed
- **larger tub** or **half-barrel**, 2, for potting on in second year
- **bamboo canes**, 12
- **stiff wire** and **pliers** or **garden twine** and **scissors**
- **pea** and **bean netting**
- **clothes pegs**

plant list
✳ **Varieties of blueberry** (***Vaccinium corymbosum***): 'Patriot' | 'Bluecrop' 'Bluegold' 'Blue Pearl'

1 Plunge the bushes in a bucket of rainwater, collected from a water butt. Wait until the bubbles stop. You'll need two varieties for the best crop yield.

3 Add some ericaceous compost to the ceramic pots, using a trowel. Blueberries can't survive unless the soil and water used are lime-free.

5 Water the blueberry plants regularly with rainwater using a watering can. Feed fortnightly in the growing season with some ericaceous fertilizer (rhododendron and azalea feed), following the instructions on the packet.

6 Notice the fiery autumn leaf colour, which is a feature of blueberries. Pick off flower buds in the first spring.

8 Before fruits ripen make a frame with three canes pushed into each tub or barrel. Connect the tops with three canes and join with wire or twine cut to length.

2 Cover the drainage holes in the pot with crocks and ask an adult to help you pour in about 2½cm/1in of gravel.

4 Plant a blueberry bush in each of the prepared ceramic pots, firming the compost lightly around the roots.

7 Allow the plants to flower in the second year. Pot on into larger tubs or half-barrels in the second year.

9 Drape the frame with netting, pulling it taut and fixing with pegs. Leave an opening for picking fruit. Open and close with pegs.

Apple and blackberry pie

These tubs will give you enough fruit to make at least one delicious apple and blackberry pie, especially if you grow a dual cooking/eating variety of apple. It'll produce fruit on its own, especially with other trees in the neighbourhood but, like most apples, it has better crops when it is grown near a type flowering at the same time. All those on our list are compatible. Bees will do the cross-pollinating for you!

you will need
- **wooden half-barrels**, 2
- **crocks**
- **gravel**
- **peat-free soil-based potting compost**
- **slow-release fertilizer granules**
- **apple tree** on **dwarfing rootstock** (*see* Plant List), 1, soaked in water
- **thornless blackberry bush** (*see* Plant List), 1, soaked in water
- **watering can**
- **secateurs**
- **manure**
- **liquid tomato food**
- **bamboo canes**, 5
- **garden twine**
- **pea** and **bean netting**
- **pegs**

FACT FILE
DWARF OR GIANT?
Apples are joined on to different types of roots (rootstocks) in a process called grafting. These rootstocks are numbered according to how vigorous or slow-growing they are. For dwarf apple trees that won't grow much above head height – perfect for patio pots – choose apples on M9 or M27 rootstocks.

dwarf apple tree

plant list
✳ **Varieties of apple** (*Malus domestica*):
  'Discovery'
  'James Grieve'
  'Katy'
  'Sunset'
✳ **Thornless varieties of blackberry** (*Rubus fruticosus*):
  'Helen'
  'Loch Ness'
  'Merton Thornless'
  'Oregon Thornless'

1 Prepare the wooden half-barrels for planting the apple and blackberry plants. Cover the drainage holes with crocks, then ask an adult to help pour in gravel to a depth of about 5cm/2in.

2 Part-fill the tubs with compost, then mix in slow-release fertilizer. Try a plant for depth – the surface of the root-ball should be 5cm/2½in below the rim of the barrel. Firm in and water.

3 Ask an adult to prune container-grown apple trees using secateurs in mid to late summer to control their height, create an open framework of branches and encourage fruiting 'spurs'.

4 This tree was pruned to create a narrow pyramid. Cut the current season's growth by about half and remaining side branches back to two buds from the bottom of the season's growth.

 = Watch out! Sharp or dangerous tool in use. = Watch out! Adult help is needed.

5 Cut to just above an outward-facing bud. Adult supervision is required. Keep tubs well watered, mulch with manure in spring and liquid feed every ten days once flowering begins.

6 Modern thornless blackberries are easy to look after, especially those with upright growing stems. Make a bamboo wigwam and tie stems to it with garden twine.

7 Juicy blackberries will be tempting for the birds, so as the crop develops, stretch fine pea and bean netting over the wigwam and secure with pegs for easier picking access.

8 Pick blackberries over two or three days, keeping fruits refrigerated until you have enough for your pie. Apples are ripe if they come away when the stem is gently twisted.

apple and blackberry pie   69

Tasty hanging basket

All the ingredients for this basket have edible parts or fragrant flowers that can also be used as a garnish or food decoration, such as the pink, ball-shaped chive heads and purple-blue lavender spikes. Nasturtium blooms, sweet viola flowers and French marigold heads are edible too, as well as being insect attractors. Keep picking the parsley, chives, thyme and marjoram for the kitchen.

you will need

- **35cm/14in wire hanging basket**
- **heavy pot**
- **recycled wool** or **coir basket liner**
- **assorted plants** (*see* Plant List)
- **moisture-retentive hanging basket compost**
- **bucket** of **water**
- **slow-releaser fertilizer granules**
- **watering can**

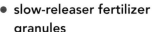

hanging basket

plant list

- ✻ **1 alpine strawberry/ frais des bois plant**
  Fragaria vesca
- ✻ **1 chive plant**
  Allium schoenoprasum
- ✻ **1 dwarf lavender plant**
  Lavandula angustifolia variety
- ✻ **4–5 French marigolds**
  Tagetes patula
- ✻ **1 golden marjoram plant**
  Origanum vulgare 'Aureum'
- ✻ **1 nasturtium**
  Tropaeolum majus

- ✻ **1 parsley plant**
  Petroselinum crispum
- ✻ **2 variegated thymes**
  Thymus 'Doone Valley'
- ✻ **4–5 violas**
  Viola Sorbet Series

alpine strawberries

1 Position a hanging basket in a pot. Unhook the chain and pull it to one side to give you room to work. Add a wool or coir basket liner. Plunge the plants in a bucket of water and wait for the bubbles to stop.

2 Half-fill the basket with moisture-retentive hanging basket compost, and plant the pot-grown nasturtium so that it trails over the edge of the basket. Plant two variegated thymes.

3 To make a pretty contrast to the orange nasturtium flowers, plant golden marjoram. This will form a spreading dome and will eventually cascade over the edge of the basket.

4 Violas have a sweet scent and are shade tolerant. Modern bedding types keep flowering for months if you deadhead them regularly. Plant little clumps between other low-growing herbs.

5 Keep the centre of the basket free so that you can plant a dwarf lavender as a specimen. Once this is in, add a chive plant. This can be split up in autumn or spring for more plants.

6 In the remaining space, squeeze in an alpine strawberry or frais des bois (strawberry of the woods). It's another shade-tolerant plant so won't mind being at the back.

⚠ = Watch out! Sharp or dangerous tool in use. 🐸 = Watch out! Adult help is needed.

7 In gaps between the basket plants, insert a few French marigolds. Deadhead regularly to keep them flowering. Ensure that you don't accidentally introduce tiny slugs or snails, which will eat them up!

8 If there's room, add parsley. Work in extra compost to fill the gaps between root-balls. Firm lightly. Reattach the chain and water thoroughly. Ask an adult to hang in a sunny spot.

TOP TIP

▶ To save planting space, you could sow nasturtium seeds into the compost. The seedlings will come up quickly and should flower well.

tasty hanging basket

Edible flowers

Colourful flowers and petals are fun to use in cooking. Many can be eaten raw as unusual additions to salads.

you will need

- **range** of **edible flowers** (see Plant List)
- **shallow container**
- **colander**
- **mixed salad leaves**, rinsed
- **salad bowl**

plant list

Culinary herbs and vegetables (annual)
- ✳ **Basil**
  Ocimum basilicum
- ✳ **Borage/star flower**
  Borago officinalis
- ✳ **Rocket**
  Eruca vesicaria subsp. *sativa*

Culinary herbs and vegetables (perennial)
- ✳ **Chives**
  Allium schoenoprasum
- ✳ **Culinary mint**
  Mentha spp. and cvs.
- ✳ **Culinary sage**
  Salvia officinalis
- ✳ **Dill**
  Anethum graveolens
- ✳ **Garlic chives/ Chinese chives**
  Allium tuberosum
- ✳ **Marjoram/oregano**
  Origanum spp. and cvs.
- ✳ **Rosemary**
  Rosmarinus officinalis
- ✳ **Thyme**
  Thymus spp. and cvs.

Annual flowers
- ✳ **Cornflower**
  Centaurea cyanus
- ✳ **French marigold**
  Tagetes patula

- ✳ **Nasturtium**
  Tropaeolum majus
- ✳ **Pot marigold**
  Calendula officinalis
- ✳ **Sunflower** (petals)
  Helianthus annuus
- ✳ **Viola/pansy**
  Viola spp.

Perennial flowers
- ✳ **Bee balm**
  Monarda didyma and cvs.
- ✳ **Pink/carnation**
  Dianthus spp. and cvs.
- ✳ **Day lily**
  Hemerocallis spp. and cvs.

WARNING Don't confuse day lily with lily flowers, which are poisonous!

Shrubs and climbers
- ✳ **Honeysuckle**
  Lonicera periclymenum
- ✳ **Jasmine**
  Jasminum officinale
- ✳ **Lavender**
  Lavandula angustifolia cvs.
- ✳ **Rose** (petals)
  Rosa cvs.

nasturtium

1 For the best flavour and texture, pick flowers that have just opened and which aren't showing signs of ageing, such as fading, browning or shrivelling of the petals. Collect in a shallow container.

2 Nasturtiums come in a range of hot colours, including yellow, orange and red, so are great for brightening up green salads and making dishes look exotic or tropical. They have a peppery flavour.

3 Pick the heads of fully opened but not old pot marigolds. Use just the petals in cooking. These were once added to stews in the cooking pot, hence the common name.

4 White-flowered garlic chives, shown here, have a mild garlicky flavour, unlike pink-flowered chive blooms, which are more like onion. Use only very young, freshly opened flowers.

5 Normally only the leaves of rocket are eaten, but the white flowers are edible too. Other members of the family can also be tried, such as broccoli, mustard and mizuna flowers.

6 Some flowers are particularly suited for use in cake decorating or to garnish sweet cordials or fruit salads. The scented clove pinks shown here have a sweet yet spicy flavour.

⚠ = Watch out! Sharp or dangerous tool in use. 🐾 = Watch out! Adult help is needed.

7 Fresh rose petals add colours and flavour to salads. Fragrant roses usually have the best flavour for eating and tiny rose buds look great as decorations.

8 Rinse the flowers gently in a colander. Prepare the salad leaves and mix in the flowers and petals, reserving a few. Transfer to a salad bowl and garnish with the reserved petals.

FACT FILE

DO'S AND DON'TS

• Don't pick or eat any flower that you haven't checked first with an adult. **Some plants are highly poisonous!**

• Don't pick flowers from the roadside or gardens that have been sprayed with any chemicals.

• Do store flowers for a day at the most in airtight containers in the refrigerator.

Windowsill salads

Tasty mixed salad leaves are easy to grow on a windowsill even in spring and autumn when home-grown vegetables are in short supply. You can buy packets of ready-mixed salad leaves and cut-and-come-again lettuce, but you can easily invent your own mix using leftover seed. Add zing with mustard or rocket leaves and colourful lettuce, purple basil and beetroot varieties. Cutting leaves and shoots but leaving the roots allows the plants to keep growing.

you will need
- **small troughs** with **drip tray**, 1–3
- **crocks**
- **gravel**
- **trowel**
- **peat-free potting compost**
- **slow-release fertilizer granules**
- **watering can** with a **fine rose attachment**
- **packets** of **seeds** (see Plant List)

mustard and cress seeds

TOP TIP
▶ If you have any quick-growing salad or bunching onion seeds left over after planting, you can sprinkle a few in with the leafy salad and herb mix to add a subtle onion flavour. The plants don't have to be fully grown before you cut them, so you can harvest them when they are young, at the same time as the quicker-growing salad and herb leaves.

Jen

spring onions

plant list
✳ **Beetroot**
  Beta vulgaris 'Bull's Blood'
✳ **Coriander**
  Coriandrum sativum
✳ **Loose-leaf lettuce varieties**
  Lactuca sativa 'Red Salad Bowl'
✳ **Mizuna varieties**
  Brassica rapa japonica varieties
✳ **Mustard varieties**
  Brassica juncea varieties
✳ **Purple basil**
  Ocimum basilicum 'Purple Ruffles'
✳ **Rocket**
  Eruca vesicaria subsp. *sativa*

1 Set up one or more small plastic troughs with drip trays to keep the windowsill clean. Cover the drainage holes with crocks, then cover the base with a thin layer of gravel using a trowel.

2 Add potting compost, using a trowel. Mix in a small quantity of slow-release fertilizer, following instructions on the packet. The plantlets won't need liquid feeding as they are harvested so quickly.

3 To provide a good base for sowing, firm the compost lightly with your hand. You could also use a piece of wood cut to fit the size of the trough (ask an adult to help).

4 Water the compost using a watering can with a fine rose attachment so that you don't disturb the soil. Preparing the troughs is messy so do it outdoors if you can.

 = Watch out! Sharp or dangerous tool in use.   = Watch out! Adult help is needed.

5 Decide which mix of seeds you want to grow and, taking just a few seeds of each, sprinkle them evenly over the compost surface. Don't sow too thickly – the plants need room to grow.

6 Cover the seeds lightly with more compost. Place the trough on the windowsill. Keep well watered as the seedlings develop. You'll start to see signs of growth in about a week.

7 When the seedlings are a few centimetres tall, start picking the leaves with your fingers. The variety will have an influence on the taste. Mizuna, mustard, rocket and coriander are more intensely flavoured than other types.

rocket

TOP TIP

▶ For a crunchy salad sow any kind of pea in pots of moist compost about 2½cm/1in deep. Cut the shoots with tendrils when they are 7.5–10cm/3–4in tall.

Herb pyramid

This tiered planting of herbs is a clever way of cramming a lot of plants into a small space. The good drainage created by the arrangement of the pots suits most kitchen herbs. We've mixed in ornamental varieties to liven up the display.

you will need

- **terracotta pots** that **stack inside each other**, 3
- **crocks**
- **gravel**
- **trowel**
- **bucket** of **water**
- **selection** of **herbs** (see Plant List)
- **peat-free potting compost** with **added loam (John Innes)**
- **watering can**

plant list

- ✳ **Chives**
  Allium schoenoprasum
- ✳ **Common thyme**
  Thymus vulgaris
- ✳ **Cotton lavender**
  Santolina chamaecyparissus
- ✳ **Dwarf lavender**
  Lavandula angustifolia 'Hidcote'
- ✳ **French tarragon**
  Artemisia dracunculus
- ✳ **Golden marjoram**
  Origanum vulgare 'Aureum'

cotton lavender

- ✳ **Golden thyme**
  Thymus pulegioides 'Bertram Anderson'
- ✳ **Parsley**
  Petroselinum crispum
- ✳ **Pineapple mint**
  Mentha suaveolens 'Variegata'
- ✳ **Purple sage**
  Salvia officinalis 'Purpurascens'
- ✳ **Rosemary**
  Rosmarinus officinalis
- ✳ **Variegated marjoram**
  Origanum vulgare 'Country Cream'

purple sage

1 Cover the drainage hole of the largest pot with a crock and add about 2½cm/1in of gravel using a trowel. Soak the herbs by plunging them in a bucket of water until the bubbles stop.

2 Half-fill the pot with compost and set the next largest pot on top. Add a little more compost into the gap between the pots, then plant the variegated marjoram in the space.

3 In order to fit the herbs' root-balls into the narrow gap more easily, gently squeeze them into an oval shape with your fingers. Plant the golden thyme, filling round the roots with potting mix.

4 Half-fill the middle pot of the tier with compost and position the smallest pot on top. Add more compost to the gap between the second and third pots and plant the purple-leaved culinary sage there.

5 Plant the pot of chives next to the sage. The chives' narrow, grassy leaves make a fine contrast with the sage leaves and the pink chive flowers also work well with the purple foliage.

6 Continue planting up the bottom and middle tiers, adding parsley, pineapple mint and golden marjoram to the base; cotton lavender and common thyme to the middle.

 = Watch out! Sharp or dangerous tool in use. = Watch out! Adult help is needed.

7 Fill all the gaps between the plants with potting compost and finally fill the top pot. Plant the French tarragon and grey-leaved lavender, leaving room for a small rosemary plant.

8 Plant the rosemary and firm in all the plants, checking for gaps between the root-balls. Water the herb pyramid thoroughly and leave to drain. Position in full sun.

TOP TIP

▶ To be able to keep picking herbs in winter, ask an adult to help you move the pyramid into a greenhouse or cool conservatory so that the plants can continue growing.

Minty madness

With so many to choose from, you could easily have over 20 types of mint in your collection in no time. They are easy to root in a jar of water and, once potted up, the baby plants make great presents for friends or family.

you will need

- **range** of **terracotta pots**, in different shapes and sizes
- **PVA glue**
- **2½cm/1in paintbrush**, for applying glue
- **peppermint-coloured emulsion paint tester pot** or **acrylic paint**
- **artist's paintbrush**
- **selection** of **mint plants** (see Plant List)
- **bucket** of **water**
- **peat-free potting compost** with **added loam (John Innes)**
- **water-retaining gel crystals**
- **recycled plastic**
- **felt-tipped pen**
- **paints**
- **scissors**
- **wire**
- **waterproof adhesive tape**
- **watering can**
- **peppermint-coloured stone chips**

TOP TIP

► As well as smelling great, mints have a wide range of cosmetic, medicinal and culinary uses:
- Add apple mint leaves to summer fruit cordials or use sprigs to garnish desserts.
- Finely chop spearmint for mint sauce or sprinkle on to new potatoes.
- Use eau de Cologne mint to perfume bath water!

spearmint

plant list

* **Apple mint**
  Mentha suaveolens
* **Chocolate mint**
  Mentha x piperita f. citrata 'Chocolate'
* **Eau de Cologne mint**
  Mentha x piperita f. citrata
* **Lemon mint**
  Mentha piperita f. citrata 'Lemon'
* **Lime mint**
  Mentha piperita f. citrata 'Lime'
* **Pineapple mint**
  Mentha suaveolens 'Variegata'
* **Red mint**
  Mentha X smithiana
* **Silver mint**
  Mentha longifolia
* **Spearmint (garden mint)**
  Mentha spicata

eau de Cologne mint

apple mint

1 Paint all the pots with a dilute solution of PVA glue using a 2½cm/1in paintbrush. Paint peppermint-coloured stripes on to the pots using an artist's paintbrush, to emphasize the mint theme.

2 It is essential that broad-leaved mints don't run short of moisture, as this can lead to mildew. To prevent this, plunge the plants in a bucket and wait for the bubbles to stop.

3 Mix the compost with water-retaining gel crystals, then put some into the pots and plant the mints. As they grow you'll need to divide them or pot them on into larger containers.

4 Fill in down the sides of the root-balls with compost and firm lightly, leaving a gap between the surface of the root-ball and the pot rim for watering. Smell the leaves as you work.

(!) = Watch out! Sharp or dangerous tool in use.   (🐾) = Watch out! Adult help is needed.

5 A fun way to remember what all of the mints in your collection are called is to make labels that give you a clue. Draw on to recycled plastic using a felt-tipped pen, then paint.

6 Cut out the labels (adult supervision is required). Attach to wire with waterproof adhesive tape. Position the labels when dry. Here, a pineapple represents pineapple mint.

7 Ensure the pots are well watered, then group the mints in a lightly shaded corner and finish off the display by pouring peppermint-coloured stone chips around the base.

TOP TIP

▶ Mints tend to have a bad reputation for spreading if planted in the ground, so growing them in pots is a way to help control their rampant nature.

minty madness   **79**

Going bananas!

With their giant leaves, bananas add a tropical touch to your garden. The little plants you buy in garden centres can grow to 1.8m/6ft. They may not produce fruit, but still look impressive.

you will need

- **young banana plant** (*see* Plant List), 1
- **bucket** of **water**
- **crocks**
- **patio pots**, various sizes
- **gravel**
- **peat-free container** and **hanging basket compost**
- **trowel**
- **watering can**
- **soluble plant food**
- **cobbles** or **ornamental bark**, for decoration

cobbles

plant list
✱ **Patio varieties of banana:**

Ensete ventricosum

Ensete ventricosum 'Maurelii'

Musa acuminata 'Zebrina'

Musa basjoo

Musa sikkimensis

1 Choose a sheltered spot outside. Plunge the plant in a bucket of water until the bubbles stop.

2 Put some crocks in the bottom of a patio pot and add a layer of gravel for drainage. Three-quarters fill the pot with compost, then make a hole with a trowel and plant the banana plant.

3 Water the plant regularly and feed following instructions on the packet.

4 Pot into a larger container as needed, to keep pace with the stem and leaf growth. Eventually, your banana can go in a really big pot, as shown – ask an adult to help with any lifting.

5 Top the pot with cobbles or ornamental bark. When suckers develop at the base, you can grow a new banana plant by cutting it off with a knife (ask an adult to help) and potting it up.

banana

TOP TIP
▶ In winter, either move the plant into a conservatory during autumn or insulate the pot with bubble wrap, top the compost with 10cm/4in bark and wrap the main stem with hessian sacking stuffed with straw. The leaves may die off but the plant should re-shoot.

! = Watch out! Sharp or dangerous tool in use.   🐾 = Watch out! Adult help is needed.

Runner bean wigwam

Originally introduced for their pretty flowers, runner beans also produce an abundance of tasty, tender and nutritious pods if the plants are kept well fed and watered – yummy!

you will need
- **digging fork** or **spade**
- **well-rotted manure**
- **2.4m/8ft bamboo canes**, 5
- **step ladder**
- **garden twine**
- **scissors**
- **small pots** and **compost**
- **runner bean seeds** (*see Plant List*)
- **watering can**

plant list
Recommended varieties of runner bean (*Phaseolus coccineus*):
'Desiree'
'Galaxy'
'Mergoles'
'Painted Lady'

runner beans, leaves and flowers

1 Dig over a section of flower border or vegetable garden and work in some well-rotted manure. Adult help may be required. This will keep the beans moist.

2 Push five long bamboo canes into the ground, making a circle about 1m/3ft across. Ask an adult to help if you find this difficult.

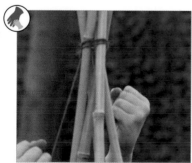

3 Standing on a step ladder if necessary (ask an adult to help you), tie the canes together at the top with garden twine to create a wigwam.

4 Fill some small pots with compost and plant a bean per pot to grow on a windowsill, in case the ones outside don't grow properly or get eaten!

5 Outside, make a hole on each side of the cane about 3cm/1¼in deep. Put one bean in each hole.

6 Water during dry weather and protect from slugs (*see page 41*). When they reach the top of the wigwam, pinch out the shoot tips. Don't allow pods to mature fully or bean production will stop.

TOP TIP
▶ Another way to ensure that bean roots have all the moisture they need is to dig a deeper planting hole, fill it with shredded recycled newspaper, grass cuttings and garden compost, water, then put the soil back on top.

Monster pumpkin pet

Even if you don't manage to grow a giant pumpkin, you'll have fun with this sprawling animal. For a really impressive pumpkin on Hallowe'en, grow one of the big boys, such as 'Atlantic Giant'. But, if you prefer sweet little pumpkins, which are better for eating, try 'Baby Bear'.

you will need

- **small pots**, 3
- **peat-free seed** and **cutting compost**
- **small dibber** or **cane**
- **pumpkin seeds**, 3
- **windowsill propagator** or **plastic bags** and **sticks**
- **13cm/5in pots**, 3
- **peat-free compost** with added loam (**John Innes**)
- **well-rotted manure**
- **border fork** or **spade**
- **trowel**
- **watering can**
- **horticultural fleece** or **cloches**
- **wires** and **canes**
- **tomato food**
- **tiles** or **bricks**
- **secateurs**

plant list
* **Varieties of pumpkin (*Cucurbita pepo*):**
'Atlantic Giant'
'Autumn Gold Improved'
'Hundredweight'
'Jack of All Trades'
'Jack-be-little'
'Baby Bear'

FACT FILE
FAMILY AND FRIENDS
The pumpkin is a member of a vegetable family called the Cucurbitaceae. Cucurbits include squashes, courgettes or zucchini, marrows, melons, gourds and cucumbers.

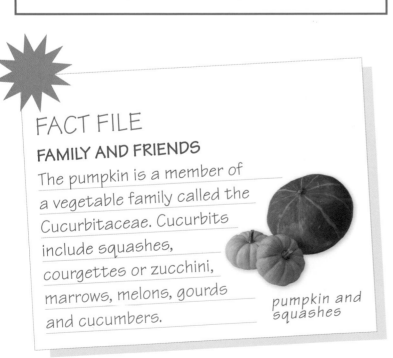

pumpkin and squashes

1 Fill three small pots with moist peat-free seed and cutting compost, then make a hole about 2.5cm/1in deep with a dibber or cane in the middle of each.

2 Sow the seeds on their edges rather than flat. Put the pots in a windowsill propagator, or cover each pot with a sealed plastic bag. Don't exclude light.

3 After the plants have germinated and grown on for a while, move into 13cm/5in pots filled with peat-free compost in a warm, light spot. Prepare the pumpkin patch outside by digging in plenty of manure with a spade or fork.

4 Plant the baby pumpkins after the risk of frost has passed in late spring or early summer. First harden off gradually over a two-week period. Dig holes in the prepared ground with a trowel and plant the pumpkins. Water.

5 Keep an eye on the weather and cover plants with horticultural fleece or large cloches during colder periods. Once the plants start to grow away, guide the stems where you need them to grow.

6 Tendrils help the plant to climb, so provide support in the form of wires and canes. Male flowers appear first on upright stems. Females (shown here) produce baby pumpkins.

! = Watch out! Sharp or dangerous tool in use.   = Watch out! Adult help is needed.

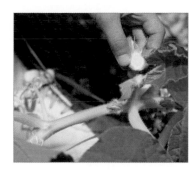

7 Water during dry spells and mulch. Feed with tomato food. Once you can see three pumpkins growing well, pick off the rest to encourage monster fruits.

8 Developing pumpkins should rest on a dry surface, not on the damp earth, otherwise they could rot. Support the fruits with tiles or bricks.

9 If the pumpkin pet is starting to get too big for its boots and is romping over other plants, ask an adult to help you cut some of the stems back with secateurs.

10 To ripen the fruits, cut off any leaves that are shading them. Leave attached to the plant until the skin is really hard.

pumpkin seeds

monster pumpkin pet   **83**

Herb wheel

A herb garden makes an attractive feature in a small vegetable plot or a sunny area of gravel. If you leave herbs to flower they attract pollinating insects, but this makes the foliage of edible kinds less tasty. A compromise is to plant two of each type, letting one flower while the other one is grown purely for picking.

you will need

- **border fork**
- **grit**, optional
- **garden compost**, optional
- **wooden wagon wheel** or **bricks**
- **loam-based potting compost** or **topsoil**
- **range** of **herbs** (*see* Plant List)
- **bucket** of **water**
- **trowel**
- **hand brush**
- **20cm/8in terracotta pot**
- **horticultural grit**
- **watering can**

plant list

✳ **Chives**
   Allium schoenoprasum
✳ **Cotton lavender**
   Santolina chamaecyparissus
✳ **Dwarf English lavender**
   Lavandula angustifolia variety
✳ **Gold variegated sage**
   Salvia officinalis 'Icterina'
✳ **Golden thyme**
   Thymus pulegioides 'Bertram Anderson'
✳ **Hyssop**
   Hyssopus officinalis
✳ **Moss curled parsley**
   Petroselinum crispum
✳ **Pineapple mint**
   Mentha suaveolens 'Variegata'

✳ **Purple sage**
   Salvia officinalis 'Purpurascens'
✳ **Rosemary**
   Rosmarinus officinalis
✳ **Variegated marjoram**
   Origanum vulgare 'Country Cream', 'Gold Tip'
✳ **Variegated thyme**
   Thymus 'Doone Valley'

gold variegated sage

rosemary

1 Dig over the area chosen for the wheel using a border fork. Break up any large clumps of soil to improve drainage. Fork in grit and garden compost if the soil is a heavy clay type. Adult supervision is required.

2 Level the ground and ask an adult to help you position the wagon wheel. This provides planting pockets that keep the plants separate. If you can't get one, ask an adult to help you make a replica out of bricks.

3 Fill in the empty wheel sections with loam-based potting compost or topsoil. This will give the young plants a chance to root freely. Firm lightly and level off with your hands.

4 Plunge the herbs in a bucket of water and wait for the bubbles to stop. Use a trowel to make holes. Plant the golden thyme, cream variegated marjoram and purple sage.

5 Continue, placing the herbs to create as much contrast in colour, leaf shape and texture as possible. Plant the parsley, yellow variegated marjoram, cotton lavender and variegated thyme.

6 Plant the chives and yellow variegated sage. Finish with hyssop, the variegated mint and lavender. Firm in the herbs. Using a hand brush, sweep excess soil from the wheel.

 = Watch out! Sharp or dangerous tool in use.   = Watch out! Adult help is needed.

7 Plant a small rosemary plant in a 20cm/8in terracotta pot filled with a gritty soil mix. Place the pot in the centre of the wheel to act as a focal point. You could also use lavender or a bay tree.

8 Add a layer of horticultural grit to the surface of the compost in the rosemary pot. It will help to highlight the foliage and keep the neck of the plant dry. Water the wheel.

TOP TIP
▶ To keep your plants healthy, pick the leaves and soft stems of the edible kinds frequently, especially chives, parsley and mint.

Chequerboard plot

If you only have a little corner to garden in, then dividing it up into squares can help you make the most of the space. Choose dwarf and compact vegetable and herb varieties, which will crop in a very small space and won't grow so tall that they overshadow their neighbours. Keep a note of what you sow in each of the squares so that you remember to sow or plant vegetables from different groups the following season.

you will need

- **border fork**
- **wheelbarrow**
- **manure** (at least 3 years old) or **garden compost**
- **slow-release fertilizer granules**, suitable for edible plants
- **1.2m/4ft canes**, 8–10
- **tape measure** or **ruler**
- **garden twine**
- **scissors**
- **trowel** or **dibber**
- **assorted plants** (*see Plant List*)
- **bucket of water**
- **recycled plastic bottle cloche(s)** (*see page 41*)
- **fleece**
- **watering can**

plant list

- ✳ **Baby beetroot**
  Beta vulgaris 'Boltardy'
- ✳ **Common thyme**
  Thymus serpyllum
- ✳ **Compact cabbage**
  Brassica oleracea var. capitata 'Golden Acre'
- ✳ **Dwarf broad bean :**
  Vicia faba 'The Sutton'
- ✳ **Dwarf curly kale**
  Brassica oleracea var. acephala 'Starbor' F1
- ✳ **Dwarf pea**
  Pisum sativum 'Little Marvel'
- ✳ **Garlic chives**
  Allium tuberosum

- ✳ **Lettuce**
  Lactuca sativa 'Little Gem'
- ✳ **Mini courgette**
  Cucurbita pepo 'Bambino' F1
- ✳ **Radicchio**
  Cichorium intybus
- ✳ **Round carrot**
  Daucus carota 'Parmex'
- ✳ **Salad onion**
  Allium cepa 'White Lisbon'
- ✳ **Radish**
  Raphanus sativus 'Cherry Belle'
- ✳ **Viola**
  Viola Sorbet Series

TOP TIPS

▶ 1.2m/4ft wide raised beds (shown here) are perfect for growing vegetables, especially on poor ground with thin soil or where the ground is heavy and poorly drained. Fill the space created by the raised edges with topsoil, garden compost and manure.

▶ You don't have to dig to cultivate, just keep beds topped up with compost.

▶ You can easily work from the edges of the raised area, which stops the beds getting compacted.

1 Fork a wheelbarrow load of manure or garden compost into the area you are going to cultivate. Adult help may be required. This is important if the ground had crops on it last year.

2 Add some slow-release fertilizer to give plants a steady supply of feed. Peas and beans are able to make their own fertilizer and they leave nutrients in the soil after they die down.

3 Lay out four 1.2m/4ft bamboo canes and use a tape measure or ruler to set them 30cm/12in apart. If you like, you can make the squares slightly larger or lay them out differently.

4 Place the set of vertical canes down on top of the horizontal ones, set out at the same distance apart. Use garden twine to join the canes together where they cross.

 = Watch out! Sharp or dangerous tool in use.  = Watch out! Adult help is needed.

5 Use a trowel or a dibber to make planting holes for seedlings and plantlets. Soak the various plants before planting out by plunging them in a bucket of water until the bubbles stop.

6 As well as planting home-grown seedlings and strips of vegetable plants bought from garden centres, sow quick-maturing salad seeds, such as lettuce. You don't have to sow in rows.

7 Plant flowers, such as violas, in some of the squares to attract pollinating bees and beneficial insects, which can help control pests. Pot marigolds are also a good choice.

8 Use plastic bottles as mini cloches to protect seedlings from cold and slugs. Surround carrots with a barrier of fleece to keep off carrot fly. Water plants often during warm weather.

Flower power

Here you will find how to grow a wide variety of colourful and fragrant blooms to brighten your garden, at the same time giving bees and other beneficial insects a treat. There are quirky containers for growing pretty or scented plants, and as well as potted patio displays there are mini garden schemes and border plantings to try.

Potty about flowers

Sow quick-and-easy hardy annual flowers in pots to brighten up dull parts of the garden, such as a driveway or paved area.

you will need

- **large**, **colourful plastic containers** or **planters**
- **utility knife** (for adult use only)
- **colour-coordinated hardy annual seed mixtures** (see Plant List)
- **trowel** or **dustpan**
- **gravel**
- **peat-free potting compost** with **added loam (John Innes)**
- **watering can** with a **fine rose attachment**
- **horticultural grit**

horticultural grit

plant list

- **Californian poppy**
  Eschscholzia californica
- **Clarkia**
  Clarkia elegans
- **Cornflower**
  Centaurea cyanus
- **Godetia**
  Godetia grandiflora
- **Love-in-a-mist**
  Nigella damascena
- **Mallow**
  Lavatera trimestris
- **Mallow-wort**
  Malope trifida
- **Poached egg plant**
  Limnanthes douglasii
- **Pot marigold**
  Calendula officinalis
- **Shirley poppy**
  Papaver rhoeas
  Shirley Series
- **Tickseed**
  Coreopsis tinctoria

1 Ask an adult to cut a few pieces out of the base of each container using a utility knife, if necessary. Without holes, water makes the compost soggy and will drown the plant roots.

2 Choose seeds to go in coloured containers. We've used a red mix to go in an orange one and an orange mix to go in a purple one.

3 Using a trowel or dustpan, pour several centimetres (inches) of gravel into the bottom of each tub, then fill with compost and water well. Adult help may be required.

4 Sow by pouring the seeds out on to the flat of your hand. You will see that there are small and large seeds.

5 Space out a selection of the larger seeds on the surface of the compost (each flower has a differently shaped seed).

6 Scatter the smaller seeds thinly between the larger ones. You will probably have enough seeds for two tubs and dividing the seeds will help prevent sowing too thickly.

7 Cover the seeds with a thin layer of grit, using a dustpan. The tiny seedlings will soon appear. Water as required.

mallow

marigold

 = Watch out! Sharp or dangerous tool in use.   = Watch out! Adult help is needed.

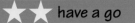
Giant dahlia

Dahlias are show-offs! Tall, big and colourful, they will give your garden or patio a totally tropical feel!

you will need

- **dahlia tuber**
  (*see* Plant List)
- **small seed tray**
- **soil-less seed** and **cutting compost** with **added Perlite**
- **25cm/10in pot**
- **peat-free potting compost** with **added loam (John Innes)**
- **watering can**
- **bamboo canes** (various sizes)
- **soft garden twine**
- **grit** or **fine gravel**
- **clay pots**, (5cm/10in, 35cm/14in and 40cm/16in in diameter, for potting on

- **crocks**, for potting on
- **gravel**, for potting on
- **general flowering plant liquid fertilizer**
- **liquid tomato food**

plant list
* **Tall large-flowered types of dahlia (*Dahlia*):**
  'Admiral Rawlings'
  'Café au Lait'
  'Gallery Art Nouveau'
  'Grenadier'
  'Kenora Sunset'
  'Kidd's Climax'
  'Zorro'

1 Put the tuber into a seed tray filled with slightly moist seed and cutting compost to start the tuber growing and plump it up. Keep on a windowsill or in a frost-free greenhouse until it sprouts green shoots.

2 Plant the tuber in a 25cm/10in pot so that the shoots are just poking up through the compost.

3 Alternatively, plant the tuber halfway down the pot to start with and keep adding compost as the shoots grow (but don't bury the tips).

4 As it gets bigger in late spring, start to harden it off, putting outdoors for a few hours a day. Or, use a cold frame and increase ventilation gradually (see page 13).

5 Put a cane into the pot to support the growing plant. You will need to replace this with a taller cane as the plant grows. Tie the stem on gently using soft garden twine.

6 Pinch out the main shoot tip with your thumb and forefinger as the plant grows to encourage side branches.

7 Water and cover the compost with grit. This helps stop slugs and snails eating the plant.

8 Continue watering and feed with general liquid fertilizer. Pot on into progressively larger pots when the roots start to poke out of the drainage hole. Switch to tomato food when the plant begins flowering.

Super sweet peas

Sweet peas are hardy annual climbers that flower all summer long. Some grow very tall and are best planted out in borders but it's easy to find room for shorter types on the patio. There are even mini sweet peas that can be grown in hanging baskets! Though often sold in packets of single colours, mixtures usually have a good range of shades – mostly pastels with some darker and more vivid colours. Make sure your variety is recommended for fragrance!

you will need

- **scissors**
- **kitchen paper roll centres**, cut in half by an adult
- **seed tray**
- **seed** and **cutting compost**
- **recycled plastic container**, 1, cut in half by an adult
- **sweet pea** (*Lathyrus odoratus*) **seeds**, compact variety with an ultimate height of 90–120cm/3–4ft
- **recycled plant label**
- **watering can** with a **fine rose attachment**
- **clear film**
- **barrel** or **tub**, with drainage holes
- **gravel**
- **peat-free potting compost** with **added loam** (John Innes)
- **trowel**
- **1.8m/6ft bamboo canes**, 5
- **garden twine**
- **training wire** or **twine**

FACT FILE

HEAVYWEIGHT BEES

Sweet peas and other members of the pea and bean family have a characteristic flower shape. The upright part of the flower is called the standard and the lower part, the keel. Being big and heavy, bumble-bees find it relatively easy to force the bloom open to reach the pollen and nectar.

bumble-bee

sweet peas

1 Snip the ends of kitchen roll centres a few times, with adult supervision. Bend the flaps in to make bases. Position in a seed tray, then use a container cut in half to pour compost into the tubes.

2 Firm the compost lightly with your fingers. To sow, simply push a seed 1cm/½in deep into each of the tubes with your finger and re-cover the hole with compost.

3 To remember exactly what type of sweet pea you have sowed, you could add a hand-made plant label recycled from a plastic container (see page 124).

4 Water the tubes in the seed tray using a watering can with a fine rose. Stretch clear film over the pots and tray to act like a mini greenhouse and place on a cool windowsill.

 = Watch out! Sharp or dangerous tool in use.   = Watch out! Adult help is needed.

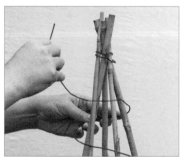

5 Remove the clear film when the seedlings appear. When each plantlet has two to three leaves, pinch out the growing tip with your thumb and forefinger to encourage bushy growth.

6 Prepare a barrel or tub by covering the drainage holes with 10cm/4in gravel and filling with compost. After hardening off plantlets (see page 13), plant, spacing up to 15cm/6in apart.

7 Add five bamboo canes spaced equally and tied at the top to make a wigwam. You will need to guide the young stems and climbing tendrils to the supports to begin with.

8 For extra support, tie a piece of training wire to the base of one of the canes then wind it up and round like a coiled spring. Tie off at the top by winding round several times.

super sweet peas   93

Succulents in a strawberry planter

Traditional strawberry planters made from terracotta are ideal for growing your very own curious collection of succulents (fleshy plants, often evergreen, that store water in their leaves) and other drought-resistant types, including many different alpines.

you will need
- terracotta strawberry pot
- crock
- loam-based potting compost (John Innes No. 2)
- horticultural grit
- trowel
- **succulents**, 9 (or enough to fill all the planting holes)
- **watering can**
- **decorative grit** or **fine gravel**

plant list
- ✳ **Cobweb houseleek**
  Sempervivum arachnoideum
- ✳ **Common stonecrop**
  Sedum acre
- ✳ **Echeveria**
  Echeveria secunda var. *glauca* *
- ✳ **Houseleek**
  Sempervivum 'Commander Hay';
  S. tectorum
- ✳ **Purple broadleaf stonecrop**
  Sedum spathulifolium
  'Purpureum'
- ✳ **Stonecrop**
  Sedum spathulifolium
  'Cape Blanco'
- ✳ **White stonecrop**
  Sedum album 'Coral Carpet'

* keep frost free

FACT FILE
HENS AND CHICKS
Houseleeks (*Sempervivum*) are very easy to grow and can stay in the same pot for years. There are lots of different leaf colours and forms to choose from. Houseleeks are sometimes called hen and chickens because of the way the mother plant produces lots of babies all around it. They need very little soil and can even be planted between tiles on a roof!

houseleeks

1 Bring all your 'ingredients' together so that you have everything to hand when you start planting. Check when you buy that your strawberry planter doesn't have any fine cracks or chips.

2 Cover the drainage hole in the pot with a crock – this could be a piece of broken terracotta pot or tile – to stop the hole from getting clogged up with soil.

3 Mix up loam-based compost, such as John Innes No. 2, with some horticultural grit (about one-quarter grit to three-quarters soil). Use a trowel to add it to the pot.

4 Fill up to the bottom hole in the strawberry pot with soil. Take the first plant out of its pot and feed the root-ball through from the outside in. The roots mustn't be visible.

 = Watch out! Sharp or dangerous tool in use. = Watch out! Adult help is needed.

5 Add the other plants on this lowest level, resting the root-balls on the surface of the compost. Next, work more compost around the roots and fill to the next level of holes.

6 Having planted up the middle row of holes in the same way, plant the top row of holes. Firm the compost lightly to keep the plants in place and prevent them falling out.

7 Use a larger, more eye-catching specimen to plant in the top of the strawberry planter. Ask an adult for help to move the pot to its home, then water to settle the soil.

8 Put a decorative layer of grit or fine gravel on the top of the pot around your specimen plant to finish it off and give the planting a sunny, Mediterranean garden feel.

succulents in a strawberry planter 　　95

Flowering wellies

When you have grown out of a pair of Wellington boots, why not turn them into fun containers for plants? You just need to create a few drainage holes, fill them with soil and plant away!

you will need
- **wellington boots**, 1 pair
- **utility knife**
  (for adult use only)
- **trowel**
- **gravel**
- **peat-free potting compost**
  with **added loam** (John Innes)
- **plants** (see Plant List)
- **bucket** of **water**
- **watering can**

plant list
Summer
- ✱ **Swan river daisy**
  Brachyscome multifida
- ✱ **Trailing geranium**
  Pelargonium cvs.
- ✱ **Trailing petunia**
  Petunia Surfinia Baby Pink Morn
- ✱ **Twin spur**
  Diascia 'Ruby Field'

Winter/Spring
- ✱ **Double daisy**
  Bellis perennis
- ✱ **Dwarf daffodil**
  Narcissus 'Tête-à-tête'
- ✱ **Hardy primrose**
  Primula Wanda hybrids
- ✱ **Mini cyclamen**
  Cyclamen Miracle Series

1 Ask an adult to cut a few small holes round the base of the boots, using a utility knife. Cut the holes just above the thick sole of the wellington boots to provide drainage. It is a good idea to rest the boots on an upturned pot to cut the holes.

2 Using a trowel, fill the foot of the boots with gravel for drainage and to stop the boot falling over.

3 Next add compost to the boots. You'll need to work it well into the foot and ankle parts of the boots with your hand.

4 Plunge the plants in a bucket of water until the bubbles stop. Remove from their pots.

5 Carefully lower the plant in the top of the boots. There should be enough compost to support the plant at the right height.

6 Add more compost to fill the gaps around the root-ball, then firm in.

7 Stand the boots in a sheltered spot out of direct sun. Water cyclamen under the leaves, only when the compost feels a little dry.

 = Watch out! Sharp or dangerous tool in use. = Watch out! Adult help is needed.

Bags of blooms

These plastic-coated canvas carrier bags are great for using as plant containers for the summer. You'll find them in all shapes, sizes, colours and patterns. These have a different pirate picture on opposite sides.

you will need

- **plastic-coated canvas carrier bags**, 2
- **scissors**
- **bedding** or **patio plants** (*see* Plant List), enough to fill the bags
- **bucket** of **water**
- **peat-free potting compost** with **added loam (John Innes)**
- **trowel**
- **watering can**

plant list

- ✳ **African marigold**
  Tagetes erecta 'French Vanilla'
- ✳ **Bidens**
  Bidens ferulifolia
- ✳ **Busy Lizzie**
  Impatiens Accent Series
- ✳ **Fibrous-rooted begonia**
  Begonia sempervirens
- ✳ **French marigold**
  Tagetes patula
- ✳ **Geranium**
  Pelargonium (Zonal)
- ✳ **Trailing verbena**
  Verbena Tapien Series

* Nip off the faded flowers to keep plants blooming.

1 Ask an adult to help you cut out two or three small holes in the bottom of each bag using scissors. This will allow excess water to run out.

2 Plunge the plants in a bucket of water until the bubbles stop.

3 Half-fill each bag with potting compost using a trowel.

4 Leave enough room for the root-balls to be planted (try them in the bags for size). Allow a few centimetres/inches free at the top for watering.

5 Take the soaked plants (here a marigold) out of their pots and position in each of the bags.

6 Fill the gaps round the roots of the plants with more potting compost and firm in lightly using your fingers.

7 Make sure the surface of the root-ball is just covered but don't pile soil up round the neck of the plant or bury any leaves. Water with a watering can.

TOP TIP

▶ To help keep larger bags upright, add several centimetres/inches of gravel.

Flower friends

Some common plant names include a person's name and and it's fun to collect a quirky group of 'friends' together. You could even make name tags to put in their pots, if you like.

you will need
- **trowel**
- **gravel**
- **colourful glazed pots**, 3
- **peat-free potting compost** with **added loam (John Innes)**
- **plants** with **people's names** (*see Plant List*)
- **split cane** with **protector**
- **watering can**

compost

gravel

plant list
✳ **Black-eyed Susan**
   Thunbergia alata
   Suzie hybrids
✳ **Busy Lizzie**
   Impatiens New
   Guinea hybrids
✳ **Creeping Jenny**
   Lysimachia nummularia
✳ **Flaming Katy**
   Kalanchoe blossfeldiana
✳ **Jacob's ladder**
   Polemonium
✳ **Sweet William**
   Dianthus barbatus

1 Using a trowel, put a layer of gravel in the bottom of each of the pots, for drainage.

2 Add enough compost to allow the surface of the root-balls to sit about 2cm (¾in) below the rim of the planter. This makes watering easier.

3 Position the flaming Katy plants. Squeeze a couple of extra plants in for a bold display.

4 Plant the tall, annual climber black-eyed Susan in a separate pot. You can grow this from seed in spring or buy plants to train up canes.

5 Top up the compost in all the pots, working it down the edges.

6 Insert the cane in the pot containing the black-eyed Susan. Check that a suitable cane protector is in place. Water thoroughly and stand in a warm, sheltered spot.

TOP TIP
▶ These plants can also be grown on a well-lit windowsill or in a conservatory (sunroom). Pinch off fading blooms and use a liquid feed for flowering plants every two weeks. Water flaming Katy sparingly.

 = Watch out! Sharp or dangerous tool in use.   = Watch out! Adult help is needed.

Buckets of bells

The plants in this pretty collection are all members of the same family. To highlight this and to make the most of the blue flowers, plant them up in contrasting yellow and orange buckets.

you will need

- **bellflower plants**
  (*see Plant List*)
- **bucket** of **water**
- **colourful metal buckets**, 3
- **15cm/6in nail**, 1
- **hammer**
- **trowel**
- **gravel**

- **peat-free potting compost** with **added loam (John Innes)**
- **bamboo canes**, 3
- **soft garden twine**
- **watering can**
- **liquid flowering plant food**

plant list

✳ **Italian bellflower**
  Campanula isophylla 'Stella Blue'

✳ **Milky bellflower**
  Campanula lactiflora

✳ **Trailing bellflower**
  Campanula poscharskyana

  campanula

1 Soak the plants in a bucket of water until the bubbles stop rising.

2 Ask an adult to help you make drainage holes in the buckets by turning them upside down, positioning the nail and tapping it with a hammer until it pierces the metal.

3 Using a trowel, add a layer of gravel to cover the drainage holes and help water to escape, then part-fill the bucket with potting compost.

4 Ease the pots from the root-balls of the plants. Put the campanula (the tall one) into the large bucket.

5 Fill round the edges of the root-ball with more compost, leaving a gap below the rim of the bucket to allow for watering. Firm the compost lightly with your fingers.

6 Add a wigwam of bamboo canes fixed together at the top.

7 Gently tie soft garden twine around the wigwam and the plant to support the tall bellflower stems.

8 Plant up the other little buckets in the same way and water all of them. Stand in a cool, well-lit spot. Deadhead and feed and water regularly.

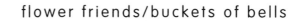

Potted perfumes

Fragrance makes being out in the garden even more enjoyable. A collection of perfumed flowers and herbs is a particularly nice idea for a sitting area. Of course, there are many more scented plants than those used here. Make a point of smelling flowers that you come across and try to describe what they are like and if they remind you of other things, such as lemons or apples.

you will need
- **assorted fragrant plants**
  (see Plant List)
- **bucket** of **water**
- **animal-shaped terracotta planters**, 2
- **loam-based potting compost**
  (John Innes No. 2)
- **trowel**
- **terracotta bowl**
- **crock**
- **gravel**
- **horticultural grit**
- **watering can**
- **assorted pots**

variegated apple mint

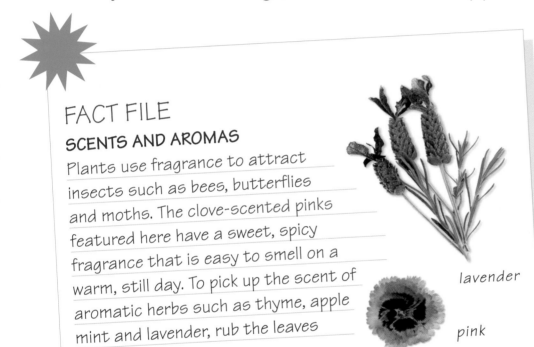

FACT FILE
SCENTS AND AROMAS
Plants use fragrance to attract insects such as bees, butterflies and moths. The clove-scented pinks featured here have a sweet, spicy fragrance that is easy to smell on a warm, still day. To pick up the scent of aromatic herbs such as thyme, apple mint and lavender, rub the leaves between your fingers.

lavender

pink

plant list
* **2 clove-scented pinks**
  Dianthus
* **3 dwarf English lavenders**
  Lavandula angustifolia 'Hidcote'
* **2 French lavenders**
  Lavandula pedunculata subsp. *pedunculata*
* **2 thymes**
  Thymus pulegioides
* **1 variegated apple mint**
  Mentha suaveolens 'Variegata'

1 Plunge all the plants in a bucket of water until the bubbles stop. This ensures that the compost is moist through to the middle. Take the first clove-scented pink from its pot.

2 Unlike glazed or plastic-lined pots, the terracotta cat planters we used are small and porous so won't need extra drainage. Add a little compost with a trowel.

3 Position the pink on the compost, in the centre, then add extra compost as required to fill any gaps round the edges, leaving a small gap for watering. Firm in lightly.

4 Choose a pink with a different petal colour and pattern from the one you have just planted and plant in the second container, repeating the method described.

    = Watch out! Sharp or dangerous tool in use.   = Watch out! Adult help is needed.

5 Next, prepare a terracotta bowl for planting by covering the drainage hole with a crock and adding some gravel with a trowel to ensure good drainage.

6 Add compost. Most herbs hate getting too damp so add grit to the compost if you use a glazed pot. This terracotta one will lose moisture through the sides so won't get too damp.

7 Remove the lavender from its plastic pot and plant it in the bowl. The surface of the root-ball should be just under the lip of the bowl to allow space for watering.

8 Add two more plants, then fill in the gaps with compost, and water. Continue planting up other plants. Thyme grows well in terracotta pots but use a glazed container for mint.

Potty about bulbs

Providing a splash of colour, spring bulbs put on a fabulous display and look especially good in pots.

you will need

- **crock**, 1
- **pot** (we used a tall pot, which we decorated, but they can be any shape or size you like)
- **gravel**
- **peat-free potting compost** with **added loam (John Innes)**
- **trowel**
- **spring bulbs**, 1 packet (we used grape hyacinth)
- **watering can**

bulbs

plant list

- ✳ **Dwarf daffodil**
  Narcissus 'Tête-à-tête'
- ✳ **Dwarf iris**
  Iris 'Joyce' (Reticulata)
- ✳ **Dwarf tulip**
  Tulipa 'Red Riding Hood'
- ✳ **Early crocus**
  Crocus chrysanthus
- ✳ **Grape hyacinth**
  Muscari armeniacum
- ✳ **Siberian squill**
  Scilla siberica

1 Grape hyacinths and other bulbs like good drainage, so place a piece of crock over the hole in the bottom of a pot to stop it clogging with soil.

2 Cover the crock with a layer of gravel, then half-fill the pot with compost, using a trowel.

3 Space out about 12 little grape hyacinth bulbs evenly on the surface of the compost, as shown, with the pointed ends facing upwards.

4 Other bulbs may be larger and require more space; follow instructions on the packet.

5 Cover the bulbs with more compost, nearly filling the pot to the top. Firm the top of the compost lightly with your fingers.

6 Water well and leave to grow in a sheltered spot outdoors. Don't allow the compost to dry out through the winter.

FACT FILE

GRAPE HYACINTHS

▶ With intense blue flowers and a sweet, musky scent, grape hyacinths are a good source of nectar for insects coming out of hibernation.

muscari

 = Watch out! Sharp or dangerous tool in use.   = Watch out! Adult help is needed.

Baby busy Lizzies

In early spring you can buy special little seedlings and rooted cuttings, often called 'plugs', that are cheaper than normal-sized bedding plants.

you will need
- **plastic trug** or **container**
- **utility knife** (for adult use only)
- **crock**
- **gravel**
- **trowel**
- **peat-free potting compost** with **added loam (John Innes)**
- **busy Lizzie (*Impatiens*) plug plants**, 2 small packs
- **watering can**

TOP TIP
► You can use these plants to get a head start if you have a light, frost-free spot, such as a conservatory (sunroom) or greenhouse. They will grow quickly under cover.

1 Ask an adult to cut a hole in the base of the trug or container using a utility knife. Next, cover the hole with a crock. Add gravel, using a trowel.

2 Fill the plastic trug or container almost to the top with compost, leaving a small gap.

3 When you are ready to plant, carefully remove the plug plants from the gel-filled container.

4 Gently separate the plug plants by pulling them apart from each other very carefully with your hands. Try not to break the delicate little roots.

5 Space out the plugs and begin planting them about 12cm/4in apart. You can scoop out the compost using your fingers.

6 Lightly firm the compost around the plugs, making sure that the surface is level. Water using a can with a fine rose attachment.

7 Keep the trug in a warm, light place until there is no more risk of frost.

8 From late spring, ask an adult to put the trug out for increasing amounts of time during the day, bringing it in at night.

watering can, gloves and trowel

Barrel of chocolate

This dark-leaved combination of plants with chocolate in their name has a surprise: the flowers of one plant actually smell of chocolate too! Called chocolate cosmos, this is a tender perennial that grows from a tuber. In a warm, sheltered spot it will flower all summer if you deadhead spent blooms regularly.

you will need
- **wooden barrel**
- **crocks**
- **trowel**
- **gravel**
- **plants** (see Plant List)
- **bucket** of **water**
- **peat-free potting compost** with **added loam** (John Innes)
- **watering can**

watering can with a fine rose attachment

FACT FILE

CHOCOLATE SCENTS

If you are a real chocoholic you might want to try other chocolate-scented plants besides the cosmos. The yellow-bloomed chocolate daisy (*Berlandiera lyrata*) is the chocolatiest of them all. The scent is released at night but you can still smell it in the morning. Rub the leaves of the chocolate mint (*Mentha* x *piperita* f. *citrata* 'Chocolate') for a delicious aroma of chocolate peppermint creams!

chocolate-scented cosmos

plant list
* **3 chocolate cosmos**
  Cosmos atrosanguineus
* **1 coral flower**
  Heuchera 'Chocolate Ruffles'
* **1 white snakeroot**
  Eupatorium rugosum 'Chocolate'

Heuchera 'Chocolate Ruffles'

1 Cover the drainage holes in the wooden barrel with crocks, then use a trowel to add 8–10cm/3–4in gravel.

2 Plunge the plants in a bucket of water and wait for the bubbles to stop.

3 Pour in a couple of buckets of compost to three-quarters fill it. You'll need quite a lot of compost for this large container. Ask an adult to help you if necessary as the bucket will be heavy. Leave enough room to plant.

4 As this wooden barrel planter will eventually stand against a wall, the tallest plant, the snakeroot, needs to go in first, towards the back. Make sure the surface of the root-ball is about 2.5cm/1in below the rim of the barrel.

5 Plant the chocolate cosmos. They will make more of a show if they are quite close together.

6 Add the other plants, making sure you fill in between the roots with compost as you go.

 = Watch out! Sharp or dangerous tool in use. = Watch out! Adult help is needed.

7 Plant the frilly leaved heuchera in the remaining space. All the plants in the barrel should be planted at the same level below the rim as the snakeroot. This allows water to pool on the surface of the compost, then soak in.

8 Carefully feel under the plant's leaves with your fingers to check where the gaps are and then add more compost as necessary, working it in between and around the plants. Firm the compost lightly with your hand.

9 Water the plants thoroughly so that the compost is nice and moist. Watering also helps to wash compost into any gaps that you have missed, so you may need to check and add some more compost later.

10 Allow the barrel to drain, then ask an adult to help you move it into position on a patio or some other sunny spot in the garden.

11 Keep your eyes open for slug and snail damage. Water frequently in dry weather.

wooden barrel

Everlasting flowers

Dried flowers make long-lasting arrangements. You can dry any blooms, but ones that are naturally dry or papery are especially suitable.

you will need

- scissors
- garden twine
- hammer
- nail or hook
- vase, (optional)

plant list

- **Big quaking grass**
  Briza maxima
- **Globe thistle**
  Echinops ritro
- **Lavender**
  Lavandula spp. and varieties
- **Masterwort**
  Astrantia major
- **Ornamental grasses**
  Miscanthus
- **Pearly everlasting**
  Anaphalis triplinervis
- **Statice**
  Limonium sinuatum
- **Sea holly**
  Eryngium spp. and varieties
- **Strawflower**
  Bracteantha bracteata
- **Yarrow**
  Achillea millefolium

1 Pick a dry day when the dew has disappeared. Using scissors, cut flowers with long stems. Adult supervision is required.

2 Prepare the separate bunches of flowers by removing all the foliage and clustering the flower heads together. Cut the stems to the same length.

3 Tightly tie each bundle with garden twine. The stems will shrink as they dry and may come loose otherwise. Leave a long piece for hanging.

4 Find a cool, dry, airy place for hanging the bunches. You may need to ask an adult to hammer in a nail or hook.

5 Hang up the bunch of flowers by the long piece of twine you left loose.

6 Depending on how large and full of moisture the flowers are when you cut them, it could take several weeks before they are dry enough to take down to arrange in a vase or hang up indoors or outside.

TOP TIP

▶ Try to pick perfect flowers for drying. Ones that aren't fully open work best because flowers continue to develop during the drying process and may drop their petals. Fully dry flowers are firm and unyielding.

 = Watch out! Sharp or dangerous tool in use. = Watch out! Adult help is needed.

Spring drift

Seeing bulbs pushing their way through the ground lets you know that spring is on its way. Plant early varieties in a lawn to create a cheerful scene.

you will need
- **spring bulbs** (see Plant List) at least 2 large packets
- **bulb planter**, preferably long-handled

crocus

plant list
- ✳ **Daffodils**
  Narcissus cvs.
- ✳ **Drooping star of Bethlehem**
  Ornithogalum nutans
- ✳ **'Dutch' crocuses**
  Crocus vernus types
- ✳ **Early yellow crocus**
  Crocus x *luteus* 'Golden Yellow'
- ✳ **Grape hyacinths**
  Muscari armeniacum
- ✳ **Siberian squill**
  Scilla siberica
- ✳ **Snakeshead fritillaries**
  Fritillaria meleagris
- ✳ **Snowdrops**
  Galanthus nivalis
- ✳ **Species crocus**
  Crocus tommasinianus

1 Take handfuls of bulbs and throw them randomly on to the lawn.

2 Using a long-handled bulb planter, make holes of an appropriate depth for each bulb. The hole should be 2½–3 times deeper than the length of the bulb. You may need to ask an adult to help you.

3 As you work, the bulb planter will squeeze out a circular plug of turf and soil taken from the previous hole. Hold the plug to one side and put a bulb in the hole.

4 Replace the turf plug, and continue making holes and planting with all the bulbs.

5 Lightly tread the turf plugs back into position to leave the lawn level.

6 After the crocuses have flowered in spring, water in liquid tomato food and then allow about six weeks for the leaves to die down before mowing. The bulbs then build reserves for next year's display.

TOP TIP
► When planting larger bulbs in a lawn, rather than planting them individually, lift patches of turf with a spade. Loosen the bottom of the hole with a border fork, plant the bulbs, then replace the turf. Adult supervision is required.

everlasting flowers/spring drift **107**

Little and large sunflowers

Cheap to buy and fun to grow, you could have a competition to see which of your family or friends can grow the tallest sunflower? Some, such as 'Russian Giant', will tower over you, reaching 2.4m/8ft or more. To get a head start, grow several seedlings and select only the tallest and strongest-looking ones.

you will need

- **trowel** (optional)
- **8cm/3in plant pots** or **yogurt pots**
- **peat-free seed** and **cuttings compost**
- **dibber** or **bamboo cane**
- **sunflower seeds** (see Plant List)
- **tray** of **water**
- **plastic bags**
- **ties**
- **13cm/5in pots**
- **peat-free compost** with **added loam** (John Innes)
- **old fork**
- **watering can** with a **fine rose attachment**
- **flowering plant food**

FACT FILE

BIRD FOOD

Tall, large-flowered sunflowers make tasty treats for seed-eating birds, such as finches, if they are left to produce seed-heads. Once the seed has ripened, you can either leave the heads on the dying stems or cut them off and hang them from the bird table using wire.

sunflower

plant list

✷ **Dwarf sunflowers** (*Helianthus annuus*):
'Big Smile'
'Dwarf Yellow Spray'
'Little Dorrit'

✷ **Tall sunflowers** (*Helianthus annuus*):
'Moonwalker'
'Russian Giant'

1 Using a trowel or your hands, fill 8cm/3in plant pots or yogurt pots with seed compost and firm the compost lightly with your fingers.

2 Use a dibber or cane to make a hole 1.5cm/½in) deep. Repeat with the other pots.

3 Sow the seeds, then cover with compost. Stand in a tray of water until the compost darkens

4 Cover with the plastic bags, tied at the top to act like a mini greenhouse. Grow on a windowsill. Remove the covers once the seedlings appear.

5 When the seedlings have developed two or three pairs of leaves, they need potting on.

6 Half-fill 13cm/5in pots with potting compost. Ease the seedlings out of their pots using an old fork. Hold the seedlings by a leaf and support the roots.

7 Position the seedlings gently in the centre of the larger pots, adding enough compost to cover the roots.

8 The seedlings should be planted at the same depth in the bigger pots as they were when they were in the smaller pots.

    = Watch out! Sharp or dangerous tool in use.   = Watch out! Adult help is needed.

9 Firm in lightly with your fingers and then water the seedlings with a watering can fitted with a rose attachment.

10 Grow on plants in a warm, sunny place, gradually hardening them off as the weather warms up (*see* page 13).

11 Pinch out the growing tip of dwarf types when they have five pairs of leaves to encourage side shoots.

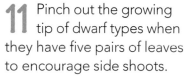

12 Plant dwarf varieties in pots and tall ones in borders, where they will need support. Water often and feed once a fortnight with flowering plant food.

little and large sunflowers **109**

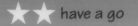
Black and white garden

This chequerboard arrangement is created using plants with black blooms or leaves contrasted with white flowers, white-variegated or silver foliage. As only one type of plant is used in each of the containers, you can move them around to create different patterns. To continue the display, think about swapping some of the summer plants for spring bulbs and winter bedding in autumn.

you will need
- **black** or **grey square plastic planters**, 9
- **gravel**, 1 bag
- **peat-free compost** with **added loam** (John Innes)
- **trowel**
- **bedding** and **perennial flowers** and **foliage plants** (see Plant List)
- **white pebbles**, 1 bag
- **black pebbles**, 1 bag
- **watering can**

FACT FILE
BLACK FLOWERS
So-called black plants have flowers or leaves of very dark maroon-purple. Because they are quite rare, black plants can become collector's items and they are considered the height of gardening fashion! One of the best black-flowered bulbs for spring is *Tulipa* 'Queen of Night'. And from seed, try *Pennisetum glaucum* 'Purple Majesty', a black grass commonly called millet. Birds love eating the seed-heads!

pincushion flower

plant list
- ✳ **1 cabbage palm**
  Cordyline australis Purpurea Group
- ✳ **1 calla lily**
  Zantedeschia 'Captain Palermo'
- ✳ **8–12 cinerarias**
  Senecio cineraria
- ✳ **1 coral flower**
  Heuchera 'Obsidian'
- ✳ **2 dwarf Shasta daisies**
  Leucanthemum X *superbum* 'Snow Lady'
- ✳ **3 Moroccan daisies**
  Rhodanthemum 'African Eyes'
- ✳ **3 pincushion flowers**
  Scabiosa atropurpurea 'Chile Black'
- ✳ **2 sisyrinchiums**
  Sisyrinchium striatum 'Aunt May'
- ✳ **3 violas**
  Viola 'Black Velvet'

1 Ensure the drainage holes in the pots are punched through properly. Ask an adult to help fill with 8cm/3in of gravel. Depending on the size of plant, part-fill with compost.

2 Take a viola out of its pot by tapping it smartly on the base to release the roots then tipping it into your other hand. Don't pull the plant by its neck!

3 Plant three violas together in a single container to create a good display. With larger plants you may need only one plant. The plants should not be squashed.

4 Gently lift up the stems and foliage of the violas so that you can see and feel where the gaps are and add compost to fill as necessary. Never bury leaves under compost.

 = Watch out! Sharp or dangerous tool in use. = Watch out! Adult help is needed.

5 Firm the compost lightly with your hands. Ensure that the surface of the root-ball is about 2cm/1in below the rim of the container to allow space for water to pool and soak in.

6 It can be tricky to get bedding plants out of polystyrene trays. Push your thumb through the hole underneath to ease out the plant – in this case cineraria. You can also use a pencil.

7 To strengthen this stylish colour scheme, arrange small groups of alternating black and white pebbles to make a border that goes all the way round the pots.

8 The black-flowered calla lily is the star of this arrangement and is positioned in the centre of the block. To make it stand out even more, cover the soil surface with white pebbles.

black and white garden   111

Spell your name in flowers!

If you have a patch of empty ground, you may have room to spell out your name in flowers. Make the letters quite big so that the shapes stand out clearly. Choose bushy, upright bedding plants – ones that spread too far will spoil the shape of the letters. It can take a lot of plants, especially if your name is long, so for a cheaper option, sow seed of compact hardy annual flowers.

you will need
- border fork
- rake
- slow-release fertilizer granules
- bamboo cane
- trowel
- coloured horticultural grit or **washed sand**
- dwarf chrysanthemums or **other bedding plants** (*see* Plant List), 40
- **bucket** of water
- **watering can** with a **fine rose attachment**

plant list
* **Ageratum**
  Ageratum 'Blue Danube'
* **Compact container and bedding petunias**
  Petunia (multiflora types)
* **Dwarf chrysanthemum**
  Chrysanthemum paludosum 'Snowland'
* **Dwarf tobacco plant**
  Nicotiana Merlin Series
* **Fibrous-rooted begonia**
  Begonia semperflorens
* **French marigold**
  Tagetes patula
* **Sweet alyssum**
  Lobularia maritima 'Snow Crystals'

TOP TIP
▶ To sow your name, rather than using ready-sprouted plantlets, carry out Steps 1 and 2. Then pour some hardy annual seeds into the palm of your hand and, taking small pinches of seed, thinly sow along the line of the lettering. Continue until all the letters have been sown, and then use horticultural grit to lightly cover the seeds. Water with a watering can fitted with a fine rose attachment. Try sweet alyssum *Lobularia maritima* 'Snow Crystals') or candytuft (*Iberis umbellata*). They will take about 8 weeks to grow.

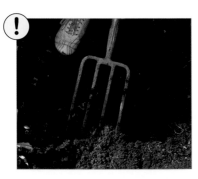

1 Fork over the area to be planted. Level and rake in some slow-release fertilizer (following the instructions on the packet). Adult supervision is required. Mark out your name with a bamboo cane.

2 Use a trowel to make the markings for the letters wider and deeper. If you are not happy with the shape and size of the name, you can just rake over the markings and start again.

3 To make the letters stand out even more clearly, carefully trickle pale-coloured horticultural grit or washed sand along the grooves. Use your hands or fill a plastic bottle and pour.

4 Plunge the bedding plants in a bucket of water until the bubbles stop. You may need to hold them under the water if they are quite dry and floating. Set out enough plants to cover one letter.

 = Watch out! Sharp or dangerous tool in use.   = Watch out! Adult help is needed.

5 Dig holes for each of the plants with a trowel. As the ground has been forked over this should be quite easy to do. Plant the soaked plants in the holes and firm in lightly with your hands.

6 Continue to plant the remaining letters or your name, spacing the flowers out to allow a little room for growth but making sure that you can still clearly see the shape of the letter.

7 Water the whole name with a watering can fitted with a fine rose attachment. This will help to settle the soil round the plant roots. If any roots are showing after watering, add a little more soil.

VARIATION
• A twist on the theme would be to mark the outline of an animal, such as a rabbit, using plastic lawn edging strip and sow inside the margin with grass seed.

spell your name in flowers! **113**

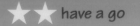
Autumn rainbow

This rainbow-like feature is planted with late summer and autumn plants for instant effect and will last until the first hard frost. You could also do a summer version. If you are happy to wait a few weeks for flowers to appear, save money by using young bedding plants.

you will need
- **border fork**
- **garden rake**
- **slow-release fertilizer granules**
- **plant selection** (*see* Plant List)
- **bucket** of water
- **trowel**
- **border spade** (optional)
- **watering can** with a **fine rose attachment**

garden rake

FACT FILE
PRETTY BUT POISONOUS!

The orange-berried winter cherry included here is grown purely for decoration. Like many of its relatives, it is poisonous to eat. Its family, the *Solanaceae*, includes some familiar fruit and veg – potato, tomato, sweet pepper, chilli pepper and aubergine.

Never eat anything unless an adult has told you that it is safe to do so!

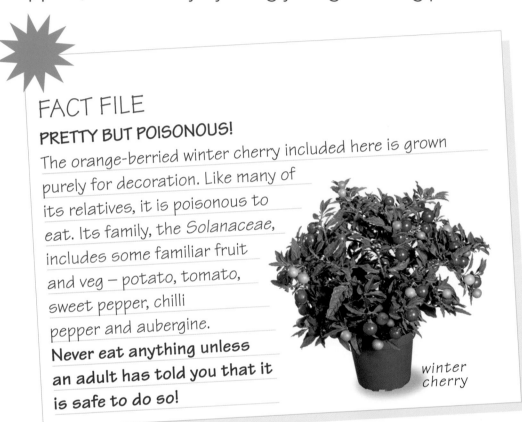

winter cherry

plant list
* **Autumn bedding viola**
  Viola Sorbet Series
* **Busy Lizzie**
  Impatiens New Guinea hybrids
* **Dwarf Michaelmas daisy**
  Aster novi-belgii cvs.
* **Heather**
  Calluna vulgaris (blue-dyed)
* **Winter cherry**
  Solanum pseudocapsicum
  (poisonous!)

WARNING – The winter cherry fruits are poisonous if eaten! You could use orange mini chrysanthemums, autumn crop pot marigolds (*Calendula*), or orange violas as alternatives.

1 Fork over the earth, then rake in some slow-release fertilizer, following packet instructions. Adult supervision is required. Plunge the plants in a bucket of water until the bubbles stop. Dig holes in an arc and plant the violas.

2 Alternatively, ask an adult to help you dig a shallow, curved trench with a spade and, after removing the pots, place all the violas in together. Draw soil dug out from the hole or trench back around the plant roots.

3 Take care to gently feel for gaps around the plants with your fingers and work the soil in between. Firm the soil lightly with the flat of your hand. Repeat for the rest of the violas so they are all firmed in.

4 Set out the next row of plants. In this case we've chosen orange-berried winter cherry (*see* Fact File and the Plant List). You won't need as many of these plants as the small bedding violas.

 = Watch out! Sharp or dangerous tool in use.   = Watch out! Adult help is needed.

5 After planting the winter cherry, add a row of the red, large-flowered busy Lizzie plants from the New Guinea hybrid group. For a hardier alternative, plant a staggered double row of scarlet red mini cyclamen.

6 Settle the soil after planting the busy Lizzies, then plant a staggered row of blue-dyed heathers. The dye is harmless and eventually fades! Leave enough room for a few purple flowers.

7 Select a range of lilac and violet-blue mini Michaelmas daisies to plant between the red busy Lizzies and blue heathers. Finish planting all the remaining rainbow flowers. Water in well.

VARIATION
• Use the following plants to make a summer rainbow: French marigolds, pot marigolds, bedding salvias, Swan river daisies and ornamental sage.

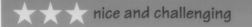

Spiral maze

Make a secret hideaway with this spiral maze of canes and tall flowers. Stepping-stones lead to the centre of the spiral and the prize, a blue glazed ball! You will need adult help to make it, as the paving slabs are heavy, but once it is in position you can sit back and watch it grow! Change the plants in following years, if you like. Aromatic ground-cover plants, such as creeping thymes, Corsican mint or mind-your-own-business would be good.

you will need

- **tall herbaceous perennial flowers** (*see* Plant List), assorted
- **ground cover plants**, assorted (*see* introduction, optional)
- **bucket** of **water**
- **border fork**
- **broom handle** or **hoe handle**
- 2.1–2.4m/7–8ft **bamboo canes**, 20
- **heavy-duty training wire**, 1 reel
- 30cm/1ft square **paving slabs**, 5
- **glazed** or **terracotta ball**
- **iridescent glass** or **acrylic decorations**, 1 small bag

hoe

glass decorations

FACT FILE

TALL FLOWERS

Purple top verbenas are perfect for this small maze because they are so light and airy and take up very little room. They also support themselves and flower for months on end in summer and autumn. Mulching with dry chipped bark helps to insulate the roots from frost damage.

purple top verbena

plant list

✳ **5 pincushion flowers**
Scabiosa atropurpurea 'Chile Black'
✳ **1 pink hyssop**
Agastache barberi
✳ **10 purple top verbenas/ purple top vervains**
Verbena bonariensis

1 Soak the plants in a bucket of water until the bubbles stop. Fork over the earth. Mark out a spiral in the area using a broom or hoe handle. Adult supervision is required.

2 Starting from the outside of the spiral, push bamboo canes into the ground, pushing them near their bases. Gradually bring the canes closer together towards the centre.

3 Attach the end of a reel of wire to the first cane, then with someone holding the canes upright, wind around each. To finish, wrap the wire around the cane. Adult help may be required.

4 Set out the purple top verbenas around the outer curve of the maze. Carefully plant between the canes, digging holes for each without disturbing the canes.

 = Watch out! Sharp or dangerous tool in use. = Watch out! Adult help is needed.

5 Towards the centre of the spiral, plant the shorter pincushion flowers and finally the pink hyssop or another aromatic plant, like French lavender. Firm in with your hands. Water well.

6 Ask an adult to help you lay out the five small paving slabs in an arc, as shown in the main picture. You could paint on some footsteps (*see* pages 148–9)!

7 All mazes need a surprise at the centre as a reward for finding your way. Here we've used an ball but you might choose some other kind of treasure, such as a terracotta seashell.

8 Define the curling shape at the centre of the spiral by laying out a row of glass or acrylic decorations or some white pebbles. You could also suspend wind dancers from the wire.

spiral maze

Sensations circle

This little garden will appeal to four out of your five senses. The soothing colour scheme is pleasing to the eye, as is the movement created by swaying grass seed-heads. Smooth cobbles and gravel contrast with a wide variety of plant shapes and textures inviting touch. If you rub the foliage of lavender, curry plant and minty *Agastache*, they will release scents for your nose to enjoy. Close your eyes and listen to the tinkling of the wind chime and buzzing of insects.

you will need

- **plants** (*see* Plant List), assorted
- **bucket** of **water**
- **trowel**
- **large rounded cobbles**, 3
- **shingle**, 1 small bag
- **iridescent glass** or **acrylic shapes, beads** or **marbles**, 1 small bag
- **shepherd's crook bird feeder support**
- **small windchime**

lavender

plant list

- ✳ **1 bluebeard**
  Caryopteris x *clandonensis* 'Dark Knight'
- ✳ **1 curry plant**
  Helichrysum italicum
- ✳ **1 cushion bush**
  Leucophyta brownii syn. *Calocephalus*
- ✳ **3 feather grass**
  Stipa tenuissima
- ✳ **1 hebe**
  Hebe 'Emerald Gem'
- ✳ **2 houseleeks**
  Sempervivum cvs.

- ✳ **1 ice plant**
  Sedum spectabile 'Brilliant'
- ✳ **1 Japanese silver grass**
  Miscanthus sinensis 'Yakushima Dwarf'
- ✳ **1 lavender**
  Lavandula angustifolia 'Hidcote'
- ✳ **1 leatherleaf sedge**
  Carex buchananii
- ✳ **1 pink hyssop**
  Agastache barberi form
- ✳ **1 silverbush**
  Convolvulus cneorum

1 Soak the plants in a bucket of water until the bubbles stop. Lay out a crescent with bluebeard and Japanese silver grass at the back and ice plant, feather grass, hebe and silverbush further in.

2 Add smaller, ground-hugging and rosette-forming plants such as this purple-tinted houseleek towards the centre. Try out different combinations to find the best look.

3 Having finally decided what plants are going where, dig out planting holes using a trowel. Position the plants in the prepared holes, starting with a cushion bush.

4 Carefully move the soil back around the roots to fill the gaps and ensure that the plants are at the same depth as they were in the pot. Firm lightly with your hands.

5 Continue planting in the same way, including as shown here, a feather grass, a curry plant and a group of purple-flowered lavenders. Finish with another houseleek. These will be surrounded by shingle.

6 Ask an adult to help you position the three cobbles. Stand one upright behind the hebe, but the other two either side should be partly buried to show off their domed, smooth shape.

 = Watch out! Sharp or dangerous tool in use.   = Watch out! Adult help is needed.

7 Spread a layer of shingle around the plants and cobbles to fill the centre of the circle. Take care not to bury the houseleeks. The shingle helps protect plants from getting too wet.

8 Place some iridescent glass or acrylic shapes, beads or marbles on to the shingle. The purple and coppery shades are reflected in the colours of the flowers and foliage.

9 Push in a shepherd's crook bird feeder support at an angle so that you can hang a small wind chime over the centre of the circle. Listen to different chimes to find the one you like best before buying.

Herb patchwork quilt

With this grid of stepping-stones planted with different sorts of creeping thyme, the effect is a bit like a patchwork quilt. Eventually all the plants will knit together and even start to grow over the edges of the slabs. Then, when you walk across, treading on the aromatic shoots, a wonderful scent will be released.

you will need
- border fork
- **horticultural/coarse grit**, 1 sack
- rake
- **30cm/12in paving slabs**, 5
- trowel
- **creeping thymes** (see Plant List), 15
- **bucket** of **water**
- **hand brush**
- **watering can** with a **fine rose attachment**

grit   rake   thyme

FACT FILE

ALL IN THE FAMILY

Like many herbs and aromatic plants, thymes are members of a very important group, the mint family or *Lamiaceae*. You will find mint family members used for cooking and for making medicines and most are also powerful bee attractors. Have a look at lavender, sage, rosemary, marjoram and catmint flowers to see if you can spot the family resemblance.

rosemary

plant list
✳ **5 Doone Valley thymes**
  Thymus 'Doone Valley'
✳ **7 lemon thymes**
  Thymus pulegioides 'Aureus'
✳ **3 woolly thymes**
  Thymus pseudolanuginosus

1 Fork over the area to loosen the soil, and mix in a sack of course grit. Level with a rake. Adult supervision is required. Ask an adult to help you lay out a rough chequerboard pattern of slabs.

2 Use a trowel to score around the edge of the paving slabs so that you will know their position when the slabs are lifted. Alternatively put a plastic plant label in each corner to mark out the area.

3 Ask an adult to lift the slab and then scrape away the soil evenly with a trowel to a depth of about the thickness of the slab. Replace the slab and check that it is solidly in place and doesn't wobble.

4 Set out the thymes, keeping the groups of each kind together so that when they grow they will mingle and look like one large patch. Leave a gap around the slabs, allowing room for growth.

 = Watch out! Sharp or dangerous tool in use.   = Watch out! Adult help is needed.

5 Even though thymes are drought-resistant, plunge each in a bucket of water, waiting for the bubbles to stop, before planting. Dig out a hole for each that is large enough to accommodate the root-balls.

6 Take each thyme out of its pot and put into the planting hole. Check it is at the correct depth, not too low or raised above the surrounding soil. Fill in round the roots with soil and firm lightly.

7 Soil mustn't bury any part of the creeping thyme's foliage (leaves) as this could cause rot. Use a hand brush to sweep soil off the paving slabs. Water with a watering can fitted with a rose attachment.

TOP TIP
▶ Whatever type of herb chequerboard you plant, it is essential that you weed it thoroughly beforehand and remove weeds as soon as you spot them.

herb patchwork quilt   121

Garden craft

If you want to decorate your garden and make attractive and useful objects, this chapter is stuffed full of ideas. Most projects can be made indoors or out and use natural or recycled materials, so you won't have to spend much pocket money. Ornamental features add style to the patio and some items are designed for outdoor games.

Recycled plant labels

These brightly coloured plant labels, shaped like the varieties of fruit or vegetables you may be growing, clearly show what seeds you have sown and which plants are which in the garden.

you will need

- **table protector**, such as a plastic sheet
- **plastic containers**, such as milk cartons, yogurt pots or clear plastic lids
- **scissors**
- **felt-tipped pen**
- **artist's acrylic paints**
- **artist's paintbrushes**
- **recycled plastic lid**
- **jam jar** of **water**
- **coloured lolly sticks**, **canes** or **stiff wire**
- **glue** or **adhesive tape**

TOP TIP

► If you don't have ice lolly sticks to hand, ask an adult to help you split the top of a short piece of cane and wedge the label in, or attach a piece of wire using adhesive tape, which can be pushed into the ground.

1 Cover the surface with a table protector. Cut out a flat piece of plastic from a container with scissors. Use a felt-tipped pen to draw the outline of the shape you want on to it. Cut out the shape. Ask an adult to help you.

2 Paint the label with appropriate-coloured artist's acrylic paint using a paintbrush. Here, we painted a carrot-shaped label orange and green. The paint should be nice and thick; if it is too diluted it won't stick.

3 Other shapes, such as a tomato, sunflower or this pepper, may fit nicely on a circular lid, which you don't then need to cut out. Draw the outline first with a felt-tipped pen and then fill in the shape with paint, as you did for the other labels.

4 Cut pointed ends on the labels so that they can be pushed into the compost easily. Attach other shapes to ice lolly sticks, canes or wire using glue or adhesive tape.

5 If you like, you can combine the scientific or Latin name, or the plant's common name, with painted decorations.

lolly sticks

(!) = Watch out! Sharp or dangerous tool in use. ( ) = Watch out! Adult help is needed.

Cane heads

Garden canes are often at head height and can poke you in the eye if you aren't careful. These cane tops, decorated to look like heads, fit on to the ends of canes and act as protective coverings.

you will need

- **polystyrene balls** or **shapes** (such as hearts)
- **pencil** or **short cane**
- **surface protector**, such as a plastic sheet
- **flesh-coloured artist's acrylic paint**
- **saucer** or **plastic lid**
- **artist's paintbrush**
- **self-adhesive eyes**
- **felt-tipped pens**
- **raffia** or **wool**
- **glue**
- **plastic lids**, such as those from plastic bottles or toothpaste tubes

felt-tipped pens

raffia

TOP TIP

▶ Polystyrene balls and other shapes are available at craft and art shops.

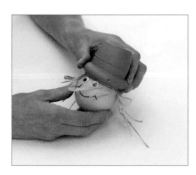

1 Place the polystyrene balls or shapes on a flat surface and push a pencil or cane into the bottom. Adult supervision is required.

2 Cover the surface with a table protector. Turning the pencil or cane, paint the 'head' using flesh-coloured artist's acrylic. Mix up the shade in a saucer or plastic lid if you don't have the right colour or use a suitable paint tester pot.

3 Stick on a pair of eyes – and draw on a mouth using red felt-tipped pen.

4 Attach a ring of hair made from bits of raffia or wool using glue. Wait for this to dry while you work on another head.

5 To hide the join where you fixed on the hair, stick on a coloured plastic bottle lid. Alternatively, draw on hair with felt-tipped pens. When the glue is dry, remove the pencil or cane and position on top of canes in the garden.

Weird and wacky gourds

Grow small ornamental gourds to dry for wacky house decorations. The weirdly shaped fruits have warty, ribbed or spiny skins, often with striped or two-tone green, yellow, orange or white colouring.

you will need

- **small pots**
- **peat-free seed** and **cutting compost**
- **small dibber** or **bamboo cane**
- **ornamental gourd seeds**
- **windowsill propagator**
- **watering can**
- **13cm/5in pots**
- **tub** or **barrel**
- **crocks**
- **gravel**
- **trowel**
- **enriched peat-free potting compost**
- **slow-release fertilizer granules**
- **liquid manure plant feed** and/or **manure mulch**
- **artist's acrylic paints** and/or **varnish** (optional, *see* Top Tip)

3 Carefully pot on larger plants to 13cm/5in pots when they are large enough to handle.

1 Fill small pots with moist peat-free seed and cutting compost, then make a hole about 2.5cm/1in deep with a dibber or cane. Sow the seeds on their edges.

2 Put the pots in a windowsill propagator. The heat provided by an electric propagator is ideal. Don't exclude light. Water occasionally, as needed.

4 Add crocks to a large tub or barrel with drainage holes, then add gravel using a trowel. Ask an adult to help you fill with enriched peat-free potting compost or add slow-release fertilizer granules.

5 Put the plants in the tub or barrel after the danger from frost or cold nights has passed. Harden off (*see* page 13) for about 3 weeks.

6 Gourds are fast-growing and spread quickly. Grow up a fence or wall if short of space. Ideally, mulch with manure. Liquid-feed frequently.

TOP TIP

▶ Harvest ripe gourds in autumn when the stems are dry and have gone brown, before the first frost. Allow them to dry out in a warm place indoors, or spread out on a groundsheet in the sun. When hard, you can paint them or just coat them with clear varnish.

(!) = Watch out! Sharp or dangerous tool in use. = Watch out! Adult help is needed.

Garden signposts

This signpost carries a message for the bumble-bees that simply says 'this way to the flowers'! Prop it up with a stone or brick or, if painting a roof tile, use the holes already in the tile to hang it up.

you will need
- **table protector**, such as a plastic sheet
- **reference picture(s)**
- **paper**
- **chalk**
- **clean, dry slate**, 1 piece, such as a roofing tile, a flat stone or matt surfaced tile
- **white, yellow, black, lilac** and **orange artist's acrylic paints**
- **fine paintbrush**
- **paint palette**
- **jam jar** of **water**
- **clear, matt exterior-quality varnish** (optional, see Top Tip)
- **varnish brush** (optional, see Top Tip)

TOP TIP
▶ Acrylic paint dries to form a waterproof coating so lasts quite a long time outdoors. But, to keep your signposts in tip-top condition for longer, varnish it when dry using a clear, matt exterior-quality product and a varnish brush.

1 Cover the surface with a table protector. Using a picture for reference, sketch a design on paper, then copy it in chalk on to a piece of clean, dry slate.

2 If you make a mistake, simply wipe the slate clean with a damp cloth and start again. Repeat as necessary until you are happy with the picture.

3 Using white paint and a fine paintbrush, go over the chalk lines to make it stand out clearly.

4 When the white paint is dry, colour the insides in sections. Here, we started with the yellow parts of the bee and the centre of the flower. When those were dry, we painted the lilac petals.

5 Acrylic paint dries quite quickly on a warm day. If you put a lot of paint on thickly, it takes longer and the paint may drip, so do thin layers.

6 Don't forget to rinse your paintbrush in between colours and change the jam jar water regularly. Paint on the rest of the design.

7 For a 3D feel, use darker and lighter shades of the same paint colours to create shading around the designs. Add wing veins and dotted lines for movement, if you like.

Dogwood stars

You can make use of lovely red-barked dogwoods to make these decorative stars. Hang them up in the house or the garden as a natural decoration.

you will need
- **thin dogwood stems**
- **secateurs** or **pruners**
- **wire** or **twine**, different colours and thicknesses
- **wire cutters**
- **clear, gloss, exterior-grade varnish**
- **paintbrush**

paintbrush

coloured twine

1 Ask an adult to cut some dogwood stems for you using a pair of secateurs or pruners.

2 Shorten the stems so they are the same length, then make six bundles of three or four twigs for each hanging. Lay them in a star shape.

3 Use coloured wire or twine to bind the bundles together where they cross over.

4 Keep tension on the reel of wire or twine and wrap the wire several times around the bundles of sticks before fastening off with a knot.

5 Every point where the stems cross must be wired. Try using different coloured wire or twine for each star, or making the stars in various sizes.

6 The stems lose their sheen after a while, so paint them with varnish using a paintbrush.

TOP TIP
▶ Stars are quite easy to make, but you could also try a simple triangle or a square. Alternatively, make a grid pattern of squares and fill the spaces with hanging ornaments, such as coloured beads.

(!) = Watch out! Sharp or dangerous tool in use. (🔔) = Watch out! Adult help is needed.

Colourful pots

Have a go and brighten up the patio or deck with painted terracotta pots in lots of different designs and colours! You could also plant the containers with herbs or houseplants for a cheery indoor windowsill display.

you will need

- **table protector**, such as a plastic sheet
- **terracotta pots**
- **glue brush**
- **PVA glue**, diluted
- **emulsion paint**
- **5cm/2in paintbrush**
- **piece** of **chalk** or a **soft pencil**
- **artist's acrylic paints**
- **artist's brushes**
- **jam jar** of **water**
- **plastic paint palette**

TOP TIP

▶ If you plan to use the pots outdoors, keep the paint looking good for longer by sealing with several coats of clear, matt polyurethane varnish (exterior quality).

1 Cover the surface with a table protector. Using a glue brush, paint the inside and outside of the pots with diluted PVA glue to seal them.

2 When the glue is completely dry, paint the pot with emulsion paint using a paintbrush.

3 Leave the rim unpainted if you like. Allow the paint to dry for about half an hour.

4 Once the paint is dry, use a piece of chalk or a soft pencil to lightly sketch on your design. Here we have used a series of circles.

5 Beginning with one acrylic paint colour and a fine paintbrush, carefully paint in the outer ring. Rinse the brush.

6 Leave to dry, or, to avoid mixing wet colours but continuing to paint, fill in the most central part in another colour, such as yellow.

7 Follow with the darker colour inside the ring (we used dark blue) and finally complete the target design with another inner ring in a vivid shade such as red (used here). Paint different target designs over the rest of the pot, if you like.

8 Another simple design can be made by painting horizontal or vertical stripes.

9 Wait until the paint is dry, then plant up the pot with a plant of your choice.

Mosaic pots

The word 'mosaic' brings to mind Roman villas with their intricately laid floors depicting all kinds of elaborate scenes. But these mosaics designs are very easy and great fun to experiment with. Once you've had a go you'll soon be decorating all kinds of objects around the house and garden! Whatever object you choose though, make sure it's dry first. Why not make some individually painted and decorated pots to give as presents? You could even plant a flower in one.

you will need

- **table protector**, such as a plastic sheet
- **glue brush**
- **recycled plastic lids** or **saucer**
- **terracotta pots**
- **PVA glue**
- **glass** or **acrylic beads**
- **chalk**
- **small glue spreader**
- **exterior-quality, waterproof tile cement**, 1 small tub
- **artist's paintbrush**
- **artist's acrylic paint**
- **water**
- **lightweight, coloured foam squares**
- **small shells**
- **old CDs**, broken into pieces (see Top Tip)

an assortment of colourful beads and foam squares

TOP TIP

▶ Ask an adult to break up some unwanted CDs for you by putting them in a bag on the ground and smashing with a hammer. Use wire snippers to break the pieces into the right shape, which can then be stuck on to the pots. Wear safety goggles. The shards of CD are safer than glass to handle but can still be sharp, so take care when using them.

CDs

1 Cover the surface with a table protector. Using a glue brush, paint the inside and outside of the pots with diluted PVA glue (mix this in plastic lids or a saucer). Leave to dry. This seals the pot.

2 Decide on your design, perhaps experimenting with different shapes and patterns of bead until you find something that appeals. Draw the design on each side of the pot in chalk as a guide for gluing.

3 Begin with the central part of the pattern. Use a small glue spreader to put a small amount of exterior-quality, waterproof tile cement on to the bead. Don't use too much or the excess with ooze out.

4 Press each bead down firmly and wipe off any excess cement with the spreader. Once each side has been completed, finish off with a narrow band of smaller beads spaced evenly round the rim.

(!) = Watch out! Sharp or dangerous tool in use.   (⚠) = Watch out! Adult help is needed.

5 For something different, paint a terracotta plant pot with cream artist's acrylic paint. Apply a second coat if necessary and leave to dry. There's no need to seal with PVA as this pot won't be used outdoors.

6 Use PVA glue to stick lightweight, coloured foam squares around the rim of the pot. Mix up the colours to give a bright finish. Wait until the pot is completely dry before moving it or the squares may slide.

7 Another variation on the theme is to again use a painted pot but this time to create a decorative edge with small shells. Attach them in a row or around the rim, using waterproof tile cement.

8 A simple mirrored mosaic design can be made using pieces of broken CDs (see Top Tip). Work out your design and draw round it on paper to remind yourself of the position before gluing with PVA.

mosaic pots   131

Mini pebble pictures

These chunky little wall plaques are a fun way to show off your favourite stones and pebbles and, if you want something more colourful, you can add iridescent glass or acrylic beads and marbles too. You can also buy small bags of polished pebbles in black or white as well as more natural shades. These pictures are based on simple flower shapes, but you could make up funny faces, cartoon figures or abstract patterns too.

you will need

- **table protector**, such as a plastic sheet
- **rigid plastic storage containers**, 2
- **clear film**
- **ready-mix mortar**, 5kg/12lb bag
- **bucket**
- **trowel**
- **rubber gloves**
- **piece** of **stiff plastic**
- **thin wire**
- **pebbles**
- **marbles**
- **glass** or **acrylic beads**
- **hand sprayer**

rubber gloves

trowel

TOP TIP

▶ The ideal pebbles or beads for this project are ones that are slightly flattened and oval or circular in shape. Instead of putting them in flat-side down, push them in on their edge or narrow end in. This means that the mortar has more pebble or bead to grip on to, making the finished picture secure.

glass beads

1 Cover the surface with a table protector. Line a couple of rigid plastic storage containers with clear film. You could also use recycled plastic packaging, such as margarine tubs.

2 Ask an adult to mix together some ready-mix mortar in a bucket with just a little water, using a trowel. It should be stiff, not sloppy. Wear gloves and don't touch the mortar.

3 Half-fill the lined plastic storage containers with the mortar mix, leaving room for the pebble pieces in the top. Press the mixture down firmly with a stiff piece of plastic.

4 Form a piece of wire into a loop with long ends. Push the ends into the mortar. When the mix hardens this will give you something to hang the pebble mosaic picture with.

(!) = Watch out! Sharp or dangerous tool in use. (👤) = Watch out! Adult help is needed.

5 Gather together pebbles, marbles and beads and work out what patterns you want to use in each container. Simple patterns work best. Push in the pieces to at least half their depth.

6 The further the decorations are pressed into the mortar, the less likely they will be to fall out. Spray the finished mosaic with water to clean off any cement dust.

7 Dry flat and leave to harden for 24 hours. Once hard, tip out into your hand; they should fall out easily. Pull off the clear film. Hang the finished mosaics in the house or garden.

TOP TIP

▶ Hang in a protected part of the garden, such as on a house wall. Don't leave them lying flat, or water can collect and freeze, causing damage.

Mary Mary…

How does your garden grow? If you want to be like Contrary Mary and decorate it with silver bells and cockleshells, here's how! You might want to find your own shells or you can buy several different types, such as the mother-of-pearl lined abalone, from craft shops.

you will need

- **small bells**
- **shells**, assorted sizes, colours and shapes,
- **fine nylon twine** or **fishing twine**
- **short bamboo canes**
- **glue**
- **rounded gravel** or **shingle**
- **pebbles** or **cobbles**

FACT FILE

SEASIDE PLANTS

Plants that grow along the beach tend to be low-growing, with adaptations that prevent them losing moisture from their leaves due to the wind and salt spray. Seaside plants often have small white, yellow, blue or purple flowers and silver, grey or blue leaves, and succulent or grassy foliage (see Plant List).

sea holly

plant list

- ✳ **Blue mist shrub, bluebeard**
  Caryopteris X clandonensis
- ✳ **Cotton lavender**
  Santolina chamaecyparissus
- ✳ **Feather grass**
  Stipa tenuissima
- ✳ **Hardy plumbago**
  Ceratostigma willmottianum

- ✳ **Lamb's ears**
  Stachys byzantina 'Silver Carpet'
- ✳ **Moroccan daisy**
  Rhodanthemum 'African Eyes'
- ✳ **Ornamental sedge**
  Carex flagellifera
- ✳ **Red valerian**
  Centranthus ruber
- ✳ **Rock rose**
  Cistus corbariensis

- ✳ **Russian sage**
  Perovskia atriplicifolia 'Blue Spire'
- ✳ **Sea holly**
  Eryngium maritimum
- ✳ **Thrift**
  Armeria maritima
- ✳ **Stonecrop**
  Sedum spathulifolium 'Cape Blanco'

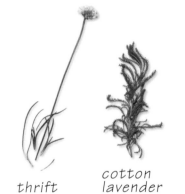

thrift   *cotton lavender*

1 Gather together all your ingredients for this project, which combines little silver bells (the sort normally stitched on to clothing) with shells. Abalones have convenient holes in them.

2 Use the naturally occurring holes in your shells or ones created by erosion to thread through fine nylon twine. Make a knot to stop the shell or bell sliding along the line.

3 It helps to line up the shells and bells in advance to make it easier to thread them on to the twine. This is quite a fiddly job and you might need some adult help.

4 Push a series of equally spaced bamboo canes into the ground along the edge of a border, then string the garland across them making loops or swags of shells and bells.

 = Watch out! Sharp or dangerous tool in use.   = Watch out! Adult help is needed.

7 Use large cobbles and smaller pebbles to edge a border next to the gravel area to create more of a beach effect.

8 If you like, position pots of plants that have small scale-like leaves, furry or succulent leaves, or grassy growth.

white cobbles

VARIATION
• You could also decorate the seaside corner with driftwood, a ceramic starfish (take it in for the winter), or fish made from recycled metal.

5 If you like, cap the canes with glued-on shells to make them easier to see and less likely to poke you in the eye! Use smooth shells, such as cowrie or cone-shaped limpets.

6 Enhance the seaside effect by adding more shells, especially any that didn't have holes in that you weren't able to use for the garlands. They work well with rounded gravel or shingle.

Wind chimes

This quirky wind chime is a test of ingenuity. Can you find suitable objects, small metal bits and pieces, lying around the house, garage or shed? Do ask permission before taking anything, especially items such as keys, which may still be in use. Some metals change colour over time. Pure iron rusts, turning brown or orange when hung outdoors. Copper eventually goes from shiny orange-brown to matt blue-green as it reacts with the atmosphere. Aluminium, chrome-plated items or galvanized pieces won't change.

you will need
- **unused keys**
- **springs** or **coils**
- **nuts**, **bolts** and **metal washers**
- **small bells**
- **foil food containers**
- **chopping board**
- **ballpoint pen**
- **cookie cutters**, several, of different sizes
- **coins**, several
- **craft scissors**
- **table forks** or **short bamboo canes**, 2
- **wire**
- **nylon fishing line**

TOP TIP
► To make coils and springs out of types of wire, take a fat marker pen and slimmer pens that are round, not ridged in cross section. Wind the wire tightly round each pen and cut to length with wire cutters. Slip the coil off and stretch slightly. Adult supervision is required.

1 Gather together a range of small metal objects that can be hung together to form a mobile or wind chime. Try out the sound of the materials clanging against each other to get a good combination.

2 Foil packaging is a great material because one or both sides are usually plain silver or gold. Wash out the containers and then cut to form sheets of thick foil. Adult supervision is required.

3 Lay the foil flat on a chopping board or artist's cutting board and, using a ballpoint pen, draw round cookie cutters or coins or create simple shapes, such as hearts.

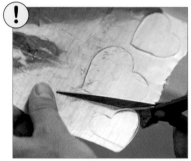

4 Cut out the shapes with a pair of scissors. Turn the foil piece as you go to make cutting easier. Don't use the best scissors as you can blunt the blades. Adult supervision is required.

5 If you want to make the shapes even more attractive, use a ballpoint pen once more and score your design on the reverse. It is easy to mark a line just inside the outline.

6 Put a pair of old forks across one another and wrap wire round them to form the frame from which the pieces of the wind chime will hang. You can use crossed bamboo canes.

! = Watch out! Sharp or dangerous tool in use.   = Watch out! Adult help is needed.

7 Make a hole in each of the foil shapes, then get all the materials ready to hang by threading them with nylon fishing line. Tie a firm knot to secure to the mobile and leave a long end for attaching.

8 Hang the crossed forks at a convenient height to work using a piece of wire. Attach the ends of the nylon threads holding the objects to the crossed forks.

9 Space the objects out evenly and hang them at different heights so they create a tiered effect and jangle against each other in the wind. Ask an adult to hang in a safe place.

small metal objects

Wind dancer

This delicate wind dancer will move in the slightest breeze because it weighs so little. The thin wire frame is almost invisible, which means that the natural elements used – pine cones, shells and feathers – appear to float in mid-air.

you will need
- **pine cones**
- **feathers**
- **shells**, such as abalone
- **pin**
- **nylon fishing line**
- **scissors**
- **wire**

1 Gather all the ingredients together. You may be able to pick up pine cones and feathers on local walks or family hikes through the woods but craft shops also sell a range of natural materials.

2 Each piece will need to be attached to the wire frame. To do this with shells, ask an adult to make a hole with a pin, take a piece of nylon line and pass one end through a hole. Knot firmly and leave a long free end.

3 To attach a pine cone, wrap the nylon line around under the scales and tie off tightly to prevent it slipping. Tie feathers around the 'stalk'. Knot several times to secure.

4 Make a lightweight frame using a reel of wire. The best way to do this is to create a zigzag of wire with a small loop at each 'elbow' or turn. These loops are used to attach the objects.

5 Mix up the different elements for your wind dancer so that you don't end up with the same things hanging together. Fix a shell to the wire loop with the free end of the nylon line.

6 Attach the small pine cones and feathers in the same way. Don't use heavy items, such as large, closed pine cones or big shells as this will pull the zigzag frame out of balance.

VARIATION
- As an alternative to a wind dancer, you can make a furry spider sitting on its web. Hang it on a wall or suspend from a piece of string.

you will need
- **twigs**, 3
- **coarse parcel string**
- **furry pipe cleaners**
- **pine cone**
- **self-adhesive eyes**

1 Bind the twigs together at the centre with parcel string to create six spokes.

2 Use the same string to make the web. Keep tension on the string as you wrap it round each spoke. Tie off firmly.

3 Make the legs by pushing pipe cleaner pieces through the scales of the pine cone. Stick on a pair of eyes and fix the finished spider to the web with fine wire.

spider wall hanging

 = Watch out! Sharp or dangerous tool in use.   = Watch out! Adult help is needed.

7 Slowly pick up the structure, arranging the hanging pieces so that they are dangling free from the frame. Gently bend the wire frame into a sort of spiral so that the pieces hang away from each other.

8 You might find it easier to work out the balance of the wind dancer and to thread more pieces on to spare loops if the frame is already hanging up in a temporary position.

9 Once you are happy with the mobile, hang it in its final spot so that the elements can move freely in the breeze. The canopy of a shed or summerhouse, as here, is ideal.

shells

feathers

CD screen

This decorative screen made from bamboo canes and recycled CDs is like a giant outdoor mobile! Use it in the vegetable garden to keep birds off your crops or as a backdrop to flowers. It's amazing how many old or unwanted music or recordable CDs you can collect just by asking adults to save them for your project. When hung outdoors, the surface that isn't printed on catches the light and shows all kinds of rainbow colours, like oil on water.

you will need

- 1.8–2.1m/6–7ft **bamboo canes**, 8
- **thick garden wire** or **garden twine**
- **wire cutters** or **scissors**
- **pliers**
- **unwanted CDs**
- **drill**, with very fine drill bit (for adult use only)
- **nylon fishing line** or **thin, coloured parcel twine**
- **cane toppers**, (see page 125)

garden twine and scissors

FACT FILE

FLOWERING CLIMBERS FROM SEED

Your CD screen can also work as a frame for growing colourful flowering climbers, such as the hardy annual nasturtium and sweet pea. After the last spring frost, sow runner beans directly into the ground, which you have forked over.

Start Spanish flag and canary creeper seeds in pots on a warm window ledge in early spring following instructions on the packet.

WARNING – Spanish flag seeds are poisonous.

nasturtium

sweet pea

---

1 Push three pairs of crossing bamboo canes into the ground. Try to make the angles as even as possible. Be careful when moving them into position to keep the ends away from people's eyes.

2 If the ground is very hard, hold the canes close to the bottom so that the cane doesn't snap or bend when you are pushing it in. Ask an adult to help you if you are having difficulty.

3 Join the canes where they cross over with pieces of thick garden wire or twine, cut to length with wire cutters or scissors. Ask an adult to cut the wire. Twist and tighten with pliers.

4 Balance a bamboo cane across the top and attach the three pairs of canes to it to create a series of large diamond shapes and smaller triangles. This is definitely a two-person job!

5 Push in an upright cane at both ends. Attach the top cane to them to create a strong framework. It needs to be able to stand up to strong winds and the weight of climbing plants.

 = Watch out! Sharp or dangerous tool in use.   = Watch out! Adult help is needed.

6 Ask an adult to drill small holes into each of the CDs. Then thread through nylon fishing line or thin, coloured parcel twine, knotting it to prevent it slipping.

7 Use the two long free ends of line to attach each CD to the framework. Position one CD to hang in the middle of each of the small triangular spaces along the top.

8 Hang as many CDs on to the frame as you like. Tie the line shorter or longer so they hang at different levels. It doesn't matter which way the CDs hang. Add cane toppers.

TOP TIP
▶ You can hang all sorts of natural bits and pieces from this screen, provided they are light enough, or even strips of coloured fabric or plastic.

CD screen 141

Spooky Jack-o'-lantern

Whether you are planning to surprise visitors at a Hallowe'en party with home-grown Jack-o'-lanterns or just want to join in the seasonal fun of pumpkin carving, this project will give you all the help and advice you'll need. Of course you must ask permission from an adult before you begin and you'll probably need some grown-up help along the way. If you are lucky, your Monster Pumpkin Pet (see page 82) might even produce a fruit that is big enough to carve!

you will need
- **large pumpkin**
- **medium sharp knife**
- **bowl**
- **felt-tipped pen**
- **small sharp knife**
- **bucket** or **bowl**
- **night light** or **small candle**
- **matches**

bowl   *pumpkin*

TOP TIP

► To make a tasty snack from the pumpkin seeds, heat the oven to 180°C/350°F/Gas 4. Scoop out the seeds and rinse in a colander. Spread the clean seeds out thinly on a baking tray so that they roast evenly. Drizzle with olive oil and lightly salt. Roast for about 10 minutes or until light golden brown, shaking occasionally so they brown evenly. You need to keep a close eye on them as they can burn easily. Cool and store in an airtight container. Sprinkle over salads, or eat on their own as a delicious snack.

pumpkin seeds

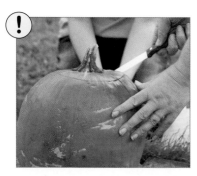

1 Find a ripe pumpkin and ask an adult to help you cut the 'lid' off the fruit. Leave the stalk as a handle. Take great care with knives and don't use them unless you have permission.

2 Angle the cut so that you can fit the lid back on neatly afterwards. Remove the solid flesh directly beneath the lid. It can be used in soups or to make pumpkin pie!

3 The next step is a bit gross! Pull out all the slimey stuff and pumpkin seeds and put them into a bowl. You will need this later if you want to make a yummy snack (see Top Tip).

4 Wash and dry your hands and the knife. Check the skin of the pumpkin is dry, then draw on a face with a felt-tipped pen. Make the features big and simple.

ⓘ = Watch out! Sharp or dangerous tool in use.   ⓐ = Watch out! Adult help is needed.

5 Ask an adult to help you to cut out the eyes, nose and mouth. You might want to use a smaller knife for greater cutting control. Set the pumpkin on a bucket or bowl to steady it.

6 Once you have finished cutting, press the segments back into the hollow insides with your thumbs. You might need to do a little bit of neatening up afterwards with the knife.

7 With permission from an adult, light a night light or small candle and pass it through the mouth. Carefully guide it into position with your other hand. Be careful not to burn yourself!

8 Replace the pumpkin lid with the stalk set at a jaunty angle. Once it has gone dark you'll really be able to see the flickering candle, the scary eyes and eerie orange glow.. Spooky!

spooky Jack-o'-lantern   **143**

Friendly scarecrow!

The beauty of this scarecrow is that he is 100 per cent recycled! You shouldn't need to buy any of the materials listed below. They are all things that you can normally find in the house, garage, shed or garden. Do ask permission from an adult first though. Another plus point is that the scarecrow can easily be dismantled and stored under cover for the winter. Use him to brighten up your veg plot – he may even scare off a few crows!

you will need
- **wooden battens**, 2
- **nails**
- **hammer**
- **plain pillow cases**, 2
- **stuffing material**, such as plastic bags, bubble-wrap packaging, recycled newspaper etc
- **flesh-coloured acrylic paint**
- **paintbrush**
- **wool**
- **scissors**
- **parcel tape**
- **pencil**
- **black marker pen**
- **garden twine**
- **old clothes**, such as a shirt, trousers, scarf, gardening gloves and a hat
- **plastic refuse sacks**
- **old wellington boots**, 1 pair
- **piece** of **wire**
- **fabric flower** (optional)

TOP TIP
▶ Choose whatever theme you like for your scarecrow and even dress him or her up differently during the year or change the hairstyle, for instance, by attaching long woollen plaits. If you can't find wooden battens to nail together, you can make the frame from twigs and tree branches bound together with strong twine.

Hallowe'en scarecrow

wellington boots

1 Find a long piece of wooden batten (head height or taller) and another shorter piece to fix for the shoulders and arms. Ask an adult to help you nail them together using a hammer.

2 Pack a pillowcase with stuffing and gather the material at the back to make a round shape. Paint the face with flesh-coloured acrylic paint. Attach wool for the hair with parcel tape.

3 Draw on the face – big eyes, nose and mouth – with a pencil. Go over with a black marker pen so that you can see the features clearly. Attach the head to the frame with garden twine.

4 Hammer the frame into the ground and begin to dress the scarecrow. Start with an adult's shirt. Fill a large plain pillowcase with plastic stuffing for the body.

 = Watch out! Sharp or dangerous tool in use.   = Watch out! Adult help is needed.

5 Use the top two corners of the pillowcase to tie the body round the neck of the scarecrow. You can hide the join with a scarf. Tie some twine round the middle to shape the waist.

6 Make sausage-shaped stuffing for the arms and legs using refuse sacks filled with newspaper and tied off. Tie off the legs of the trousers and stuff. Stuff the arms, then do up the cuffs.

7 Stuff gloves to make the hands and fix to the ends of the batten. Attach the trousers with twine – the buttoned-up shirt will hide the join. Put the stuffed legs into a pair of wellies.

8 Add the finishing touches, such as a straw sun hat. Attach with wire to stop it blowing off. You can also give the scarecrow a buttonhole using a fabric flower.

friendly scarecrow!   145

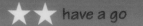
Time for a bath

A supply of fresh drinking water is almost as important for birds as food. Always keep your new birdbath clean and topped up. It might be something you can do for them every other day. Birds also need to take care of their feathers by taking regular baths in shallow water. Seeing them splash about in specially created 'puddles' is a treat for any bird lover! Well-kept plumage (that's another name for feathers) keeps birds warm and dry.

you will need

- **tarpaulin** or **piece** of **plastic sheeting**
- **flat, rigid board**
- **gloves**
- **sharp sand**
- **Savoy cabbage**
- **ready-mix mortar**, 5kg/11lb bag
- **bucket**
- **water**
- **trowel**
- **clear film**
- **watering can**

VARIATION

- Any heavy, shallow dish that won't blow away can be used to make a birdbath for birds to drink from and bathe in. A terracotta or glazed ceramic plant pot saucer is ideal. Use pebbles to make a gently sloping ramp round one half of the dish so that other small creatures, such as frogs, toads and mice can reach the water!

Step 1

Step 2

1 Cover the ground with a tarpaulin and use a flat board to work on. Wearing gloves, make a smooth dome of moist, sharp sand. Compact with your hands. Adult supervision is required.

2 Take off the large outer leaves from a Savoy cabbage. Lay them over the mould with the undersides facing upwards, as shown here. Fill in any gaps by overlapping smaller pieces.

3 Ask an adult to mix together some ready-mix mortar in a bucket with a little water, using a trowel. Put on to the mould. It should be 4–5cm/1½–2in thick. Do not touch the cement.

4 Cover well with sheets of clear film and leave to dry. It will take between two to three days to dry, or more if the weather is cold and damp. Check the mortar is hard before moving.

 = Watch out! Sharp or dangerous tool in use.   = Watch out! Adult help is needed.

5 Pull off the clear film and, with adult help, lift the bowl up off the sand mould. Remove the leaves and set the bath in position. Fill with water and watch the birds flock to it!

FACT FILE

FINE FEATHERS

After bathing, birds spend a lot of time preening with their beaks. They have a special gland at the base of the tail that secretes an oil, which they work over the feathers to make them waterproof. Feathers are edged with tiny hooks and preening 'zips' the feathers together.

preening bird

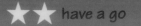
Footstep path

This is a stepping-stone path with a difference – you get to walk in your own footprints! Your left and right feet are used as templates for these brightly coloured designs and the canvas is also most unusual – how often do you get to paint on stone or concrete? Be as creative as you like with the patterns and colours. If the stepping-stones are laid on green grass, bright reds, oranges and vivid pinks will show up particularly well.

you will need

- **paper**, 2 pieces
- **coloured pencils**
- **scissors**
- **stone** or **concrete paving slabs** (30 x 30cm/12 x 12in), 5 or 6
- **acrylic paints**
- **artist's paintbrushes** (assorted)
- **clean water**
- **recycled plastic lids**, 2
- **jam jar** of **water**
- **kitchen paper**

coloured pencils

scissors

acrylic paints

TOP TIPS

▶ Ask an adult to set the stones in position only when they are completely dry, and don't try walking on them for a day or two – wait for the paint to harden. Lay them on the surface of the ground or cut out square shapes to drop the slabs into, making them level with the ground.

▶ Although the paint will last well in the summer months, it needs protection from damp and cold to extend its life. Seal the painted surface with two coats of exterior-quality varnish or a clear sealant.

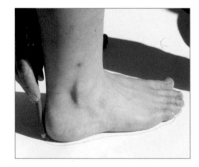

1 Take off your shoes and socks. Stand on a piece of paper and use a coloured pencil to draw round your feet. It's easier to do one at a time on separate sheets. Don't forget the toes!

2 Cut out the footprint to create a template. Adult supervision is required. You can use the same template for both feet. Simply flip over the cut-out to create the template for the other foot.

3 Use the template to transfer the outline to a stone or concrete paving slab using a coloured pencil that shows up well. Slabs usually have a smooth side that's best for painting on.

4 We drew our feet on the diagonal, which looks more interesting. Use a thick, dark acrylic paint and a paintbrush to form the outline of the foot. Dilute the paint slightly if it is too thick.

 = Watch out! Sharp or dangerous tool in use. = Watch out! Adult help is needed.

5 Using recycled plastic lids as palettes and to keep colours from running into one another. Start to paint your patterns. Make them as fun as you like, though simple designs work best.

6 Fill inside the outline of some feet with solid colour, then, if you like, you can also paint around the outside in a different shade. Give the outline band a fuzzy or smudged edge.

7 Add texture by waiting until the base coat has dried, then using a different colour to apply a pattern. Here we have dots but you could use wavy or straight lines, a criss-cross pattern etc.

VARIATION
• Although feet work well, you could paint any other shapes you like on the stepping stones, such as stars, hearts, arrows or swirls.

footstep path   149

Miss Muffet's tuffet

You can have much more fun with a grass dome than the Miss Muffet of nursery rhyme fame did! Use it as a seat or perch, as a high point from which you can survey your realm, as a pitching mound or as sanctuary in a game of tag. Provided your foundations are very well compacted you can build bigger ridges and mounds or even snake-like shapes using relatively inexpensive builder's rubble and hardcore and a covering of topsoil.

you will need
- **thick gloves**
- **bricks**
- **rubble**
- **wheelbarrow**
- **gravel** or **hardcore**, 1–2 tonnes
- **spade**
- **topsoil**, 1 tonne
- **grass seed**, general purpose or hard-wearing mix
- **garden rake**
- **watering can** with a **fine rose attachment**

wheelbarrrow

heavy-duty gloves

TOP TIP
▶ When part of a lawn is dug up to make way for a new feature, don't get rid of the turf – turn it into a mound! Put the turf pieces (called 'sods') upside down, packing them together neatly in a series of circles. Gradually build up the mound. Tread it down, cover with soil and use any remaining turf to cover the mound, grass-side up. Water well.

turf sod

1 Wearing thick gloves, ask an adult to help you lay down a foundation using any spare bricks or concrete building blocks, broken tiles or any other building rubble that won't rot down.

2 Try to arrange the construction under the mound as solidly as possible, leaving few gaps. Next, pour on several wheelbarrow-loads of gravel or hardcore. Hardcore is cheaper.

3 Compact this loose material well. Ask an adult to help you, especially if building larger mounds. Using a spade, add about a tonne of topsoil. It doesn't have to be top-quality.

4 Compact the mound again with your feet. This is the fun part! It must be solid enough for you to stand on without moving. A flat top is more practical than a rounded one.

(!) = Watch out! Sharp or dangerous tool in use.   (🖐) = Watch out! Adult help is needed.

5 Smooth over the mound, using the back of a spade. Adult supervision is required. Avoid using your hands, as in topsoil that hasn't been sieved there are sometimes pieces of glass.

6 Sprinkle the mound with grass seed. This germinates best in mid spring or early autumn, when the ground is warm and moist, but it will sprout in summer if you keep it watered.

7 Lightly rake over the mound, trying not to disturb the soil too much. This lightly covers the seed, putting it in closer contact with the soil. If patches don't germinate, you can reseed.

8 Pat down with your hands, pressing the seed lightly into the soil. If it doesn't rain in the next couple of days, water carefully. Grass should appear within 5–10 days.

Miss Muffet's tuffet   151

Flower arbour

Arbours are great places to sit and chat to your friends or watch birds or other animals in your garden. They are normally quite expensive, but this one uses a cheap, flat-packed arch set against a fence that acts as the arbour's back wall. With clematis planted on both sides, the arch will soon be covered with lush growth.

you will need

- **flat-pack metal garden arch**
- **small screwdriver**
- **bamboo measuring cane**
- **clematis cultivars** (*see Plant List*), 2
- **bucket** of **water**
- **spade**
- **well-rotted garden compost** or **manure**
- **watering can**
- **chipped bark**
- **planks** of **wood**
- **saw** (for adult use only)
- **bricks** or **building blocks**
- **garden twine**
- **scissors**

plant list

✳ ***Clematis viticella* cultivars:**

'Etoile Violette'

'Madame Julia Correvon'
'Prince Charles '
'Ville de Lyons'

TOP TIP

▶ Late summer- and autumn-flowering clematis can be pruned hard in late winter to around 30cm/ 12in from ground level, preferably just above a pair of buds.

clematis

1 You will need adult help to build the arch. Lay out all the pieces on the ground. Follow the instructions to slot the pieces together. Secure screws with a screwdriver. Stand the arch in position.

2 Ask an adult to cut a cane to the width of the arch. Lay the cane down and use it to space the legs correctly. Push the legs into the ground, holding them near their bases.

3 Plunge the clematis plants in turn in a bucket of water. Wait for the bubbles of air to stop. Dig a hole on one side of the arch for the first plant using a spade and try the clematis plant for size.

4 Place a cane across to check the depth. Large flowered clematis are set 5–7cm/2–3in) deeper than the surrounding soil. This helps them recover if they get clematis wilt disease. Others are planted as normal.

5 *Clematis viticella* hybrids are disease-resistant, but to improve the soil, mix a good quantity of well-rotted compost or manure into the soil dug out of the hole.

6 Plant, working the soil well in round the roots. Firm with your hands not with your foot – you don't want to compact the soil as this could affect rooting. Water and mulch with bark.

 = Watch out! Sharp or dangerous tool in use.   = Watch out! Adult help is needed.

7 Find some wooden planks to make a seat with. Try them for size and ask an adult to help cut them down if necessary. Make the legs using piles of bricks or building blocks.

8 Clematis climb with twining leaf tendrils and need plenty of support to grow up over the arch. Tie garden twine to the lowest horizontal bar and, keeping it taut, wind around the bars and tie off.

9 Repeat on both sides of the arch. Attach the clematis stems on to the twine. Train the clematis to climb over the arch, tying it in at regular intervals as it grows to provide support.

Living wigloo

This living structure is based on the shape of an igloo but is made from willow – hence the name 'wigloo'! Even before the wigloo is fully grown, you can start to use it as a den. Cover the ground with a waterproof groundsheet and bring in a blanket and some old cushions. Until the walls have knitted together, you can create shade and privacy by draping the willow frame with an old sheet. Make sure you keep the wigloo well watered in the first year.

you will need
- **long-handled pruners**, for adult use only
- **deep bucket** of **water**
- **rope** or **hosepipe**
- **hand shears**
- **secateurs** or **pruners**
- **spade**
- **stout stick** or **stake**, 1
- **rubber mallet** or **lump hammer**
- **watering can**
- **strong garden twine**
- **waterproof groundsheet**, 1
- **outdoor blanket**, 1
- **old cushions**

TOP TIPS
▶ Willow has an amazing ability to root. Keep fresh-cut stems in a deep bucket of water until ready to use. These 'wands' will last many days like this.
▶ In spring, when the buds sprout, remove at least half of the young shoots to allow the roots to develop properly.

WARNING – Don't plant willow near buildings, drains or sewers, as the roots can cause damage.

soaking willow

1 Ask an adult to help you cut some long, unbranched willow wands from a willow tree using long-handled pruners. Put them in a bucket of water until required.

2 Using a piece of rope or hosepipe, mark out a rough circle in a reasonably sunny part of the garden. Ideally the ground should be quite moisture-retentive. Clay soils are ideal.

3 Ask an adult to help you cut down any weeds within the circle with hand shears and secateurs or pruners. Dig a narrow trench all around the edge of the circle using a spade.

4 Use a stout stick or stake to make a series of pilot holes. Knock the stick or stake into the ground using a rubber mallet or lump hammer. You may need adult help.

 = Watch out! Sharp or dangerous tool in use. = Watch out! Adult help is needed.

5 Make sure the holes are evenly spaced, 20–30cm/8–12in apart. Holding a wand towards the base to stop it bending, push it into the hole. Drive it in as far as it will go. You may need adult help.

6 When these upright willow wands are all in position, move the soil back into the trench, tread in firmly with the weight on your foot and water with a watering can.

7 Starting halfway down, draw two wands across one another and tie with twine. Continue the criss-cross pattern towards the top of the wigloo. Cut off unwanted branches.

8 To make the doorway, check there's enough room for you to crawl through and ask someone to hold the stems together temporarily while you do this. Firmly tie the crossing stems over the doorway.

9 Continue to weave in the side shoots. Eventually, the wigloo will knit together as a solid dome and will just need trimming a few times a year, in winter and late summer.

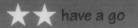
Weave a fence

This border edging is particularly useful for containing sprawling plants next to a lawn. You can make the fence any length you want – just hammer in more stakes. The plant list shows some of the most suitable plants for cutting and weaving but you can experiment. For the best colour development, cut after or just before leaf fall.

you will need
- **2.5 x 2.5 x 45cm/1 x 1 x 18in wooden stakes**
- **lump hammer**
- **secateurs** or **hand pruners**
- **plant stems** (*see* Plant List)

plant list
- **Golden willow**
  Salix alba var. *vitellina*
- **Hazel**
  Corylus avellana
- **Orange stemmed dogwood**
  Cornus sanguinea 'Midwinter Fire' or 'Winter Beauty'
- **Red barked dogwood**
  Cornus alba 'Sibirica'
- **Scarlet willow**
  Salix alba var. *vitellina* 'Britzensis'
- **Yellow stemmed dogwood**
  Cornus sericea 'Flaviramea'
- **Yellow variegated dogwood**
  Cornus alba 'Gouchaultii' or 'Spaethii'
- **White variegated dogwood**
  Cornus alba 'Elegantissima'

WARNING – Willows and the moisture-loving dogwoods should not be planted near drains or sewers as their roots can block the channels.

FACT FILE
COLOURFUL DOGWOODS
Variegated *Cornus alba* have dark, cherry-red stems. 'Sibirica' has eye-catching lacquer-red shoots and 'Midwinter Fire' and 'Winter Beauty' glow with sunset colours. *Cornus stolonifera* 'Flaviramea' has bright mustard yellow growth. Cutting some or all stems back to near ground level in spring (stooling or coppicing) generates more colourful stems next autumn.

dogwood

1 Ask an adult to help you drive in a row of equally spaced wooden stakes using a heavy lump hammer. Space them approximately 30–45cm/12–18in apart depending on the length of stems cut.

2 Since secateurs or pruners can be dangerous, ask an adult to help you cut a big bundle of long, straight, flexible stems from trees such as suckering shrubs or coppiced trees. Strip off any leaves.

3 If the branches are forked or have side shoots, ask an adult to cut these off to leave a single unbranched stem. These will be easier to weave in and out of the stakes and won't catch on anything.

4 Collect together bundles of freshly cut stems and take them to where you are making the fence or edging. If you leave cut stems to dry out, they can become brittle, so work with fresh stems.

 = Watch out! Sharp or dangerous tool in use.   = Watch out! Adult help is needed.

5 Weave the stems in and out of the stakes, making sure that you work behind and in front of neighbouring stakes and don't miss any out. For the row above, switch to weave the other way round.

6 This is much easier to do with two people, as one can hold the stem in place while the other finishes weaving with it. Overlap the joins when putting in the row above, for extra strength.

7 Press the stems down as you go so that the layers of stems are lying close against each other. Mix as many differently coloured stems as you can find to make the fence look more attractive.

TOP TIP
▶ If you don't have any suitable shrubs to prune, buy dried willow wands from craft or willow weaving companies and soak before use to make them flexible.

Wildlife gardening

This chapter reveals different ways
to discover more about the creatures
that share our gardens and how to
encourage them to stick around.
You can make habitats for all sorts of
animal life, both large and small, as
well as feeding stations and even
places for them to nest or hibernate.
So, get planting, and your blooms
will soon be buzzing!

Backyard safari

There's no need to travel to exotic places looking for wildlife – your backyard is full of exciting creatures and minibeasts! Use an old tin or jar to hold creatures safely while you investigate them with a magnifying glass, but remember to return them to their homes afterwards. Adult supervision is required, and great care should be taken if potentially harmful animals could be near.

you will need
- **magnifying glass** or **hand lens**
- **notebook**
- **pencil**
- **camera**
- **binoculars**
- **guidebook** or **wildlife identification sheets**

magnifying glass

FACT FILE

ON THE SNAIL TRAIL

Garden snails and slugs are nocturnal, living in cool shade. They eat flowers, leaves, fruit and decaying matter. Slime or mucus allows them to travel over rough surfaces. In autumn, snails hibernate, sealing up their shells. The fastest snails are speckled garden ones, which can move up to 55m/55yd per hour, while other land snails only move at about 60cm/24in in an hour.

garden snail

WILDLIFE WISE

Although many animals that are found in gardens are harmless, some may not be. Do not touch anything unless an adult says you can, and take extra care if you know there are any dangerous creatures where you live. Adult supervision is always required.

1 Carefully lift stones and pebbles and slates to see what animals are hiding underneath. It's best not to lift small creatures as you might crush them. Afterwards, put the stone back as it was.

2 Use a magnifying glass to find out about the creatures you find. What shape, size and colour are they? How many legs can you see? Try drawing the animal or take a picture.

3 Rotten logs and tree stumps are great places to look for minibeasts. Search under pieces of loose bark. You may find tunnels and boreholes left by burrowing worms and larvae.

4 There are many kinds of spider living in the garden. See how many species you can find and make a note of where you find them. Some have beautiful markings and make intricate webs.

(!) = Watch out! Sharp or dangerous tool in use. = Watch out! Adult help is needed.

5 Some creatures, such as beetles and ants, quickly run for cover when disturbed. Others, such as slugs, snails, caterpillars and woodlice, move slowly, allowing you to observe them quite easily.

6 A pair of binoculars is useful for looking at birds and larger animals, such as squirrels, especially those sitting up high. Keep yourself hidden from view, still and quiet.

7 Butterfly and other wildlife identification sheets are really useful for working out what you are looking at. Choose one that is suitable for the area you live in.

8 If you come across a nest, such as this robin's nest, in long grass, be very careful not to disturb it. Do not touch it as your smell could scare birds off!

Cardboard box hide

You can have hours of fun with this easy-to-make bird hide. Based on a giant cardboard box, some adhesive tape and left-over paints, the project is cheap to make and you'll soon be getting to know the different visitors to your garden. Make yourself comfortable in the hide by sitting it on a thick sheet of plastic to stop damp coming up from the soil and by kneeling on some old cushions.

you will need
- large cardboard box
- chalk
- parcel tape
- **utility knife** (for adult use only)
- **decorating sponge**, cut into pieces
- **paint tray** or **shallow dish**
- **dark green, light green** and **light brown artist's acrylic paints**
- **hanging bird feeders**
- **face paints** (optional)
- **binoculars** (optional)
- **plastic sheeting**

FACT FILE
MUSIC TO YOUR EARS
Birds are particularly active and vocal during the spring and early summer nesting period. They start to sing as the days get longer and only a few birds sing in the winter. You can tell various bird species' call or song even if you can't see them. Listen carefully and you'll soon learn which is which.

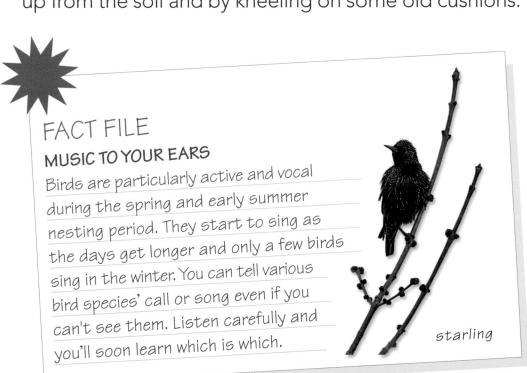

starling

TOP TIP
▶ Take a field guide with identification pictures with you into the hide and a pair of binoculars for observing birds in more detail.

binoculars

1 Draw circular, square and rectangular holes in the front of the box using chalk. Remember, when the flaps are closed, some holes will need cutting through two layers, so you need to draw these too.

2 Use parcel tape to strengthen the box and seal up spare flaps for rigidity. Put the box on its side and ask an adult to remove one of the flaps at the back and cut out the holes with a utility knife.

3 Use a piece of chalk to sketch on different leaf shapes to create the camouflage design. Your aim is to make the hide blend in as much as possible with the background, so look closely at the foliage in your garden.

4 Use a piece of decorating sponge to daub on some green paint around the design. Rinse out the sponge and add some pale green paint, then repeat with some light brown. You don't have to be too careful.

(!) = Watch out! Sharp or dangerous tool in use. (🦉) = Watch out! Adult help is needed.

5 Finally, paint on some streaks of black to look like leaf shadows. For camouflage to work, you need both light and dark areas and colours, as these help break up the outline of the hide.

6 Place the hide among greenery or against a similar-looking backdrop to the painted camouflage design. Hang bird feeders in front of the hide at least a week before you start using it.

7 Move slowly and enter the hide from the back. Open or close the main flap to give you different views. Once inside, keep as quiet and still as possible. Green and black face paints will camouflage your features.

8 Be patient! It may be a while before birds and animals come back to the area. Wear dark, dull coloured clothing when you go bird-watching. They won't see you as easily if you blend in.

9 Protect the hide from rain and damp with clear plastic sheeting or store it undercover when it is not in use by removing the tape and folding the box flat. It can then be kept easily in a shed or garage.

Make a bird table

This bird table can be made from any leftover scraps of wood. It can be hung from a tree branch, suspended from a pergola or even hooked over one arm of a rotary washing line. Swinging high above the ground and in a relatively open position, birds should be safe from cats and can eat to their hearts' content.

you will need

- **2cm/¾in square long piece** of **wood**
- **square piece** of **plywood**
- **pencil**
- **saw** (for adult use only)
- **hammer**
- **long galvanized nails**
- **drill**, with a drill bit (for adult use only)
- **screw eyes**, 6
- **pliers** or **small screwdriver**
- **plastic sheeting**
- **exterior-quality matt varnish**
- **jam jar**
- **old paintbrush**
- **strong rot-proof twine**
- **scissors**

nails. pliers, twine, jam jar of varnish, paintbrush plywood, wood, screw eyes and hammer

TOP TIPS

▶ If the nails are slightly too long and poke through, ask an adult to turn the table upside down and, while resting on a solid surface, knock the protruding nail flat against the wood.

▶ Clean the table regularly. Remove any old, uneaten food after a few days and use a stiff brush to remove debris.

▶ Don't put loose peanuts on the table during the nesting season (spring to mid summer) as there is a risk that parents might try feeding them to nestlings and the babies can choke on them.

▶ Make sure there is food out in early afternoon and first thing in the morning in cold weather. This helps keep birds warm through the night and to warm up quickly again after sunrise.

bird table

1 Divide the square length of wood into four pieces that will fit around the square plywood base. Mark where to cut with a pencil. Ask an adult to saw them and hammer in the nails.

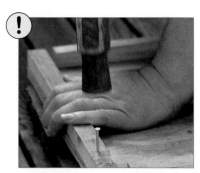

2 Leave a small gap at diagonally opposite corners to allow water to drain from the table. Ask an adult to drill several holes through the plywood base for additional drainage.

3 Ask an adult to make a small hole near each of the four corners using a hammer and nail. These will allow the screw eyes to go into the wood more easily and reduce splitting.

4 Screw in four screw eyes by hand then, if you want to tighten them up more, use a pair of pliers or thread a small screwdriver through and twist. Ask an adult to help.

5 Spread out some plastic sheeting to protect the work surface. Pour a little varnish into a jam jar and then paint all surfaces of the bird table. Allow to dry, then repaint.

6 With adult supervision, cut four lengths of twine long enough to come together above the table and to make a loop for hanging. Attach each to a screw eye with several knots.

7 Bring together the strings and make sure the table hangs level. Allowing enough room for the birds to fly in, knot the strings together. Tie another knot to create a hanging loop.

8 Work a couple of screw eyes into the ends of the edging strip. These can be used for attaching fat snacks or hanging bird treats. Hang up the table and add food.

make a bird table   165

Feed the birds

Help the birds that live in or pass through your garden by putting out a range of foods for them. Different birds are adapted to eat certain types: some have fine beaks designed for eating worms and insects; others, such as finches, have stout, seed-crushing beaks. Birds get used to knowing they have food, so keep putting it out!

you will need
- **assorted bird food** (see Fact File)
- **ground feeder tray** or **bird table**
- **fat ball hanger**
- **peanut feeder**
- **mixed seed feeder**
- **niger seed feeder**
- **container**
- **bottle brush**
- **scrubbing brush**
- **mild detergent**

FACT FILE
WHAT'S ON THE MENU?
- **Mealworms** These freeze-dried grubs can be used dry or soaked in warm water for 15 minutes.
- **Fat snacks** A blend of fat and mixed seed wrapped in mesh, fat snacks can be hung on twigs or from special feeders.
- **Black sunflower seeds** Black sunflower seeds won't swell up with water and block feeders.

mealworms

fat snacks

black sunflower seeds

- **Peanuts** These are a great source of fat and protein. Don't put whole nuts on a bird table during the nesting season as baby birds can choke.
- **Niger seed** Rich in oil, this is a favourite food of goldfinches. Use with a special feeder.
- **Mixed seed** Supply this general food in hanging feeders or on bird tables.

peanuts

niger seed

mixed seed

1 Some birds are more comfortable feeding on the ground but to keep food clean and contained, use a ground feeder tray which has a fine mesh that allows water to drain through.

2 Site trays and bird tables in a relatively open area away from bushes where predators can lie in wait. They do also require some cover to retreat to if danger threatens.

3 Hanging feeders are used by relatively agile birds that can grip the sides. A variety of fat snack feeders is available. Hang from pergolas, archways and trellis or in shrubs and climbers.

4 One of the most popular foods is black sunflower seed. Fill the special seed feeders to the top as they will soon be emptied. Check occasionally that the outlets haven't become blocked.

(!) = Watch out! Sharp or dangerous tool in use. 🐾 = Watch out! Adult help is needed.

7 Store food in a cool, dry place, protected from mice, and always wash your hands after dealing with the food and the feeders. Clean away debris beneath hanging feeders and bird tables.

5 Peanuts are taken by a wide range of birds, especially in winter, and also by squirrels. Use a metal holder with an outer mesh guard to prevent squirrels gnawing through.

6 A good bird feeder will come apart for cleaning and the removal of stale food. This is very important with peanut feeders as mouldy peanuts are toxic. A swivel hanger deters squirrels.

8 Though it is often recommended that you feed only in winter, there are times when birds can't find enough wild food. Provide a variety of foods and plenty of clean water.

TOP TIPS

▶ Always throw away old food before refilling and regularly clean feeders with brushes and mild detergent.
▶ Wash your hands after handling feeders.

Bird feast

Berries are a great natural food for several bird species. This feeding and watering station includes berries plus extra types of food for birds that don't eat berries, and the shrubs will eventually grow to form cover for roosting and nesting.

you will need

- **shrubs** and **plants** (*see* Plant List)
- **bucket** of **water**
- **border fork**
- **border spade**
- **trowel**
- **shallow dish** or **bowl**
- **watering can**
- **bird feeder hangers**
- **bird feeders**
- **fat snacks**
- **peanuts**
- **spike** or **cane** (optional)
- **chipped bark** (optional)

plant list
- ✳ **1 barberry**
  Berberis thunbergii f. *atropurpurea*
- ✳ **1 cotoneaster**
  Cotoneaster conspicuus 'Decorus'
- ✳ **1 firethorn**
  Pyracantha 'Golden Charmer'
- ✳ **1 laurustinus**
  Viburnum tinus
- ✳ **1 pheasant berry**
  Leycesteria formosa 'Golden Lanterns'
- ✳ **5 thymes**
  Thymus 'Doone Valley'

FACT FILE

COTONEASTER KNOW-HOW
This shrub is best known for its crops of ornamental berries, which are gorged on by local garden birds as well as visiting migrants. Cotoneasters are also good bee and hoverfly plants, bearing hundreds of nectar-rich blooms.

WARNING – Many berries are poisonous to humans.

cotoneaster

1 Plunge all the plants in a bucket of water and wait for the bubbles to stop. Fork over the ground to break up any clods. You may need adult help. Remove all visible weeds and weed roots. Set out the plants.

2 Place the tall firethorn about 45cm/18in from the fence and angle the top of the plant in towards it. If you plant too close, it may not get enough water. Arrange the rest of the plants according to height.

3 Dig a hole for the cotoneaster. The plant shown here is slightly potbound. If you see this, gently loosen a few of the roots to encourage them to spread once planted.

4 Replace the soil using a trowel, firming in around the root-ball with your hands. Repeat for all the other shrubs. Next, set a shallow dish or bowl into the ground .

5 Plant the creeping thyme plants around the birdbath to cover the bare ground. These plants will attract bees, which will also pollinate the berrying shrubs. Water all the plants.

6 Push hanging bird feeder supports into the soil and attach two types of feeder – the one shaped like an apple contains peanuts and the other is designed for fat snacks.

168   wildlife gardening   = Watch out! Sharp or dangerous tool in use.   = Watch out! Adult help is needed.

7 Pour water into the birdbath. This shallow dish is ideal for birds to drink from and bathe in and will be easy to clean out frequently. Use a soft hand brush and watering can for cleaning.

8 If you have some windfall apples, push a few on to a long spike or cane for the birds to peck at and enjoy. Ask an adult to help you, as the cores can be quite hard.

TOP TIP
► To keep down weeds after planting this permanent shrub border, cover the ground with a mulch of chipped bark to 5–8cm/2–3in deep.

bird feast 169

Hanging bird treats

In cold weather garden birds can keep warm by eating high-energy foods such as this hanging fat, fruit, seed and nut snack. You can also crumble one on a bird table.

you will need
- **suet**, ½ packet
- **pan**
- **wooden spoon**
- **bird seed**
- **fresh peanuts**
- **raisins**
- **aluminium foil**
- **scissors**
- **old plastic plant pot** or **yogurt pot**
- **garden twine** or **string**

TOP TIP
► To speed things up, put the filled container into a plastic bag and place it into the freezer for about 30 minutes so that the melted fat solidifies quickly.

1 Melt the suet in a pan. Stir with a wooden spoon until clear and liquid. Adult supervision is required.

2 Remove the pan from the heat and add bird seed, some broken-up peanuts and a few raisins. Stir. The mixture should be quite stiff. Allow to cool.

3 Cut out a circle of aluminium foil to fit in the base of a pot. Adult supervision is required.

4 Twist a length of garden twine or string to make a thick cord. Make a large knot at one end. This will stop the fat snack falling off the hanger.

5 Holding the knot at the bottom of the pot with the string upright, carefully spoon the fat and seed mixture into the pot and firm it down with the back of the wooden spoon. It should be well compacted.

6 Stand the pot outside to cool and set.

7 When the mixture is hard, remove the snack from its pot and peel off the foil base. Make a loop in the string and hang up.

twine

 = Watch out! Sharp or dangerous tool in use. = Watch out! Adult help is needed.

Butterfly food

Butterflies feed from the sweet nectar of flowers, but in autumn they also like sugars produced by rotting fruit.

you will need

- **forked twig**
- **plastic water bottle**
- **scissors**
- **drawing pins** or **notice board pins**
- **red cloth** or **plastic**
- **overripe banana** or **other fruits**

rotten apple

plant list

- ❋ **Black-eyed Susan**
  Rudbeckia fulgida
- ❋ **Globe thistle**
  Echinops ritro
- ❋ **Goldenrod**
  Solidago varieties
- ❋ **Ice plant**
  Sedum 'Herbstfreude'
  (syn. 'Autumn Joy')
- ❋ **Joe Pye weed**
  Eupatorium purpurea

- ❋ **Michaelmas daisy**
  Aster frikartii 'Mönch'
- ❋ **Purple coneflower**
  Echinacea purpurea
- ❋ **Purple top verbena/ vervain**
  Verbena bonariensis

purple top verbena

1 Find a reasonably long stick with a few prongs that will support the base of a plastic bottle. The bottle will need to be wedged among the branches.

2 Push the stick into the ground among some late-flowering perennials (see Plant List).

3 Cut off the base of the bottle with a pair of scissors to make a shallow container. You may need to ask an adult to help you.

4 Wedge the container into the branched stick. If necessary, fix it more securely with a drawing pin.

5 Ask an adult to help you cut some ribbons of red cloth or red plastic with a pair of scissors. They should be about 2.5cm/1in thick and 10cm/4in long.

6 Butterflies love red! Attach ribbons to the tops of the cut branches using drawing pins.

7 Fill the container with pieces of overripe banana or rotten fruit. You can also buy a nectar substitute, which has to be diluted and soaked in cotton wool.

8 Retreat to a safe distance and wait for the butterflies to arrive!

Create a wild lawn

If a weed-infested lawn is left to grow long, you'll find all kinds of flowers coming into bloom – a treat for bees and hoverflies. Try adding some bulbs and other wild flowers.

you will need
- **long-handled bulb planter**
- **low-growing spring bulbs** (*see Plant List*), 1–2 bags
- **trowel**
- **lawn 'weeds'** or **wildflower 'plugs'** (*see Plant List*)

plant list

bulbs
- ❋ **Crocus**
  Crocus tommasinianus
- ❋ **Grape hyacinth**
  Muscari armeniacum
- ❋ **Snake's head fritillary**
  Fritillaria meleagris

wild flowers
- ❋ **Autumn hawkbit**
  Leontodon autumnalis

- ❋ **Bird's-foot trefoil**
  Lotus corniculatus
- ❋ **Common daisy**
  Bellis perennis
- ❋ **Oxeye daisy**
  Leucanthemum vulgare
- ❋ **Ribwort plantain**
  Plantago lanceolata
- ❋ **Self heal**
  Prunella vulgaris
- ❋ **Yarrow**
  Achillea millefolium

1 Check the bulb packet for the planting depth and take out circles of turf to the right depth using a long-handled bulb planter.

2 You may need an adult to help you make more holes. Choose an area where grass can be longer.

3 Plant one or two bulbs in each hole. You could alternate which type of bulb you put in the holes so you create a mixed flower effect.

4 Repeat until you have planted bulbs in each of the holes.

5 Replace the turf plugs as you go and firm in with your foot.

6 To plant extra wildflower plugs or young, pot-grown plants, dig out a chunk of turf with a trowel or bulb planter and press the plant firmly into the space.

TOP TIP
► To encourage more wildflowers, don't use any kind of fertilizer. Mow the lawn in autumn and after the bulbs have died down in spring and a few times in summer. Let the plants drop seed.

 = Watch out! Sharp or dangerous tool in use.   = Watch out! Adult help is needed.

Grow a wildlife hedge

Plant a hedge with native shrubs and trees that have nectar-rich flowers, berries, fruits and nuts. This will feed the wildlife and offer safe roosting and nesting spots.

you will need

- **border spade**
- **border fork**
- **well-rotted garden compost** or **manure**
- **slow-release fertilizer granules**

chipped bark

- **mixed bare-rooted country** or **wild hedging shrubs** or **trees** (see Plant List)
- **bucket** of **water**
- **measured stick** or **cane**
- **secateurs**
- **watering can**
- **chipped bark**

plant list

- **Blackthorn/sloe**
  Prunus spinosa
- **Dog rose**
  Rosa canina
- **Elder**
  Sambucus nigra
- **Field maple**
  Acer campestre

- **Hawthorn**
  Crataegus monogyna
- **Hazel**
  Corylus avellana

  WARNING – Some native hedgerow plants are poisonous if eaten.

1 Ask an adult to help you dig a trench to a spade's depth. Fork in well-rotted compost or manure.

2 Sprinkle slow-release fertilizer granules on to the soil following packet instructions. This will mix in when you replace the soil.

3 Half an hour before planting, remove the outer wrapping protecting the hedge roots and soak in a bucket of water.

4 Mark a stick or cane with the correct planting distance (about 25–30cm/10–12in).

5 Use this to space the plants in the trench.

(!)

6 Trim overlong roots with secateurs (adult supervision is required) and spread them out. Holding the stem upright, work soil back round the roots. This is a two-person job.

7 Plant the hedging plants at the same depth as they were originally planted – you will see a dark stain on the stems.

8 Firm in lightly with your foot and water. Mulch with chipped bark to prevent weeds growing.

Make a mini meadow

It's easy to create your own patch of meadow in the garden. All you have to do is prepare an area of earth and sow annual flower seeds, which look pretty and also attract insects. Try to use plants that grow wild near where you live, as insects will like these best.

you will need
- **border fork**
- **soil rake**
- **hardy annual seed** (see Plant List)
- **sand** (optional)
- **stick** (optional)
- **watering can**

corn marigold

field poppy

annual mallow

plant list

- **Annual mallow**
  Lavatera trimestris
- **Californian poppy**
  Eschscholzia californica
- **Corn chamomile**
  Chamaemelum nobile
- **Cornflower**
  Centaurea cyanus
- **Corn marigold**
  Chrysanthemum segetum

- **Field poppy**
  Papaver rhoeas
- **Love-in-a-mist**
  Nigella damascena
- **Meadow cranesbill**
  Geranium pratense
- **Nasturtium**
  Tropaeolum majus
- **Pot marigold**
  Calendula officinalis

FACT FILE
CORNFLOWERS

Before wheat or corn seed could be purified, and before the introduction of weedkillers, cornfield annuals were a familiar sight, benefiting many different creatures. Some farmers are now beginning to re-introduce the flowers into their fields to great benefit. It is known that they secrete a root substance that actually helps wheat to grow.

cornflower

1 Fork over the ground to loosen the soil and break up large any large clods. Remove all visible weeds and weed out roots. Rake level and work the soil to create a fine crumb-like surface. Adult supervision is required.

2 Buy a mixture of cornfield flower seeds or make up your own mix combining plants from the Plant List. You can also add hardy annuals to perennial flower borders to increase nectar levels.

3 The traditional way of sowing cornfields was to scatter the seed by hand in a wide sweeping motion called 'broadcasting'. To see where you've been and to sow the seed more evenly, consider mixing it with sand.

4 An alternative to broadcasting your seed is to mark out patches in the soil using a stick and sowing just one variety in each patch. This still gives a natural look but the colours are solid blocks rather than all mixed up.

5 Many hardy annuals need light before they germinate so be careful not to bury the seed with soil as you walk about sowing it in areas that have not yet been sown.

7 Water the area with a watering can if the weather is particularly dry and sunny and repeat later if the young plants appear to be struggling with drought. Keep on top of weeds, removing them as soon as you see them.

6 Once you have sown all the seed, lightly rake over the whole area and, to bring the seed in close contact with the soil, gently press down the earth with the flat side of the head of the rake.

8 To get cornfield annuals to flower the following year, in spring, the old meadow must be forked over. This triggers germination. Sprinkle extra seed to guarantee displays.

9 You could also sow perennial wildflower mixtures for a permanent meadow that includes plants that tolerate less vigorous grasses, such as meadow cranesbill and the lesser knapweed (illustrated).

TOP TIP
▶ You can sow cornfield annuals in large wooden barrels, plastic tubs and large clay or glazed pots. Keep well watered throughout the growing period.

make a mini meadow   175

Buzzing blooms

Plant bee-friendly flowers rich in pollen and nectar and you will be helping these creatures to thrive. In addition, the more bees that visit your garden and pollinate your flowers, the bigger your crops of fruit and vegetables will be! Bees are especially attracted to single rather than double blooms, in blue and purple, white and yellow. They can even see flower shapes and patterns that show up in ultraviolet light, which are invisible to humans.

you will need
- **border spade**
- **grit** (optional)
- **perennials** (see Plant List)
- **bucket** of **water**
- **bamboo cane**
- **border fork**
- **watering can** with a **fine rose attachment**

pincushion flower

purple top verbena

plant list
S= small; M=medium; T= tall

* **Bee balm**
  Monarda didyma M–T
* **Bidens**
  Bidens ferulifolia S
* **Borage/starflower**
  Borago officinalis M
* **Catmint/catnip**
  Nepeta 'Six Hills Giant' M–T
* **Cosmos**
  Cosmos bippinatus T
* **Cranesbill**
  Geranium 'Johnson's Blue' M
* **Fiddleneck**
  Phacelia tanacetifolia S–M

* **Hollyhock**
  Alcea rosea T
* **Jacob's ladder**
  Polemonium caeruleum M–T
* **Lavender**
  Lavandula angustifolia 'Munstead' M
* **Lupin**
  Lupinus (blue/purple spp./hybrids) T
* **Penstemon**
  Penstemon (pink flowered cvs.) M–T
* **Pincushion flower**
  Scabiosa atropurpurea 'Chile Black' M
* **Pink hyssop**
  Agastache barberi M

* **Purple top verbena**
  Verbena bonariensis T
* **Rosemary**
  Rosmarinus officinalis T
* **Sage (ornamental and culinary types)**
  Salvia spp./cvs. M–T
* **Snowdrop**
  Galanthus spp./cvs. S
* **Squill**
  Scilla spp./cvs. S
* **Sunflower**
  Helianthus annuus T
* **Thyme**
  Thymus spp./cvs. S

1 Choose a sunny spot and turn over the soil, breaking up clods. If necessary, work in grit to improve drainage. Ask an adult to help. Plunge the plants in a bucket of water and wait for the bubbles to stop.

2 Plant the border in sections so that you have room to work. Lay out the plants with the lower growing ones towards the front and taller plants towards the back.

3 Once you are happy with the position of all of the plants, dig the first planting hole with a spade, making it wider than the pot, but the same depth as the height of the pot.

4 Try the pot for size in the hole. It shouldn't be too shallow, as this will make the plant vulnerable to drying out, or too deep, as this can cause rotting. Adjust as necessary.

 = Watch out! Sharp or dangerous tool in use. = Watch out! Adult help is needed.

FACT FILE

HONEY VERSUS BUMBLE

Bumble-bees are among the first insects to appear in late winter and survive on early spring flowers, such as bulbs, alpines and wild plants. It is not warm enough for honey bees until later in spring. Bumble-bees are large, rounded and furry and honey bees are elongated, with smooth bodies. Only honey bees make honey.

honey bee

bumble-bee

5 Carefully take the plant out of its pot. You might struggle if the plant is very well rooted. Tap the base sharply on a hard surface to loosen or ask an adult to help.

6 Plant, then check that the top surface of the root-ball is at the same level as the surrounding soil – lay a cane across the hole to check, if you like. Backfill with loose soil.

7 Firm the soil with your hands, checking that you have filled all the gaps. Continue planting all the plants, then level the surrounding soil using a border fork.

8 Water the plants in thoroughly. To extend the border, follow the same method, perhaps repeating blocks or swathes of the same varieties, or introduce different plants.

Butterfly pots

Even a small collection of flower-filled pots will attract butterflies, especially if you plant them with their favourite plants, such as the well-named butterfly bush.

you will need
- **assorted plants** (see Plant list)
- **bucket** of **water**
- **assorted pots**, 5
- **crocks** or **pieces** of **polystyrene**
- **gravel**
- **trowel**
- **peat-free potting compost** with **added loam (John Innes)**
- **watering can**
- **kneeler**

plant list
- ✳ **Black-eyed Susan**
  Rudbeckia fulgida var. *sullivantii* 'Goldsturm'
- ✳ **Butterfly bush**
  Buddleja davidii 'Empire Blue'
- ✳ **Dahlia**
  single flowered cv.
- ✳ **Ice plant**
  Sedum 'Herbstfreude' (syn. 'Autumn Joy')
- ✳ **Joe Pye weed**
  Eupatorium purpureum
- ✳ **Scabious**
  Scabiosa caucasica
- ✳ **Verbena**
  Verbena 'Temari Burgundy'

ice plant

1 Plunge your chosen plants in a bucket of water and wait for the bubbles to stop.

2 Prepare the pots by covering the drainage holes with crocks made from pieces of broken pot or pieces of polystyrene.

3 Cover the crocks with a layer of gravel. A large pot like this will need about 5cm/2in for good drainage.

4 Ask an adult to help you tip in enough compost to three-quarters fill the pots, or use a trowel. Try your largest plant in them for size.

5 Position the Joe Pye weed at the back of the pot, then add the black-eyed Susan. These plants flower at the same time and enjoy the same moist conditions, so can be planted together.

6 Fill in around the root-balls with more compost, ensuring there are no gaps. Check that the surface of the compost is about 2½cm/1in below the rim of the pot to allow for watering.

7 Plant the butterfly bush in its pot in the same way. This shrub is fast-growing but won't mind being in a pot for a couple of years. You may find seedlings coming up in paving cracks later on.

8 Continue planting the other pots in the same way. Most of the flowers featured are hardy, but many annuals, such as French marigolds, and tender patio plants, such as this verbena, are great butterfly attractors.

(!) = Watch out! Sharp or dangerous tool in use. = Watch out! Adult help is needed.

9 Dahlias are some of the biggest show-offs in summer and autumn. Butterflies prefer single varieties with an open centre like the one shown here, which allows them easy access to the nectar.

TOP TIP

▶ Early butterflies need to feed on spring flowers after hibernating. You can help them by growing bulbs and rockery plants including grape hyacinth, crocus, aubrieta, heathers and yellow alyssum as well as honesty, forget-me-nots and early blooming wild or hedgerow flowers.

butterfly on heather

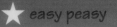
Hoverfly hotel

These pots of citrus-coloured blooms will be a magnet for hoverflies. Often mistaken for wasps or honey bees, hoverflies are completely harmless. You'll find them visiting many of the same flowers as bees and butterflies but they especially like yellow, orange and white blooms, daisies and heads made up of many tiny flowers.

you will need
- **assorted plants** (see Plant List, we used pot marigolds and tickseed plants)
- **bucket** of **water**
- **pieces** of **polystyrene**
- **blue glazed pots**, 2
- **gravel**
- **trowel**
- **peat free-potting compost** with **added loam (John Innes)**
- **watering can**
- **liquid plant food**

plant list
- **Black-eyed Susan**
  Rudbeckia fulgida
- **Common daisy**
  Bellis perennis
- **Fennel**
  Foeniculum vulgare
- **Feverfew**
  Chrysanthemum parthenium
- **Masterwort**
  Astrantia major
- **Milfoil**
  Achillea 'Moonshine'
- **Pot marigold**
  Calendula officinalis
- **Poached egg plant**
  Limnanthes douglasii
- **Stonecrop**
  Sedum spurium
- **Sunflower**
  Helianthus annuus
- **Sweet alyssum**
  Lobularia maritima
- **Tagetes**
  Tagetes tenuifolia 'Lemon Gem'
- **Tickseed**
  Coreopsis grandiflora 'Early Sunrise'

FACT FILE
GARDENER'S FRIEND
Adult hoverflies pollinate flowers just like bees and their eggs hatch into larvae, which eat huge numbers of greenfly or aphids as well as other common garden pests. Luring adult hoverflies into the garden with their favourite blooms is an easy and natural way of reducing problems on plants such as roses.

adult hoverfly

1. Plunge the plants in a bucket of water and wait for the bubbles to stop. Place broken-up chunks of polystyrene in the bottom of one pot. Add a couple of handfuls of gravel.

2. Cover with compost, nearly filling the pot but allowing space for the root-balls. Ease the young plants out of their tray, pushing your thumb through the drainage holes.

3. Choose young, vigorous plants with a few unopened flower-buds and a good root system. Avoid pot-bound plants. Space the plants out and fill the gaps in between with compost.

4. Prepare a second container, following the same method as before. Add a small amount of compost and try plants of tickseed (*Coreopsis*) for size. Remove from their pots.

 (!) = Watch out! Sharp or dangerous tool in use. = Watch out! Adult help is needed.

5 Place the first plant in the pot. The top of the root-ball should be about 2.5cm (1in) below the top of the pot. Add or remove more compost to adjust the level if necessary.

6 Add a few more plants, spacing them equally. If you like, you could also grow these plants from seed, sowing them in early spring on a warm windowsill.

7 Finish planting, carefully working more compost into the gaps between the root-balls. Lift the leaves, taking care not to bury them. Firm with your fingers and water.

8 Both the pot marigolds and the tickseeds will only keep flowering if you pinch off the fading flowers regularly and prevent them from setting seed. Water regularly and feed every two weeks.

pot marigold

Bumble-bee beds

An old buried teapot offers a gentle bumble-bee a home where she can raise her young female worker bees and later male drones and young queens in safety.

you will need
- **old teapot**
- **cotton wool balls, kapok** or **soft dried moss**
- **trowel**
- **silicone sealant**
- **bulbs** (see Plant List)
- **logs** and **dried leaves**

bumble-bee

crocus

grape hyacinth

plant list
* **Crocus**
  Crocus chrysanthus varieties
* **Dead nettle**
  Lamium maculatum 'White Nancy'
* **Glory of the snow**
  Chionodoxa luciliae
* **Grape hyacinth**
  Muscari armeniacum
* **Lungwort**
  Pulmonaria saccharata
* **Siberian squill**
  Scilla sibirica
* **Viola**
  Viola Sorbet Series

1 Choose a teapot with a rough interior so that the bee is able to grip. Ones with a broken spout are ideal as the way in will be wider. Fill the pot loosely with soft bedding material, such as cotton wool balls, kapok stuffing or dry mosses, and replace the lid.

2 Find a sheltered spot – under a hedge, where the ground is slightly banked is ideal. Dig a hole for the teapot with a trowel.

3 Seal the lid with sealant. Bury the pot, covering the lid but leaving the tip of the spout protruding.

4 Plant around the spout with early bulbs and perennials so that the queen has plenty of food close by.

5 Arrange the logs to shelter the spout from rain and scatter leaf litter to cover the ground planted with bulbs.

FACT FILE
SLEEPY QUEENS
Bumble-bee queens hibernate over winter and in early spring search for a nest site, such as gaps under stones, under untidy hedges or in abandoned burrows.

 = Watch out! Sharp or dangerous tool in use. = Watch out! Adult help is needed.

Lacewing lodge

Along with ladybirds, lacewings are a gardener's friend. Some green lacewing adults overwinter in bark crevices and our 'hotel' mimics that hideaway.

you will need

- **large plastic bottle**
- **scissors**
- **corrugated cardboard**
- **pliers**
- **heavy-duty, plastic-coated training wire**

FACT FILE

adult lacewing

APHID LIONS

Lacewing adults have transparent, veined wings, bright green or brown bodies and golden eyes. They lay hundreds of eggs and the larvae, nicknamed 'aphid lions', feast on garden pests, such as greenfly, so they are a gardener's friend!

1 Wash out a large plastic bottle and leave it to air dry. It needs to be completely dry. Leave the cap on but carefully cut off the base of the bottle with a pair of scissors. You may find the cutting tricky to start so ask an adult to help you.

2 Roll up some pieces of thin corrugated card, such as the type used for packaging, and push the roll into the base of the bottle. The cardboard should be a snug fit to create plenty of warm spaces for the insects to crawl into.

3 To prevent the cardboard working its way out over time, carefully puncture a hole on either side at the base with the tip of the scissors and feed through some stiff garden wire to act as a barrier. Twist the two ends together so they are secure.

4 To allow the bottle to be hung up outdoors, loop and twist some stiff wire around the neck, under the rim. If necessary tighten the wire by twisting the ends with a pair of pliers. Leave a long piece of wire free to attach to the support.

Log garden

This little fernery makes an interesting feature for a shady wild corner and will make a cosy home for all sorts of minibeasts, such as insects, amphibians and small mammals. Ideally it should be kept moist, so water if it gets dry.

you will need

- **logs** and/or **tree branches**
- **wedges** of **wood**
- **fern selection** (*see Plant List*)
- **bucket** of **water**
- **peat free-potting compost** with **added loam** (John Innes)
- **leaf mould**, home-made (optional)
- **trowel**
- **bark pieces** or **chippings**
- **twisted branches** or **roots**, **driftwood**, or **pine cones**

plant list

* **Common polypody**
  Polypodium vulgare
* **Copper shield fern**
  Dryopteris erythrosora
* **Hard shield fern**
  Polystichum aculeatum
* **Japanese painted fern**

Athyrium niponicum var. *pictum*
* **Scaly male fern**
  Dryopteris affinis
* **Soft shield fern**
  Polystichum setiferum Divisilobum Group

FACT FILE

DINOSAUR PLANTS

Ferns go back 360 million years and would have been the main ground-cover plant when dinosaurs roamed the earth! They reproduce via spores, usually produced in clusters on the back of their fronds – have a look! The spores are so tiny that they float round the world on air.

fern frond

1 Lay out a series of long logs or tree branches in a shady spot. Raise them up with wedges of wood to create planting pockets. You may need adult help. Soak the ferns in a bucket of water.

2 Fill the gaps between the logs with compost. Ferns don't need any extra fertilizer, but you could add some home-made leaf mould to make the soil more like that of a woodland.

3 Lay out all the ferns, working out which combination of leaf form and texture looks best. Take the soft shield fern out of its pot giving the base a tap on a hard surface if it sticks.

4 Dig a hole in the compost with a trowel and put the fern in it. Fill round the roots with compost and firm gently with your hands. Take care not to bury any fronds.

5 The soft shield fern and the copper shield fern are both evergreen, so the leaves will remain attractive all through the winter. The copper shield fern's fronds are pinky-orange when young.

6 For decoration and to fill gaps between the ferns, prise pieces of bark from logs using a trowel. The best way to do this is to turn the trowel upside down, wedge it under a loose corner, then lift.

7 Work the bark that you have collected in around the plants. If you don't have enough, use decorative chipped bark mulch. This will help to keep down weeds and retain moisture.

8 Look out for pine cones, interestingly shaped pieces of branch or root (even driftwood from the beach) and use them to add the finishing touch to your 'fernery'.

FACT FILE
DINO GARDEN
lizard
Lizards are descended from dinosaurs and many can lose their tails to escape a predator, then regrow a new one.

Wildlife wall

You can build this wildlife wall or habitat stack anywhere in the garden but somewhere close to a wild area, perhaps with a nearby pond or mini meadow, would be ideal. Though you'll need to buy the gabion cages, the contents won't cost you anything if you use all kinds of recycled materials. The name of the game is to create lots of nooks and crannies, some big, some small, to suit a wide range of minibeasts and other creatures.

you will need
- **thick gloves**, 1–2 pairs
- **large gabion cages** (45 x 45cm/18 x 18in), 2
- **small gabion cages** (30 x 30cm/12 x 12in), 3
- **logs**
- **tiles, slates** or **broken paving slabs**
- **bamboo canes** or **hollow twigs**
- **plastic** or **clay drainage pipes**
- **pebbles, cobbles** or **building rubble**
- **house bricks**
- **secateurs**
- **pliers**

FACT FILE

CREATURE FEATURE

With a range of different-size 'homes' to move into, all kinds of creatures could take up residence in your wall. Some will relish the cool dampness of the log pile. Others, such as young frogs, toads and mice, will use the wall to hibernate or shelter in. Hunters, such as spiders, ground beetles and centipedes, can find 'dinner' hiding in the crevices, and larger predators will forage around the edges.

field mouse

centipede

1 Wearing gloves, ask an adult to help you arrange the pre-assembled gabion cages side-by-side to create a wall-like effect. Gather together all the materials you have salvaged or scavenged to go into the containers.

2 If space or the position of the wall doesn't allow you to lift the lid right back or prop it open, you'll need someone to hold it while you stack the contents inside the cages. Be careful! House bricks are heavy.

3 Swap over and give each other a turn at filling the gabion cages. Logs make ideal filler material as they offer homes for creatures that bore into the rotting wood as well as for those that shelter between.

4 Tiles such as these old clay roof tiles can be layered in with other materials, such as rubble, bricks and clay drainage pipes, to create a network of spaces of different sizes. Experiment with different combinations.

 = Watch out! Sharp or dangerous tool in use.   = Watch out! Adult help is needed.

5 Loose pebbles or rubble creates another type of habitat or home for minibeasts. Fill the cage right up to the top. If you don't have enough cobbles, fill the centre with bricks, say, and work the cobbles around.

6 Add some hollow sticks including bamboo canes cut into sections (ask an adult to help you cut them up), which will be used by many hibernating insects and may even become nest sites for solitary bees in spring.

7 Carefully lower the lids down on to the filled cages. The spiral fixing acts like a hinge, allowing you to open and close the cage easily. To lock the cage shut, ask an adult to twist in another spiral opposite the 'hinge' using pliers.

TOP TIP

▶ To assemble gabions, hold two pieces at right angles and twist a spiral through so it catches both sides of the panels. Continue, connecting five sides. Leave the last as a hinged lid.

wildlife wall **187**

Mini wildlife pond

This pond will be a wildlife magnet and in spring and summer you'll have some great backyard safari moments as frogs dive for cover and birds queue up for a bath. Position it next to some long grass or evergreen plants so that creatures have somewhere to hide. You must ask adult permission before making this pond, and it is not suitable if there are very young children around.

you will need

- spade
- large black plastic container (around 30 x 65cm/12 x 26in)
- gravel
- straight piece of wood
- spirit level
- house bricks
- large cobbles
- small cobbles and pebbles
- small pieces of turf
- marginal plants (see Plant List), soaked in a bucket of water

plant list
* **Marsh pennywort**
  Hydrocotyle vulgaris
* **Miniature bulrush/dwarf reedmace**
  Typha minima

Warning!

Ponds or water features are not recommended in gardens with children under the age of six as they can drown in even very shallow water. Children should never be around water of any type or depth without adult supervision at all times.

FACT FILE
POND VISITORS

A tiny pond such as this can attract a surprising number of animals. All kinds of insects will fly in for a drink, a frog or two will soon take up residence and the glint of water will also attract dragonflies on the look out for their next meal.

Birds not only drink but also bathe, standing on the pebbles. And at night hedgehogs and other nocturnal creatures will call by.

green dragonfly

1 Using a spade, dig a hole just large enough to slot the container into. The reservoir tanks you can buy for self-contained water features are ideal for creating mini ponds. Adult supervision is required.

2 Try the container for size. The base should rest evenly on the soil at the bottom of the hole so that it is properly supported. The rim should be level with or just below the soil. You may need adult help.

3 To create the pond floor and encourage aquatic or water-dwelling creatures to inhabit it, fill the base of the container with washed gravel to a depth of about 5cm/2in. Ask an adult to help you.

4 Check that the pond is level by placing a piece of wood across and resting a spirit level on it. The moving bubble should be right in the middle. Next build a simple stack of bricks in the container.

   (!) = Watch out! Sharp or dangerous tool in use.   🧤 = Watch out! Adult help is needed.

5 Check the bricks are secure, then top them with one large cobble. Add smaller cobbles and pebbles to camouflage the bricks and create a ramp for easy access. Fill the pond with water.

6 The cobbles allow creatures to get safely into the water and if they fall in, to help them scramble out again. Blend the container edge in by covering it with some large and small cobbles.

7 If the pond is next to a lawn, squeeze in some small pieces of turf and low-growing weeds or wild plants to create easy access to the water and camouflage the hard rim of the container.

8 Create platforms with submerged bricks for the marginal (pond edge) plants to sit on. The surface of the pots should be just below the water. Fence off the pond so young children cannot go near it.

mini wildlife pond 189

Frog in a bog!

Bog gardens offer a safer alternative to ponds so are more suitable for gardens where young children play, although adult supervision is still always required. Even though there is no open water, the bog attracts a wide range of wildlife, including frogs and other amphibians that relish the damp, leafy cover. Several of the bog plants also supply nectar and pollen so the bees and hoverflies will be happy.

FACT FILE
FRIENDLY FROGS

Frogs are very popular with gardeners as they catch lots of insects with their sticky tongues and gobble them down. They love ponds and bog gardens, such as this one and may return year after year to breed.

plant list
* **Loosestrife**
  Lythrum salicaria 'Blush'
* **Houttuynia**
  Houttuynia cordata 'Chameleon'
* **Japanese sweet flag**
  Acorus gramineus 'Ogon'
* **Astilbe**
  Astilbe 'Sprite'
* **Golden groundsel**
  Ligularia dentata 'Desdemona'
* **Giant rhubarb**
  Gunnera manicata
* **Cardinal lobelia**
  Lobelia X *speciosa* purple form

you will need
* spade
* **tarpaulin** or **ground sheet**
* **plastic sheeting** or **pond liner**
* **bricks**
* **scissors**
* **border fork**
* **wheelbarrow**
* **well-rotted manure, spent mushroom compost** or **garden compost**
* **assorted bog plants** (see Plant List)
* **bucket** of **water**
* **trowel**
* **chipped bark**
* **logs** or **tree branches**
* **home-made sign** or **frog sculpture**
* **hosepipe** or **watering can**

Japanese sweet flag

Warning!

Ponds or water features are not recommended in gardens with children under the age of six as they can drown in even very shallow water. Children should never be around water of any type or depth without adult supervision at all times.

1 Ask an adult to help you remove pieces of turf from the lawn with a spade, then dig out a shallow bowl shape, putting the excavated soil on to a waterproof sheet or tarpaulin for later use.

2 Spread out a large sheet of heavy-duty plastic or pond liner over the hole and move it around to fit the contours. Weight it down with bricks and trim to size with scissors.

3 Use a border fork to puncture the liner a few times. Ask an adult to help you add several wheelbarrow loads of manure, mushroom compost or garden compost, using a spade.

4 Mix the compost with the excavated soil and fill the hole back to the level of the lawn or a little higher – the mixture will sink over time.

5 Meanwhile, plunge each plant in a bucket of water, waiting until the bubbles stop.

6 Begin to put the plants into the ground, digging out holes for the roots using a trowel.

 = Watch out! Sharp or dangerous tool in use.   = Watch out! Adult help is needed.

7 Position the plants in the holes. Fill round the roots with soil and firm in lightly with your hands. This colourful houttuynia will send out runners and spread to fill a large area.

8 Mulch with bark and add rustic logs to create a natural-looking margin. You could also use rockery stones or large rounded cobbles to fit in with the surroundings.

9 You could add a sign to let the frogs know it's a good place to be! (*See* page 127.) Alternatively, find a frog ornament or sculpture and set it among the plants.

10 Water the bog garden with a hose. The soil needs to be wet but don't turn it into a pond! Fence off the bog securely so that young children cannot go near it unsupervised.

wheelbarrow

frog in a bog!   191

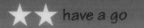

Brilliant bird sanctuaries

A sanctuary is a place of safety and shelter and these bird pouches and the bird 'tepee' will give garden birds, hedgehogs, mice and voles somewhere to hunker down in bad weather. They might even use them to make nests or to hibernate in over winter. Hang the pockets close to a hedge or a cluster of shrubs or trees so that birds don't have far to fly, keeping them safe from predators.

you will need
- **stiff wire**
- **wire cutters**
- **woven bird pouches**, assorted
- **hooks, large screw eyes** or **nails**
- **hay, dry grass** or **dry moss**
- **branch poles**
- **secateurs**
- **strong, weather-resistant twine**
- **dry bracken, hedge clippings** and other **stuffing material**

FACT FILE

ROOSTING

At dusk, most birds find a safe, warm place to spend the night. Some birds, such as starlings, gather to roost in very large numbers and other normally solitary birds sometimes squeeze together in a small shelter to keep each other warm. The roosting pouches, as well as unoccupied nest boxes, may be used for roosting.

roosting bird

TOP TIP

▶ To offer even greater protection for birds in winter, hang woven bird pouches in the centre of a dense hedge or well concealed among shrubs and climbers, such as ivy or honeysuckle, growing on a warm sheltered wall or sunny fence.

1 Thread a short piece of wire through the top of a woven bird pouch or through the hanger if they have one. These can break, however, so strengthen weak hangers with extra wire if necessary.

2 Find a sheltered spot, such as an overhang from a garden shed. Ask an adult to help you tie the wire round a solid branch of a climber or shrub or hook the loop over a projecting twig.

3 Pouches come in different designs. This one has a smaller opening. You can also insert a hook under a sheltered place, such as a porch or covered veranda, and hang the pouch there. Ask an adult to help.

4 For extra protection against cold or to entice a creature to nest, you can put in a small amount of soft, dry hay or grass or dry moss. Don't overfill or there won't be room for the birds!

⊘ = Watch out! Sharp or dangerous tool in use. ✋ = Watch out! Adult help is needed.

5 To create a shelter for birds that nest near ground level or for hibernating hedgehogs, you'll need some long, straight branches to make the basic structure of a wildlife wigwam.

6 Ask an adult to help you prune off side branches with secateurs. Trees, such as birch or willow, are ideal, since the stems are long and straight. Always check with an adult before cutting branches.

7 Arrange the poles around a solid, upright tree trunk. You can build the shelter all the way round like a wigwam or just against one side of the tree. You can also use a wall or the side of a shed.

8 Push the poles into the ground a little to make them more secure, then loosely tie around the top with strong twine to hold them to the tree. Begin filling the gaps with smaller prunings or bracken.

9 Continue adding more stuffing among the branches using dry leaf litter if available. Weave in twigs to make the outer 'skin' stronger. Wind twine around the whole structure and tie off securely.

Putting up nest boxes

As well as feeding wild garden birds and providing them with fresh drinking and bathing water, you can also support them by giving them somewhere to nest. With a little help from an adult, you could put up several sturdy wooden boxes this autumn ready for the spring nesting season. It can take birds a long time to make their minds up where to nest and they may try out a box by roosting in it over winter before finally deciding whether they want to lay eggs there or not.

you will need
- wooden nest box(es)
- galvanized screw(s)
- screwdriver
- ladder (for use only under adult supervision)
- wire or polypropylene twine
- length of hosepipe
- nesting material, such as scoured wool or animal hair
- spiral hanging feeder (optional)

wooden nest box

FACT FILE

MARKING TERRITORY

You might think that birds start singing in spring purely because they are happy, but each melody actually carries an important message: 'This patch belongs to me!'. Birds usually choose a number of different vantage points from which to announce their territorial boundaries and the area within is fiercely defended. This is because If too many birds nested in the same spot, there probably wouldn't be enough food for all the nestlings. You might also notice male birds fighting or chasing each other.

wrens mark their territory by singing

---

1 Walk around your house and garden to find a good site for the nest boxes. Ideally this should be a cool position, such as on a wall or tree facing between north and east, away from prevailing wind and rain. Many garden birds prefer boxes 2–4m/6.6–13.1ft high.

2 Once you have found your site(s), choose which nest boxes you want to buy, depending on what your local birds prefer.

3 Ask an adult to fix down the lid with a screw if necessary. Some boxes can be adapted for different birds by swapping the front panel or taking out sections to give wider access.

4 Either screw a fixing into a tree (ask an adult to help, as you will need a ladder) or loop wire or twine round the trunk, cover it with hosepipe to protect the tree, and attach the box to it.

5 Hang the box on to the fixing. Notice that various box designs have different-sized access holes. This small, round entranceway resembles a hole in a tree trunk.

 = Watch out! Sharp or dangerous tool in use.   = Watch out! Adult help is needed.

8 Birds line their nests with soft material. You can help by putting out scoured wool in a spiral bird feeder or hair gathered from grooming animals, such as dogs or cats, which they will take into the nest.

6 For birds that don't mind nesting in and around buildings, such as this shed, ask an adult to screw the fixing under a sheltering overhang out of reach of predators.

7 Hook the box on to the screw fixing. An open-fronted box such as this attracts different birds. Some birds prefer to nest lower down, protected by dense, thorny branches.

9 At the end of the nesting season in late summer, ask an adult to help you clean out the box ready for next year. You may need to unscrew the lid or roof of the box.

TOP TIP
▶ In more exposed sites, such as on the trunk of a tree, tilt the box forward at the top slightly to make it less likely that rain can enter.

putting up nest boxes   195

Creature comforts

In colder parts of the world many mammals and some amphibians survive the worst of winter by going into a deep sleep called hibernation. This snug shelter can be used for hibernation or just as a place to hide away.

you will need

- **bricks** or **breeze blocks**
- **rigid wooden** or **marine plywood board**
- **hay** or **dry leaves**
- **ground feeder tray** (optional)
- **water bowl** or **bird bath**

FACT FILE

FEEDING STATION

Help small mammals that don't have enough fat reserves to hibernate by feeding them from autumn until spring. Buy specially formulated feeds or contact a wildlife group for information on what to put out. Keep a shallow dish of clean water topped up.

1 Find a really sheltered spot outdoors, such as beneath a hedge or dense shrubbery or between a garden shed and wall. Make a low wall of bricks as wide as the piece of wood.

2 You may need to ask an adult to help you. Check the bricks are level.

3 Next, take a rigid piece of board or wood big enough to create a lean-to shelter and prop it up against the brick wall.

4 Make sure there is enough room for a hedgehog to squeeze under. Adjust the height of the brick wall as necessary.

5 Carefully stuff the space underneath the board with bedding hay, like the type you buy for guinea pigs and rabbits in pet shops. Alternatively, you can use dried leaves that you have gathered in the garden yourself. The board should keep everything dry.

6 Weight down the wooden board with more bricks to stop the wind lifting it or animals dislodging it. Put out some suitable food on a raised stand to help attract animals to the area so they can discover the shelter and perhaps set up home in it, if you are lucky.

(!) = Watch out! Sharp or dangerous tool in use.   (🐾) = Watch out! Adult help is needed.

Wild trees from seed

Trees provide vital habitats and food for a wide range of animals, as well as helping the environment. So do your bit and plant a few seeds.

you will need
- **tree seeds**
  (see Plant List)
- **crocks** or **gravel**
- **small clay** or **plastic pots**
- **loam-based seed compost** or **50:50 compost/leaf mould mix**
- **trowel**
- **watering can** with a **fine rose attachment**
- **wire mesh**
- **bricks**

acorns

plant list
- ✳ **Beech (mast, nuts)**
  Fagus sylvatica
- ✳ **Horse chestnut seed (conker)**
  Aesculus hippocastanum
- ✳ **Hazelnuts (cobnuts)**
  Corylus avellana
- ✳ **Oak seed (acorn)**
  Quercus robur
- ✳ **Sycamore seed (helicopters)**
  Acer spp.

horse chestnut seed

1 Remove the horse chestnut seed or conker from its prickly case. When ripe they should already be cracked open on the ground. Place some crocks or gravel in small pots, then mostly fill them with a 50:50 compost/leaf mould mix using a trowel. Plant the conker in a pot.

2 Cover the seed with 2½cm/1in compost mix, and water. Plant several seeds in individual pots in case some don't germinate.

3 Before sowing acorns, remove the cups and drop the remaining seed into a bowl of water. Discard any that float.

4 Plant in deep pots, about 5m/2in below the soil surface.

5 Put all the pots on the ground outdoors, where they will be open to the elements. Tree and hedgerow seeds germinate better after alternating periods of cold and warm.

6 Cover the pots with wire mesh weighted down with bricks to stop animals eating them

7 Seedlings appear in spring. Water regularly and pot into larger containers as needed. Plant baby trees as a wild hedge or mini woodland.

Indoor projects

When the weather is too cold or wet for gardening outdoors you can still raise a wide range of plants inside to keep your green fingers occupied. This chapter even shows how to grow windowsill crops. There are fun 'creatures' to make, bulbs to start off and exotic seeds to germinate and you'll love the indoor gardens, mini landscapes and scented gifts.

Sprouting seeds

It is really, really easy to sprout a number of different seeds to eat. They are crisp, juicy and nutty eaten raw in salads and large seeds, such as mung beans, are used in stir-fried meals. Although there are seed sprouters available, you don't actually need any special equipment. Experiment with different seeds to see which is your favourite type.

you will need
- **edible seeds** (*see* Plant List)
- **sieve**
- **glass jars**, 1 per type of seed
- **lids**, 1 per jar

plant list
- ✱ Aduki beans
- ✱ Alfalfa seeds
- ✱ Mung beans
- ✱ Mustard seeds

TOP TIP
▶ You can buy small packets of seed for sprouting from garden centres. They have all the instructions for each type attached, but once you know what to do it is cheaper to buy larger amounts of seeds and beans from health food stores and supermarkets.

mustard seeds

mung beans

alfalfa seeds

aduki beans

1 Pour a small quantity of seeds or beans into a sieve and rinse them thoroughly under cold running water. This removes dust or dirt. Pick out any tiny stones that you can see with your fingers.

2 Tip or scrape out the wet seeds or beans into a clean, recycled glass jar and half-fill the container with water. Slightly warm water helps the seed to swell faster. Leave overnight or for 12 hours.

3 You'll find the seeds have grown in size due to the amount of water absorbed. Some will not grow. Pick out these hard seeds. Different seed types grow at different rates.

4 Rinse the seeds again under cold running water. Tiny alfalfa seeds are easier to tap or flick out of a small, plastic-mesh tea strainer. Rinsing stops sprouts going mouldy.

5 Drain, shaking off excess water and transfer the seeds to a clean jar. Stand out of direct sunlight but not in the dark. Cover loosely with a lid to stop the air in the jar drying out too much.

6 You'll start to see the seeds sprout, pushing out roots. Rinse, drain and return to the rinsed-out jars every 8–12 hours. It takes the sprouts around 2–4 days to grow big enough to eat.

Plants from pips

Would you like to know what the plant that produces your favourite type of fruit looks like? It's worth trying any kind of fruit seed, not only the ones on the list below, just for the challenge of seeing if you can get them to grow.

you will need
- **fresh, ripe fruits** (*see* Fruit List)
- **chopping board**
- **sharp knife**
- **sieve**
- **small plant** or **plastic pots**, such as yogurt or dessert pots
- **scissors**
- **peat-free seed** and **cutting compost**
- **tray** or **bowl**
- **plastic bags**
- **slender garden canes**
- **elastic bands**
- **damp sand**
- **plant labels**

fruit list
- ✳ **Apple**
- ✳ **Avocado**
- ✳ **Grapefruit**
- ✳ **Kumquat**
- ✳ **Lemon**
- ✳ **Lime**
- ✳ **Orange**
- ✳ **Passion fruit**

FACT FILE
ORANGES AND LEMONS
You can grow lots of different members of the citrus family from seed – orange, lemon, lime, grapefruit and kumquat. Most of the seedlings won't grow fruit but they make fun houseplants anyway. Crush a leaf and you'll smell the orange, lemon or whatever fruit the seed came from really strongly.

oranges and lemons

1 Cut your chosen fruits in half on a chopping board using a sharp knife. Take great care and always cut downwards on to a non-slip surface. You may need adult supervision.

2 Pick out the seeds and rinse off any juice or fruit pulp by putting the seeds in a sieve and holding them under running water. The sugars in the fruit juice can cause mould to grow.

3 Gather a few small plant pots or old food containers. Make holes in the bottom of the pots for drainage with scissors, with adult supervision. Fill with compost and firm lightly.

4 Push the lemon seeds a little way down into the compost with your finger. Cover lightly with compost, stand the pots in a bowl of tepid water for half an hour, then drain.

5 Put plastic bags over the pots with canes to hold them up and secure with an elastic band. Place on a well-lit windowsill. The plastic bag acts like a mini greenhouse. Pot on when seedlings have grown.

6 Apple seeds usually need a cold snap before they will germinate. Take the seeds out of the core, mix them with some damp sand and keep in the fridge for 6–8 weeks before sowing outdoors.

(!) = Watch out! Sharp or dangerous tool in use. 🐾 = Watch out! Adult help is needed.

7 To grow an avocado pear tree, extract the stone and clean it. Plant in a pot of compost so that the bottom half is buried. The base of the seed has a crease or wrinkle.

8 After watering, put the avocado somewhere warm, such as an airing cupboard, to start the germination. The seed will start to crack. Move to a warm, well-lit windowsill and eventually pot on.

TOP TIP

▶ Always remember to label pots with the name of the plant and the date you sowed the seeds, so you don't get confused.

Potted pineapple

The great thing about this project is that you get to eat a delicious piece of pineapple first! If you are really lucky, and grow it in a warm spot, you might even grow a mini pineapple fruit.

you will need

- pineapple
- sharp knife
- chopping board
- plant pot
- 50:50 potting mix and **sand**
- garden canes
- large, clear plastic bag
- adhesive tape or an elastic band
- cactus and succulent potting compost
- water sprayer

cactus potting compost

sand

plant pot

pineapple

1 Choose a ripe pineapple with a strong, fresh green head of leaves. Ask an adult to cut the top off with a knife.

2 Carefully cut off almost all the pineapple flesh beneath the leafy top growth. Cut off the lower leaves to expose about 2½cm/1in of stout stem. Adult supervision is required.

3 Leave the cut stem to dry off for a couple of days. This will help the plant to form its roots and reduce the chance of rotting. You can eat the pineapple flesh straight away!

4 Plant the top in a pot of sandy compost. Firm in with your fingers and water lightly. The compost should be just moist.

5 Using canes for support, place a bag over the pot and secure with tape or an elastic band. Stand in a warm, light spot.

6 Steadily increase the ventilation and finally remove the bag. Spray frequently. Pot into cactus and succulent compost and grow in a warm place, such as a conservatory.

TOP TIP

▶ Trick your plant into producing fruit early – it normally takes two years. In winter seal the plant inside a clear bag with some very ripe apples or bananas for two weeks. In spring, the plant should produce a flower spike.

 = Watch out! Sharp or dangerous tool in use.   = Watch out! Adult help is needed.

Going nuts!

See how alien-like peanuts appear when they germinate. If you are lucky, you may even spot plants burying their flower pods in the soil. That's where the peanuts develop.

you will need

- **fresh peanuts** or **monkey nuts**, in their shells
- **small pots**
- **seed** and **cutting compost**
- **pencil** or **dibber**
- **tray** of **water**
- **watering can**
- **larger pots** or **tubs**
- **peat-free compost** with **added loam (John Innes)**

WARNING – Peanuts can cause a severe allergic reaction in some people, so check with an adult first.

dibber

peanuts

1 Crack open some fresh peanut shells to get to the peanuts. Discard any diseased pods and very small peanuts.

2 Fill small pots with seed and cutting compost. Use a pencil or dibber to make holes about 2½cm/1in deep and plant the peanuts, one in each hole.

3 Stand the small pots in a tray of water so that the compost can soak up all the liquid it needs from underneath.

4 Remove the pots from the tray of water once the dry surface of the compost has gone dark. This means they have soaked up enough water and don't need any more.

5 When the peanuts germinate, the two halves of the peanut appear at the surface, splitting open to reveal green seed leaves!

6 Continue growing in good light. Water occasionally. Repot into bigger pots filled with peat-free compost as necessary. When warm, harden plants off gradually (see page 13).

7 Small, yellow pea flowers appear at the base of the plant. Once pollinated, the pods push into the potting compost.

TOP TIP

▶ Peanut plants need lots of warmth to crop. In colder areas, as autumn approaches, bring tubs under glass to finish growing.

Saucer veg

Farmers usually cut off the growing tops of root vegetables before shipping them off to the shops, so you don't normally see what the leaves look like. In this project the leaves spring back to life!

you will **need**
- **fresh-looking root vegetable selection** (see Vegetable List)
- **sharp knife**
- **chopping board**
- **saucers**
- **small watering can**
- **sand** (optional)

vegetable list
* **Beetroot**
* **Carrot**
* **Parsnip**
* **Radish**
* **Swede**
* **Sweet potato**
* **Turnip**

FACT FILE

TAPROOTS

Although the vegetables listed vary in shape, they are all kinds of taproot, which is where the plant stores food and water.

turnips

1 Try to select very fresh-looking root vegetables, perhaps ones that still have leaves on or that have clusters of green buds at the top. Ones that you have grown in the garden would be ideal! Wash off any soil or dirt under cold running water.

2 Ask an adult to help you cut the tops off the vegetables using a sharp knife and cutting down on to a chopping board. Cut about 2.5cm/1in away from the top, so you have a chunky piece with a flat base. Trim off any leaves, but leave any buds.

3 Allow the cut surfaces of the vegetables to dry off for a day in a cool place. Next, place the vegetable tops, cut-side down, on saucers and put them close to a light window. Add a small amount of water to the saucer with a watering can.

4 Change the water every day. Rinse the saucer and vegetable tops in running water and discard any pieces that have started to rot. After a while, leaves will appear out of the tops.

5 When the vegetable tops have several leaves they can dry out more quickly, especially on sunny days, so it is important to top them up with water regularly. An alternative way to grow the tops is in saucers filled with moist sand.

 = Watch out! Sharp or dangerous tool in use. = Watch out! Adult help is needed.

Hyacinth in a glass

Hyacinths are very pretty and smell gorgeous. Growing them in clear glass bulb vases allows you to see the roots develop and it's exciting to watch the flower-bud slowly push through.

you will need
- **bulb vases**
- **pebbles** (optional)
- **prepared hyacinth bulbs**
- **charcoal chips**

TOP TIP
▶ Like prepared hyacinths, paper white daffodils will also root in water. Fill a glass bowl with small pebbles or beads. Plant groups of 5 or 10 bulbs, pointed end up, then add water to just below the bulb base. Keep dark for 2–3 weeks.

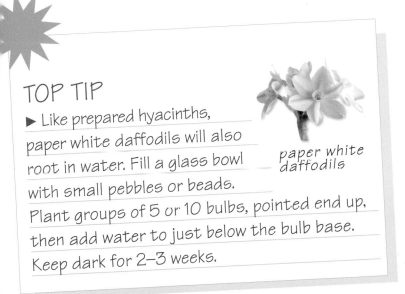
paper white daffodils

1 Fill the bulb vases with water to a level that is just below the cup-shaped bulb holder, where the vase is narrowest. Vases come in different designs and colours. Some are larger and straight-sided, in which case use pebbles to support the bulbs above water.

2 Ordinary hyacinth bulbs won't work for early indoor display. Instead, you need to use prepared ones that have been treated with a period of cold to mimic winter, which activates them. You can buy these from a garden centre.

3 Place a bulb, pointed end upwards, in the top of each container. You may want to wear gloves – they can irritate. Make sure the bulb is not sitting in direct contact with the water or it may rot. Place in a dark, cool place, around 9°C/48°F, such as a pantry or garage.

4 Move the hyacinths from the dark place into a warm, lightly shaded spot once the shoot tip has grown to around 4–5cm/ 1½–2in. Gradually introduce more light over the next few days. Charcoal chips keep the water fresh, so there is no need to change it.

Grass head man

This character can be made at any time of year and will spring into growth in just a few days. The fun continues as the grass 'hair' grows, letting you snip a variety of styles.

you will need
- **old pair** of **tights** or **stockings**
- **scissors**
- **grass seed**
- **peat-free potting compost**
- **small, coloured elastic bands**, 3
- **self-adhesive eyes**, 2
- **container**
- **saucer** or **dish**
- **small watering can**

TOP TIP
► To really soak the compost well, stand the figure in a container of water and wait for the compost to turn dark.

1 Cut off the foot section of an old pair of tights or stockings. You'll need a piece roughly 30cm/12in long. Hold the 'toe' open and put in about a dessert spoon of grass seed.

2 Add some potting compost to form the bulk of the head.

3 Press the compost down. Knot the top of the stocking. Trim away any excess with scissors. Adult supervision is required.

4 Form the nose by drawing out a lump of compost. Keep this in place with an elastic band. Repeat for the ears.

5 All the face needs now to bring it to life is a pair of eyes. Stick them on without being too neat. Wonky eyes add character!

6 After soaking (*see* Top Tip) stand on a dish on a windowsill. In a few days you will start to see the grass seed germinate.

7 Once a decent head of hair has grown, trim it with scissors to form a flat top, if you like.

8 Water the hair as needed with a small watering can. On warm sunny days, pour extra water into the saucer to act as a reservoir.

(!) = Watch out! Sharp or dangerous tool in use.   = Watch out! Adult help is needed.

Potato pets

It doesn't take long to make these cute potato pets. Try using different sizes of potato to create a family. Cut the mustard or cress for salads and re-sow on a new pad.

you will need

- **potato peeler**
- **flat-bottomed baking potato**, 1–2
- **thick wire**
- **wire cutters** or **secateurs**
- **craft foam**
- **double-sided adhesive tape**
- **coloured pompons** or **balls**, 1–2
- **self-adhesive eyes**, 2–4
- **kitchen paper**
- **small watering can**
- **mustard** or **cress seed**

TOP TIP

▶ Keep the kitchen towel moist, adding a little splash of water every day, but don't fill the potato reservoir with water or it may start to rot.

1 Use a potato peeler to carefully carve out a shallow indent in the top of a potato. Adult supervision is required. Repeat with a second potato if you like.

2 Ask an adult to cut the wire into short lengths with wire cutters or secateurs, then bend into pin shapes.

3 Make the snout using a square of craft foam, folding it into a cone and securing with double-sided adhesive tape. Attach to the potato with wire.

4 Add a pompon nose to the end of the snout using a small piece of folded double-sided tape.

5 Attach the eyes above where the snout joins the potato. Make a pair of ears from small circles of foam with a flat base. Use wire pins to form the ear shape and fix into the potato.

6 Line the carved-out indent with a piece of folded up kitchen paper.

7 Moisten the kitchen paper with water. Mustard or cress seeds germinate quickly and only need a damp surface to start them off. Sprinkle the seeds on to the paper.

8 Stand your pets on a windowsill and watch their 'fur' grow.

Weird and wacky plants

The houseplants in this collection, including the cockscomb featured in the main picture, are some of the most bizarre, both in the way they look as well as how they live in the wild. They include meat-eating plants, plants that have no roots, plants that catch and store their own water supply in a leafy vase, and plants that can rapidly move their leaves and branches if danger threatens!

you will need

- **selection** of **plants** (see Plant List)
- **plant mister**
- **shallow pot**
- **tray**
- **gravel** or **coloured glass, acrylic chips** or **gravel**
- **small watering can**
- **piece** of **wire**

sensitive plant

pitcher plant

FACT FILE

AIR PLANTS

Scientists call these amazingly tough plants bromeliads, but they get their common name from the fact that many grow on tree branches (such as Spanish moss) and seem to live on nothing but humid air and rainwater. The pineapple on page 204 is a bromeliad that grows in the ground.

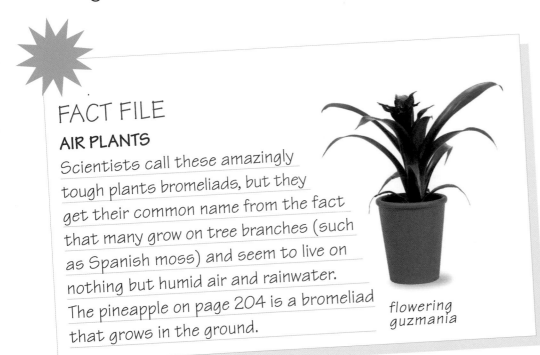
flowering guzmania

plant list

* **Bead plant**
  Nertera granadensis
* **Blushing bromeliad**
  Neoregelia carolinae 'Tricolor'
* **Common cockscomb**
  Celosia argentea var. *cristata*
* **Guzmania**
  Guzmania 'Yellow Marjan'
* **Pitcher plant**
  Sarracenia purpurea
* **Sensitive plant**
  Mimosa pudica
* **Spanish moss**
  Tillandsia usneoides

1 Have you ever seen a plant move in front of your eyes? Gently touch the leaves of the sensitive plant and watch them fold together. A bigger nudge makes the branches droop!

2 In the wild, Spanish moss hangs from tree branches in soft grey curtains. It has no roots and lives by absorbing moisture from the air. Hang from a wire hook and spray with rainwater.

3 The cockscomb is a tender annual plant with the strangest looking folded flowers. Discover how furry the crinkled heads feel by gently stroking them with your finger.

4 Both the guzmania and neoregelia are tree-dwelling bromeliads, able to collect rainwater in their leafy vases. Keep them happy on a tray of moist gravel or glass chips.

(!) = Watch out! Sharp or dangerous tool in use. (🐾) = Watch out! Adult help is needed.

5 Water these plants into the base of the leaves using a narrow-spouted watering can and rainwater. Keep the gravel tray topped with water but don't let the base of the pot stand in water.

6 This pitcher plant snacks on flies caught in its leaf traps. Once inside, the fly is slowly digested! Stand on a gravel tray and keep the mossy compost moist with rainwater.

7 This bead plant from South America produces a carpet of orange bead-like fruits. Gently touch the surface to feel how hard they are. Always water from the bottom.

FACT FILE
AIR PONDS
Some tropical frogs reproduce in the mini ponds created by the vase-shaped leaves of some tree and ground-dwelling air plants.

weird and wacky plants   211

Mini glasshouse garden

Welcome to the world of glass gardens! Even if you don't have an outside space, it is possible to create your own mini garden indoors in a glass container. Here, a special container called a terrarium is used, but you could also use a large glass jar that has a lid.

you will need
- **selection** of **houseplant tots** (*see* Plant List)
- **bucket** of **water**
- **terrarium**
- **gravel**
- **trowel**
- **houseplant compost**
- **glass decorations**, **wood** or **a shell**
- **small watering can**

FACT FILE

PERFECT PLANTS

Garden centres often have little tots or baby houseplants for sale, which are very cheap and will fit inside the miniature glasshouse. Houseplants that enjoy constant warmth and humidity and that are slow-growing and compact are ideal for terrariums and bottle gardens as they will not outgrow them too quickly. The types listed in the Plant List can all be used, so choose the ones you like best.

baby houseplants

plant list
* **Aluminium plant**
  Pilea cadierei
* **Baby rubber plant**
  Peperomia obtusifolia variegated form
* **Creeping moss**
  Selaginella martensii
* **Croton**
  Codiaeum variegatum var. *pictum* 'Gold Dust'
* **Dragon tree**
  Dracaena marginata 'Tricolor'
* **Parlour palm**
  Neanthe bella
* **Polka dot plant**
  Hypoestes phyllostachya
* **Silver lace fern**
  Pteris ensiformis
* **Spider aralia**
  Dizygotheca elegantissima

1 Plunge the plants in a bucket of water and wait until the bubbles stop. Put 2.5cm/1in of gravel in the bottom of the terrarium. Larger containers need more gravel.

2 Using a trowel, scoop up compost to transfer to the terrarium. You can fill to the bottom of the door and, if necessary, make the compost deeper towards the back.

3 Firm the compost slightly with your hand, then start planting the taller plants such as the dragon tree first, as this will go in towards the back or centre of the terrarium.

4 Put in the spider aralia next, followed by the polka dot plant. Try to place the plants to give them space to grow and to create as much contrast as possible in leaf shape and colour.

 = Watch out! Sharp or dangerous tool in use. 🐾 = Watch out! Adult help is needed.

5 The bright, golden leaves of this croton will add a splash of colour. When you look through the terrarium door it's like looking into a miniature forest of fantasy trees.

6 The rounded leaves of a cream variegated peperomia at the front of the terrarium contrast well with the spiky leaves of the dragon tree. Firm the plants in lightly with your fingers.

7 Make a kind of pathway through the plants, adding some extra colour with glass beads or, for a more natural look, add some aquarium driftwood or perhaps a shell.

8 Position the terrarium out of direct sunlight. Water very sparingly as it is easy to make the compost and plants too wet, which can lead to problems. Keep the door closed to make it more humid.

glass decorations

Safari garden

This indoor garden creates an exciting setting for your zoo animals. We've chosen a safari theme based around a watering hole in the African savannah, but you could just as easily create a steamy jungle with monkeys, snakes and jaguars. All the plants and the pool fit into a waterproof tray, which can be placed on a tabletop close to a window. Water very sparingly when the compost looks a little dry and mist with a sprayer.

you will need
- **houseplant compost**
- **waterproof container**, such as a sterilized cat litter tray
- **trowel**
- **aluminium foil**
- **houseplant tots** (*see Plant List*)
- **bucket** of **water**
- **shallow dish** of **water**
- **mist sprayer**
- **pebbles**
- **plastic safari animals**
- **narrow-spouted watering can**

plastic lion

TOP TIP
▶ If you don't have a waterproof container, use a black refuse bag to line a shallow fruit box or crate. Alternatively, to ensure your garden has good drainage, find a large plastic tray to sit the box on. If you line the box with plastic, put some holes in the base.

wooden crate

plant list
✳ **Bead plant**
   Nertera granadensis
✳ **Delta maidenhair**
   Adiantum raddianum
✳ **Dragon tree**
   Dracaena 'Janet Craig Compacta'
✳ **Pink quill**
   Tillandsia cyanea
✳ **Ribbon plant**
   Dracaena sanderiana

pink quill

1 Put some compost in a container using a trowel, banking it up towards the edges and making a space in the middle for the pool. Scrunch the edges of a piece of foil to make an oval shape.

2 Plunge the houseplant tots in a bucket of water and wait for the bubbles to stop. Water the bead plant by standing it in a shallow dish of water. Plant the three ribbon plants.

3 Balance the mini forest with an airy delta maidenhair fern. All indoor ferns like being misted with tepid water from a hand sprayer to keep the leaves from drying out.

4 The dramatic rosette-shaped dragon tree can go in next. Dragon trees are normally quite tall but this will stay neat and compact. With its dark glossy leaves feels totally tropical!

 = Watch out! Sharp or dangerous tool in use.   = Watch out! Adult help is needed.

5 Bead plants are low carpeting species producing bright orange fruits. Dig out a hole for the roots with your hand and plant so that it can grow over the edge.

6 To make it feel even more like the lush vegetation surrounding a watering hole, plant a pink quill plant. Add pebbles around the pool to look like boulders.

7 Start to add your animals – whatever African savannah creatures you may have. We've put a big elephant at the front but the zebra is hiding in the trees at the back!

8 Carefully fill the pool with water from a beaker. You shouldn't need to water the plants at this stage, but you will need to in future, using a narrow-spouted watering can.

safari garden 215

Fantasy garden

Cacti and succulents are amazing desert plants that come in all kinds of weird shapes and sizes. There are so many to choose from that it can be hard to pick out just a few plants for a collection. The ones chosen for this little fantasy garden are all easy for beginners to grow. All they need is a well-lit windowsill and only a little water. Carefully feel down with your finger into the compost and only water if it is dry.

you will need
- crock or broken tile
- terracotta bulb bowl
- soil-based potting compost
- horticultural grit
- plastic mixing bowl
- trowel
- range of cacti and succulents (see Plant List)
- kitchen paper
- dessert spoon
- blue acrylic mulch
- plastic dinosaur or monster

plastic dinosaur

FACT FILE
CLEVER CACTI
Members of the cactus family naturally live in desert areas where there is very little water, high daytime temperatures and strong sunlight. To survive, they have a thick waterproof coat, spines to stop them being eaten and sometimes light-reflecting hairs, as well as swollen stems capable of storing water.

cactus

plant list
* **Echeveria species** (in flower)
* **Fishhook cactus**
  Ferocactus latispinus
* **Good luck plant**
  Bryophyllum daigremontianum
* **Peanut cactus**
  Chamaecereus sylvestri
* **Pincushion cactus**
  Mammillaria species

WARNING – The spines of some cacti are sharp. Take great care when handling them. Avoid the *Opuntia* cactus, which has nasty irritant hairs.

1 Put a piece of crock or broken tile over the drainage hole in a terracotta bulb bowl to help stop it becoming blocked with compost. Good drainage is vital for cacti and succulents.

2 Mix together potting compost and horticultural grit in a bowl, stirring the two together with a trowel. This gritty mixture will give the plant roots plenty of drainage.

3 Add some of the mixture to the bulb bowl. Carefully take the first plant out of its pot – the leaves of some succulents can be quite brittle. Sit the two echeverias side by side.

4 Work compost around the root-balls, then add the good luck plant. This easy houseplant develops tiny plantlets complete with roots along the edges of its leaves.

 = Watch out! Sharp or dangerous tool in use.   = Watch out! Adult help is needed.

5 Though the peanut cactus may look prickly, it is quite soft. Plant it at the edge of the bowl and next to it add the pincushion cactus, scooping compost back round the roots.

6 To take the fishhook cactus with its fierce spines out of its pot, hold the 'head' with a piece of folded kitchen paper. Continue to hold the cactus like this during planting.

7 After filling in all the gaps round the root-balls and firming with your fingers, use a dessert spoon to spread fine blue acrylic mulch (or any other coloured mulch) around the plants.

8 For the finishing touch, place a dinosaur or monster figure in among the plants. The bizarre cacti and funky blue glass make the perfect fantasy landscape for a dino!

Mini farmyard

It's fun to create miniature worlds and to be able to imagine yourself walking around in them. You can put a pig in an enclosure that looks most like a muddy pigsty and settle cows, a sheep and carthorse in a mossy field. You can swap features around really easily, move and rebuild fences and pathways, create new fields, and make a twig and bark stable, perhaps, and even a corral for exercising horses. So get collecting and let your imagination run wild!

you will need
- **waterproof container**, such as a sterilized cat litter tray
- **potting compost**
- **trowel**
- **twigs**
- **aluminium foil**
- **grit** and **sand**
- **moss**
- **farmyard animals**
- **clippings** from **evergreens**
- **herb cuttings** and **seed-heads**

FACT FILE
BUILD A WALL
We've used horticultural grit to make our cobbled path but if you collect some larger stones, shingle pieces or small slate chippings, you could build a traditional-looking stone wall, if you prefer. You might need to glue the pieces with PVA glue to make the wall a bit more solid.

assorted stones

TOP TIP
▶ If you can't find any flat moss pieces to make the field, pull some grass and shred that into small pieces to cover the compost. Alternatively, pull small leaves off green coloured shrubs or herbs and overlap them to form a carpet.

1 Half-fill a waterproof tray with some dry potting compost. This will act as a base to support some of the fences and trees later on. You can also mound it up to form hummocks.

2 Build a small square enclosure for one of your farmyard animals by putting in a line of broken-up twigs. The twigs, standing in for logs, need to be about the same length.

3 Break up some larger forked twigs so that they are the same size. Plant them, evenly spaced, in a row, then rest a long thin twig across the forks to make a fence.

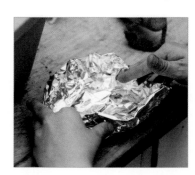

4 Take a piece of foil and mould it into a shallow dish shape. Scrunch up the edges to make it more robust. Position the duck pond in one corner of the tray and fill with water.

5 Carefully trickle some grit around the pigsty to make a cobbled pathway. You can firm it lightly with your fingers to make it lie flatter. Use sand to make a dirt track, if you like.

6 Collect a few pieces of thin carpeting moss from wood or stone in shady parts of the garden. Create the effect of a grassy meadow by patching the pieces together.

7 Add some more animals to the pasture – a cow or two, maybe some horses and foals or make it a field of grazing sheep watched over by a sheep dog. The choice is yours!

8 Use clippings from evergreen shrubs, herb sprigs and seed-heads to create hedges and trees. Because of the scale, even a small clipping looks like a big tree!

Indoor pond

If you enjoy growing indoor plants, a mini pond such as this will give you a chance to grow some really interesting and unusual types and to look after a couple of pet snails, too! During very warm weather it might be easier to manage the pond outdoors. Dig a shallow hole and put the pond into it. In early autumn lift the pond, clean it and bring it indoors as some of the plants are not hardy.

you will need

- **washing-up bowl**
- **small bucket** of **gravel**
- **selection** of **water plants** (see Plant List)
- **bucket** of **water**
- **jug** of **water**
- **Ramshorn** or **other freshwater snails**
- **scissors**

scissors

bucket of gravel

washing-up bowl

FACT FILE

UMBRELLA PLANT

One houseplant that will love spending time in your mini pond is the umbrella plant Cyperus alternifoli, a relative of the Egyptian papyrus Cyperus papyrus that was used for making paper and reed boats in ancient times. The umbrella plant reproduces from little plantlets that form in between the leaves.

umbrella plant

plant list

- ✳ **Canadian pondweed**
  Elodea canadensis
- ✳ **Fibre optic plant**
  Scirpus cernuus
- ✳ **Parrot's feather**
  Myriophyllum aquaticum
- ✳ **Water hyacinth**
  Eichhornia crassipes

1 Half-fill a clean washing-up bowl with cold water. Rinse the gravel under an outdoor tap (so the dirt stays outside), then add it to the washing-up bowl to form the base of the pond.

2 Plunge the potted water plants in a bucket of water and wait till the bubbles have stopped. This will help them to sink and stay in position. Put the fibre optic plant in one corner.

3 There's no need to take the plastic mesh pot off the plants as they are designed to let the roots grow through. Add the parrot's feather. This has finely cut floating leaves.

4 To keep the water healthy, put in an oxygenating plant that lives under the water. Canadian pondweed will grow quickly and later on you might need to pull some out.

 = Watch out! Sharp or dangerous tool in use.   = Watch out! Adult help is needed.

5 Squeeze in a small clump of water hyacinth. This strange-looking aquatic or water plant has air-filled bladders that keep the leaves above the surface of the water.

6 To help keep your mini pond healthy, add a couple of freshwater snails. They will eat the algae that grows on the walls of the bowl, keeping the bowl clean. They also look cool!

7 Top up your mini pond with water and keep it topped up as the water will be lost through evaporation. Put the pond in a light place, especially in winter. Cut back overgrown plants with scissors.

8 The peacock's feather, water hyacinth and Canadian pondweed are all potentially invasive and should not be put into outdoor pools where they might 'escape'.

TOP TIP

► You can often buy freshwater snails from aquatic or pet stores.

aquatic snail

indoor pond **221**

Ivy animals

You can buy wire topiary frames in many different designs and a small animal figure, such as this squirrel, can be made in just a couple of hours. This craft is part of a very old tradition of clipping and training plants into fun shapes called topiary. Ivy animals can be temporarily dressed up for special occasions and make great presents. Ivy is easy to grow and can take quite a lot of shade. Put on a cool windowsill out of direct sun.

you will need

- **bulb bowl** or **shallow planter**
- **crock**
- **peat-free potting compost**
- **trowel**
- **pots** of **rooted ivy** (*Hedera helix*) **cuttings**, 3
- **bucket** of **water**
- **wire mesh topiary frame**
- **pencil**
- **moist sphagnum moss**
- **pieces** of **green plastic coated wire**, 12cm/5in lengths
- **small scissors**
- **small watering can**
- **ribbon**
- **self-adhesive eyes**
- **felt nose** (optional)
- **mist sprayer**

WARNING – There is a very small chance of fungal infection from sphagnum moss. It is a good idea to wear thin latex gloves when handling moss.

TOP TIP

▶ You'll probably find many forms of English ivy (*Hedera helix*) at the garden centre or nursery, but the best for small topiary figures are ones with small, plain green leaves and only very short gaps between the leaves along the stems. These ivies stay nice and compact, are easy to train and won't overwhelm the frame.

English ivy

project equipment

1 Cover the drainage hole in the shallow bowl or pot with a piece of crock. Half-fill with compost using a trowel. Plunge the plants in a bucket of water and wait for the bubbles to stop.

2 Dig your thumbs into the centre of the ivy root-ball and open it out into a strip of cuttings. Place the strip around the edge of the prepared bulb bowl or planter.

3 Ensure you have ivies all round the edge, then add more compost to cover the roots and firm lightly with your hands. Next take the moss and start filling the wire mesh topiary frame.

4 Use a pencil to work the moss into all the hard-to-reach spaces in the frame, such as the tail. Really pack the moss in tightly as it will shrink slightly when dry and can leave gaps.

 = Watch out! Sharp or dangerous tool in use.  = Watch out! Adult help is needed.

7 Trim off any leaves that stick out too far using scissors, along with any over-long shoots. Adult supervision is required. Water to moisten the compost. Tie a ribbon bow round the neck of the animal.

VARIATION
• Creeping fig (*Ficus pumila*) grows in a similar way to ivy, rooting into the moss where the shoots touch. It is not hardy and likes being misted.

5 Put the frame into the centre of the pot. Start to train each long strand of ivy on to the frame using pieces of wire bent in half to make pins. Angle these in downwards when positioning.

6 Take the ivy stems around the main parts of the body, avoiding the head, and also secure them up and over the tail. Put extra pins in to keep the stems tight against the moss.

8 Pin on eyes and a felt nose, if you like. Mist the topiary figure regularly to keep the moss moist. Continue to pin new ivy growth on to the moss and trim back wayward shoots.

ivy animals **223**

Lovely lavender

The aromatic herb lavender has long been used to make cosmetics and toiletries. Here, it is used to make fragrant lavender bundles, which make wonderful presents to use for scenting drawers and wardrobes or simply to hang on the wall. It is best to cut the lavender in the cool part of the day if you can, so that it keeps more of its lovely scent. Try binding different types together for a multicoloured effect.

you will need
- **fresh lavender flowers,** (*see* Plant List)
- **scissors**
- **fine wire**
- **narrow parcel ribbon**

plant list
* **Varieties of English lavender (*Lavandula angustifolia*):**
  'Hidcote' (violet/blue flowers)
  'Hidcote Pink' (pink flowers)
  'Imperial Gem' (rich purple flowers)
  'Miss Katherine' (deep pink flowers)
  'Munstead' (blue-purple flowers)
  'Twickle Purple' (blue-purple flowers)
* **Varieties of French lavender (*Lavandula stoechas*):**
  L. s. pedunculata (purple flowers)
  L. s. viridis (green flowers)
* **Other types of lavender:**
  Lavandula x *intermedia* 'Grappenhall' (blue-purple flowers)
  Lavandula x *intermedia* 'Grosso' (blue-purple flowers)
  Lavandula x *intermedia* 'Hidcote Giant' (mid-blue flowers)
  Lavandula latifolia x *lanata* (dark blue flowers)
  Lavandula pinnata (blue-violet flowers)

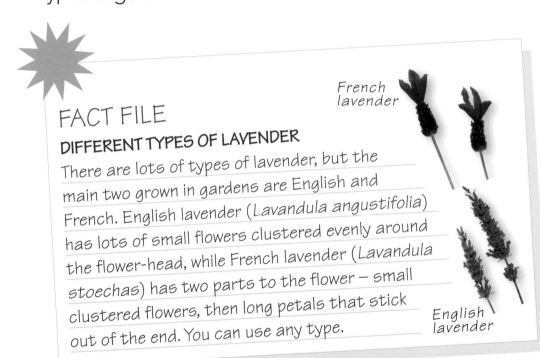

FACT FILE
DIFFERENT TYPES OF LAVENDER
There are lots of types of lavender, but the main two grown in gardens are English and French. English lavender (*Lavandula angustifolia*) has lots of small flowers clustered evenly around the flower-head, while French lavender (*Lavandula stoechas*) has two parts to the flower – small clustered flowers, then long petals that stick out of the end. You can use any type.

French lavender

English lavender

1 Using scissors, cut a handful of lavender flowers with long stems in the cool part of the day. Ones that have just begun to open up are best. Adult supervision is required.

2 Pull off the small leaves along the length of the stems. This will make it easier to bind and dry the stems. Arrange the heads to lie next to each other or form into a dome shape.

3 Take a piece of thin, flexible wire and wrap it around the stems to make a tight lavender bundle. The wiring will be covered with ribbon later so don't worry if it's untidy.

4 Tie one end of a roll of narrow parcel ribbon near the top of the stems. Make sure the knot is nice and tight as you will be pulling on it firmly as you wrap the stem.

(!) = Watch out! Sharp or dangerous tool in use.　(🐾) = Watch out! Adult help is needed.

5 Holding the roll of ribbon taut, start to wrap the stems. Overlap the ribbon as you work from top to bottom so that you can no longer see the stems. Bind in the knot and cut the end.

6 Use a pair of scissors to trim the ends of the lavender stems to the same length. Create a wire loop fixing at the stem end by wrapping wire tightly around the bundle.

7 Tie off the ribbon very firmly and trim the ends. Next take another piece of ribbon and tie a bow at the top end, towards the flowers. Leave two long tails.

8 Use the blade of a blunt pair of scissors to stretch the ribbon tails. This causes it to curl into attractive corkscrews. Ask an adult to help if you need to. Hang the bundle by the wire loop.

TOP TIP

▶ Grow lots of types of lavender in shades of purple, blue and pink so that you have plenty for cutting. You'll keep bees and butterflies happy, too.

Rosemary ring

This beautiful flower garland can be hung indoors or outside and not only looks good but smells delicious! Because rosemary is evergreen, you can make it at any time during summer or autumn. Frothy lime-green lady's mantle makes an ideal base for highlighting larger, more colourful flower-heads and rosebuds. It would make a really lovely present for Mother's Day or for someone's birthday.

you will need
- flexible twigs
- **secateurs** or **pruners**
- florist's wire
- moist sphagnum moss
- green garden twine
- rosemary sprigs
- scissors
- small flower sprigs, berries, rosebuds and rose hips
- thick wire
- hand sprayer

WARNING – There is a very small chance of fungal infection from sphagnum moss, so it is a good idea to wear latex gloves.

TOP TIPS
▶ The ring will gradually dry out but the flowers should keep their colour for quite a while. To help it look fresher for longer, hang the wreath in a cool, shaded place out of direct sunlight and mist frequently with a hand sprayer.
▶ To make a Christmas version, carefully bind holly to the ring instead of rosemary (watch out, it is prickly!). Thread in misletoe stems and some seasonal berries, such as holly berries, rose hips or viburnum berries.

plant list
✳ **Lady's mantle**
   Alchemilla mollis
✳ **Lavender**
   Lavandula varieties
✳ **Purple toadflax**
   Linaria purpurea
✳ **Rose**
   Rosa varieties
✳ **Rosemary**
   Rosmarinus officinalis
✳ **Spiraea**
   Spiraea bumalda
✳ **St John's Wort**
   Hypericum androsaemum

1 Cut some long, bendy twigs with secateurs or pruners. Ask an adult to help. Wind the twigs around into a circle. They should grip together if you tuck the ends in under another twig.

2 Wind pieces of florist's wire around the circle to help to hold it together more firmly. Tie it in five places around the ring. The wire will be covered, so you don't need to be neat.

3 Take large handfuls of pre-soaked sphagnum moss and mould it with your hands over the twig circle. Be generous with the moss as it will shrink down over time.

4 Hold the moss roughly in place by winding lengths of florist's wire around the wreath in a spiral fashion. This will allow you to hold the wreath upright.

 = Watch out! Sharp or dangerous tool in use.   = Watch out! Adult help is needed.

8 Collect flowers, fruits and rosebuds from the garden using scissors (adult supervision is required). Small, frothy or papery flowers are best. Choose colours and shapes that work together.

9 Push the flowers you have collected into the ring, tucking them among the rosemary and moss. Use thick wire to make a loop for hanging and attach it to the ring. Mist with a hand sprayer.

5 Tie one end of a roll of garden twine around the moss-covered wreath. Lift it up on to its side then, keeping the twine taut, wind it round to bind the moss to the wreath.

6 Binding the moss is difficult, so ask someone to hold the ring and turn it for you. Cut sprigs of rosemary and push them into the moss so they lie flat. Adult supervision is required.

7 Overlap the rosemary pieces, so that you cover most of the moss. You'll enjoy the aroma of the fresh rosemary leaves as you work! Wind florist's wire around to secure the sprigs.

rosemary ring **227**

Plant profiles

The following pages describe how to grow and use many of the plants included in previous chapters, so you can check where they like to live and what they like. There are sections on growing for colour and scent, plants for pots and containers, and lots of plants you can eat, including vegetables, herbs and fruits – yummy!

Planting for colour

Crocus
Crocus chrysanthus

Flowering in late winter and early spring, these colourful little bulbs are very cheering. Plant in groups at the front of the border, along the edges of pathways, in a rock garden or alpine troughs, or in bowls on the patio. Varieties include 'Blue Pearl', 'Zwanenburg Bronze' and the two-tone 'Ladykiller'.

How to grow Plant in late summer or early autumn, 5–7.5cm/2–3in deep in well-drained soil and full sun. Cut lawns six weeks after flowering.

Height and spread 7.5–10 x 5–7.5cm/3–4 x 2–3in.

Hardiness ✳✳✳ Zone 3.

Other plants Dutch crocus (*C. vernus* forms) flower slightly later and have larger blooms. 'Jeanne d'Arc' (white), 'Pickwick' (purple-and-white striped) and 'Remembrance' (purple) are good in pots and borders or naturalized in lawns (*see* page 107). Also plant the early *C. x luteus* 'Golden Yellow' in lawns.

Dahlia
Dahlia cultivars

Vibrant late summer- and autumn-flowering plants, these have large blooms in various shapes and forms. They include pompon, cactus, water lily, collerette and decorative types in reds, oranges, yellows, pinks, purples and white. Some are dazzling two-tone cultivars and many have purple-black leaves. They are perfect for large patio pots or filling border gaps.

How to grow Start tubers into growth in early spring (*see* page 91). Move outdoors from early summer, after hardening off in well-drained but moisture-retentive soil. Protect from slugs. Deadhead regularly and feed generously when in flower. May need staking or support. In colder areas, lift tubers in mid autumn, storing in a frost-free place. Otherwise, mulch well to protect from the cold.

Height and spread 60–120 x 45–60cm/24–48 x 18–24in.

Hardiness ✳ Zone 8.

Other plants Single dahlias, such as the Coltness hybrids, are good for bees and butterflies. These, and the dwarf bedding and patio types, are grown from seed.

Hollyhock
Alcea rosea

These cottage garden plants have tall spires of single or double blooms in midsummer, which take up little room. There are many shades, from dark reds to pastels. Leaves have rounded lobes. Short-lived perennials, they are usually grown as biennials (meaning they flower the second year from sowing) or annuals. Use tall varieties to give height in borders or to frame a doorway.

How to grow Sow seed in pots or trays on a windowsill in early spring (for annuals), or outdoors, in an unheated greenhouse or cold frame in early summer (for biennials). With annuals, prick out into individual pots to grow on before planting. Alternatively, buy young plants in spring. They require full sun and well-drained soil. Discard after flowering to reduce the chance of hollyhock rust disease.

Height and spread 100–200cm x 30–40cm/40–80 x 12–16in.

Hardiness ✳✳✳ Zone 3

Other plants Majorette Group, which are compact annuals with double or semi-double blooms. The tall annuals, Summer Carnival Group. Chater's Double Group, which are tall and usually grown as biennials. The nearly black *A. rosea* 'Nigra' is very dramatic and unusual.

Mexican aster
Cosmos bipinnatus
Sonata Series

This half-hardy annual produces lots of big, dish-shaped blooms in shades of pink and white all summer long. The slender stems carry frothy, divided leaves. It is great for borders.

How to grow Sow seed in pots or trays of seed compost on a warm windowsill in early spring. Prick out seedlings and grow on in good light. Harden off and plant out after the last likely frost for your area. It will grow in any well-drained soil, even if it is relatively poor, in full sun. Deadhead regularly. May need staking/support.

Height and spread 60 x 38cm/ 24 x 15in.

Hardiness ✳ Zone 7.

Other plants 'Purity' is, as its name suggests, a white form.

Ornamental onion
Allium 'Purple Sensation'

The drumstick heads of this onion family member open as the spring bulbs start to fade and early summer flowering herbaceous perennials are coming into bloom. Their vivid colour stands out well and they add height while other plants are still quite low.

▲ Spring-flowering crocus

▲ Dahlia

▲ Hollyhock

▲ Mexican aster

▲ *Ornamental onion*

▲ *Beard tongue*

▲ *Red hot poker*

▲ *Snapdragon*

How to grow Plant the pale round bulbs in autumn, 13cm/5in deep, putting three to a 25cm/10in pot. Stand in a sheltered spot outdoors but don't allow them to dry out. Alternatively, plant in groups of three or five direct in the border. In spring, when the thin green leaves appear, plant potted bulbs in gaps in the border. Leaves die before flowers open. They require full sun to light shade and any well-drained soil.
Height and spread 100 x 7.5cm/40 x 3in.
Hardiness ✳✳✳ Zone 4.
Other plants For even bigger drumsticks on tall stems try A. 'Globemaster'. For big, starry heads on short stems, grow A. *christophii* or even more starry, A. *schubertii*.

Beard tongue
Penstemon
Flowering from midsummer to mid autumn, these perennials are great value. Blooms are tubular with flared ends and often streaked inside with darker or lighter markings. Colours range from deep burgundy or purple through shades of red and pink to white. Narrow-leaved forms such as 'Schoenholzeri' (syn. 'Firebird') are generally hardier than broad-leaved ones. Best in a border with circular or daisy shaped blooms.

How to grow Grow in full sun in any well-drained soil. They are easy to propagate from shoot tip cuttings in summer. Best planted in late spring/early summer in cold areas. Deadhead flower spikes before they have finished flowering completely to encourage more spikes. Leave late seed-heads on for extra frost protection. Cut back to a low framework of branches in mid spring, just above where new growth is sprouting.
Height and spread 60–90 x 30–60cm/24–36 x 12–24in.
Hardiness ✳✳✳ Zones 6–9
Other plants For front of border positions try the pink 'Evelyn'. Bird Series include the pink and white 'Osprey' and dark purple 'Blackbird'. There are many more, including the pale pink 'Apple Blossom' and soft purple 'Stapleford Gem'.

Red hot poker
Kniphofia
These bold, late summer- to early autumn-flowering perennials from South Africa are also known as torch lilies. This is because of the shape of the flowers and the orange-turning-to-yellow colouring of many species and cultivars. Dainty, single-coloured pokers are also available. Foliage is grassy to sword-shaped and some are virtually evergreen. Good for adding an exotic feel.

How to grow They require full sun in well-drained, moisture-retentive soil, so add manure or compost to dry soils. Apply a dry mulch of bark or pine needles in autumn to protect the crowns in cold regions. Cut off old spikes at the base and tidy foliage in spring.
Height and spread 60–150 x 45–60+cm/24–60 x 18–24+in.
Hardiness ✳✳ Zone 5.
Other plants 'Samuel's Sensation' is a classic red hot poker. 'Alcazar' has vivid orange spikes and 'Percy's Pride' is greenish yellow.

Snapdragon
Antirrhinum majus
These plants are grown as half-hardy bedding specimens. Taller types are great for filling gaps in borders. You can make the flower 'mouths' open and close by squeezing, hence the name snapdragon.

How to grow They are easy to grow from seed on a warm windowsill in spring. Pinch out the tips of young plants to promote branching and more flowers. Plant out in late spring, after they have been hardened off, in any fertile, well-drained soil. Cut off the main flower spike above the lower side shoots when it has faded to encourage more spikes.
Height and spread 60–75 x 30–45cm/24–30 x 12–18in.
Hardiness ✳✳ Zone 7.

Other plants Coronette Series is resistant to the fungal disease rust, while Sonnet Series does well in rainy summers. Madame Butterfly Series has tall stems and double flowers and 'Magic Carpet' is a compact bedding or patio pot type.

Other colourful plants
* **Blanket flower** (yellow/orange/red) *Gaillardia* X *grandiflora*
* **Coneflower** (gold/orange/red) *Rudbeckia hirta* 'Marmalade'
* **Day lily** (yellow) *Hemerocallis* 'Stella de Oro'
* **Fuchsia** (pink/purple/red/white) *Fuchsia* cvs.
* **Gladioli** (pink/purple/orange/red/white) *Gladiolus* cvs.
* **Montbretia** (red) *Crocosmia* 'Lucifer'
* **Ornamental sage** (purple) *Salvia* X *superba*
* **Osteospermum** (pink) *Osteospermum* Sunny Series
* **Spider flower** (white/pink/mauve) *Cleome hassleriana*
* **Tree mallow** (pink) *Lavatera* X *clementii* cvs.

Planting for scent

Candytuft
Iberis umbellata
This quick and easy hardy annual flower (a member of the mustard family) is grown for its pretty pastel blooms and for its sweet fragrance. This is especially good in white and long-established seed mixtures. It attracts butterflies.

How to grow Rake an area of soil until it looks like fine breadcrumbs. Sow thinly, lightly covering the seed with soil. Repeat between early spring and midsummer for a succession of blooms around the garden or in pots.

Height and spread 15–30 x 15–30cm/6–12 x 6–12in.

Hardiness ✳✳✳ Zone 3.

Other plants For colour mixtures try 'Fairy' or 'Fairyland Mixed', 'Fantasia Mixed' and 'Flash', all of which have shallowly domed heads made up of many small blooms. 'Giant Hyacinth Flowered' is white with the best perfume.

Cherry pie, Heliotrope
Heliotropium arborescens
Although old-fashioned, tender perennial cultivars of *H. arborescens* have the richest perfume, seed-raised plants in a border or pots by the patio will fill the air with their sweet, spicy, vanilla scent. The deep-purple domed heads are shown off by the dark green, crinkled, glossy leaves. It is a good butterfly and moth plant.

How to grow Sow half-hardy annual seed on a warm windowsill or in a heated propagator in spring and prick out seedlings when large enough to handle into individual pots. Harden off before planting out after risk of frost has passed.

Height and spread 45 x 45cm/ 18 x 18in.

Hardiness ✳ Zone 10.

Other plants 'Marine' and the newer 'Nagano' are the main seed varieties, but 'Dwarf Marine' is a compact alternative for baskets.

Daffodil
Narcissus
If you have ever grown 'Paper White' daffodils for indoor flowering, you will know how powerfully fragrant some cultivars are. Outside, in sheltered corners of the patio or around doorways, pots and tubs of fragrant daffodils are a treat in early and mid spring.

How to grow Plant bulbs three times deeper than the size of the bulb in late summer or autumn but preferably as soon as bulbs are available. Discard any soft or very mouldy bulbs. Any good potting compost (especially loam/soil based ones) will do for containers. Avoid very dry soils. Jonquils appreciate a bed in full sun but most tolerate some shade. Deadhead after flowering and feed with tomato food at the same time to build up bulb reserves for next year. For the same reason, don't knot or cut off the leaves until at least 8 weeks after flowering.

Height and spread 15–45 x 7.5–15cm/6–18 x 3–6in.

Hardiness ✳✳✳ Zone 3.

Other plants Try the large, frilly, double-headed Narcissus 'Cheerfulness' and 'Sir Winston Churchill'. 'Sweetness' has small, deep yellow flowers and the variety 'Actaea' and *N. poeticus* var. *recurvus*, known as pheasant's eye daffodils, are creamy white with an orange 'eye'. Jonquils (*N. jonquilla*) have very dainty yellow flowers and grassy leaves.

Hyacinth
Hyacinthus orientalis
These intensely fragrant flowers can either be grown from 'prepared' bulbs designed for indoor flowering as early as Christmas, or from ordinary bulbs. The stocky flower heads, tightly packed with individual blooms, are held on short flower stems. Flowers last well in patio pots given a little shelter from wind and rain, but bulbs can also be planted with spring bedding in borders.

How to grow Plant in full sun or partial shade. For containers, choose a loam-based potting compost and ensure there is good drainage. Deadhead after flowering, feed with liquid fertilizer and leave foliage to die down to allow bulbs to build up reserves for next year's flowering.

Height and spread 20–25 x 15cm/8–10 x 6in.

Hardiness ✳✳✳ Zone 4.

Other plants For rich blues (which hide fading flowers well) choose cultivars such as 'Delft Blue' and 'Blue Jacket'. 'L'Innocence' is pure white, 'Pink Pearl' mid pink, and 'City of Haarlem' delicate yellow. 'Gypsy Queen' is pale salmon.

Night scented stock
Matthiola longipetala subsp. *bicornis*
Unlike the other types of stock, which are also scented, you grow this hardy annual species for its fragrance rather than for

▲ *Candytuft*

▲ *Cherry pie*

▲ *Daffodil*

▲ *Hyacinth*

▲ *Night scented stock*

▲ *Sweet alyssum*

▲ *Sweet pea*

▲ *Wallflower*

its amazing blooms. Sow in beds under windows or around doors or sprinkle seed in window boxes.

How to grow It prefers a sunny position in well-drained and preferably alkaline soil. Sow seed thinly in spring on to raked soil and cover lightly.

Height and spread 15–30 x 20cm/6–12 x 8in.

Hardiness ✳✳✳ Zone 5.

Other plants Brompton stocks (*M. incana* 'Brompton Mixed') are showy biennials with double blooms in pastel shades. You can buy ready grown plants in spring for flowering in summer. Ten week stocks (*M. incana* 'Ten Week Mixed') are annuals, also with double blooms, which are sown on a windowsill in early spring.

Sweet alyssum
Lobularia maritima

This hardy annual is usually white-flowered. It is often used in hanging baskets and patio beds. The tiny four-petalled blooms are massed in shallow domed heads and the sweet scent attracts lots of insects.

How to grow Sowing directly into a well-raked seedbed in spring is easiest, but you can also grow in seed trays and pots on the windowsill for planting out after hardening off. It prefers well-drained ground but tends to stop flowering and produce seed

if it runs short of water. Deadhead by clipping over with small scissors.

Height and spread 10–20 x 20–30cm/4–8 x 8–12in.

Hardiness ✳✳✳ Zone 3.

Other plants 'Snow Crystals' is longer-flowered than most, making neat domes. 'Sweet White' is very strongly scented. Pinks and mauves include Easter Bonnet Series and 'Oriental Night'.

Sweet pea
Lathyrus odoratus

Cultivated modern versions of these hardy annual climbing plants were bred more as a colourful cut flower than for their scent. However, old-fashioned seed mixtures have a stronger scent, and are usually smaller-flowered and in darker or more muted shades.

How to grow Sow in autumn or spring in long, tubular pots (*see* page 92) or directly into the ground. Plant out pot-raised plants in a sunny spot after hardening off. Prepare the ground well, incorporating lots of manure or garden compost into the bottom of the planting trench. Provide support. Alternatively, plant in tubs containing loam-based potting compost and make a wigwam to fit. Pick flowers frequently to keep them producing.

Height and spread 120–180 x 30cm/45–70 x 12in.

Hardiness ✳✳✳ Zone 3.

Other plants Varieties labelled as heritage, old-fashioned, antique or heirloom often have excellent fragrance. As well as mixtures, try the historic pink and white 'Painted Lady'.

Wallflower
Erysimum cheiri

These short-lived perennial evergreen plants flower around the same time as tulips and forget-me-nots. The fragrance not only attracts humans but also early butterflies and bees! The four-petalled flowers are often in soft 'tapestry' or old velvet colours. Taller kinds are useful for filling gaps in borders. Compact varieties do well in window boxes and tubs with dwarf bulbs.

How to grow Wallflowers are members of the cabbage family and can suffer from club root disease. However, well-drained alkaline soil will help control the problem. Buy strong-looking plants in autumn and plant firmly. You can raise your own plants from seed in an outdoor seedbed in late spring or early summer. Grow plants on and move to final flowering positions in autumn to overwinter before spring flowering. Discard plants after flowering.

Height and spread 30–45 x 30–45cm/12–18 x 12–18in.

Hardiness ✳✳ Zone 5.

Other plants Grow the compact Bedder Series, 'Harlequin' and 'Persian Carpet' in pots, troughs or front of border. 'Cloth of Gold' is a taller, single yellow variety.

Other scented plants

* **Chamomile** (creeping) *Chamaemelum nobile* 'Treneague'
* **Clove scented pinks** *Dianthus* cvs.
* **Curry plant** *Helichrysum italicum*
* **Honeysuckle** (Late Dutch) *Lonicera periclymenum* 'Serotina'
* **Jasmine** *Jasminum officinale*
* **Lavender** *Lavandula angustifolia* cvs.
* **Lemon balm** *Melissa officinalis*
* **Lemon-scented geraniums** *Pelargonium* 'Graveolens'
* **Lily** (scented types) *Lilium* African Queen Group
* **Pansy/viola** *Viola*
* **Sweet William** *Dianthus barbatus*
* **Thyme** (creeping) *Thymus* spp. and cvs.

Planting for pots and containers

Busy Lizzie
Impatiens walleriana

Cheerful busy Lizzies can brighten up any shady corner. They are ideal for patio containers since they flower from the time they are planted out in early summer until the frosts start.

How to grow The fine seed is difficult to handle, so buy plug plants instead and pot them up on a warm windowsill until the weather is warm enough to harden them off. Little deadheading is needed but, after rain, fallen petals stick to the leaves so pick off fading flowers. Red and orange blossoms show rain damage more than pastels, and doubles are less reliable outdoors. Feed and water regularly.

Height and spread 20–30 x 20–30cm/8–12 x 8–12in.

Hardiness ☀ Zone 10.

Other plants F1 hybrid series such as 'Accent' are the best for bedding. Single-coloured, coloured-edged and striped flowers or ones with a contrasting 'eye' are available along with mixtures. For sheltered spots, try New Guinea Hybrids, which have larger flowers in vivid shades and larger, often bronze-tinted or variegated foliage.

French marigold
Tagetes patula

There are many bright varieties of this easy, showy half-hardy annual to choose from. They are often golden yellow or orange, but sometimes deep red or bicoloured (have two colours). They mix well with blue and purple bedding plants. Singles rather than full doubles are better for attracting insects such as hoverflies, but any are useful for discouraging white fly.

How to grow Sow the large seed on a warm windowsill in early spring. Prick out seedlings and harden off before planting out after the risk of frost has passed. Look out for slugs. Deadhead frequently.

Height and spread 15–25 x 20–25cm/6–10 x 8–10in.

Hardiness ☀ Zone 9.

Other plants Also try the larger hybrid Afro-French marigolds, such as *Tagetes* 'Zenith Mixed', and the low domes studded with flowers of *Tagetes* 'Lemon Gem'.

Geranium
Pelargonium

If you aren't able to water plants regularly, geraniums, properly called pelargoniums, are great for sun-drenched pots. There are types to suit all kinds of container and colour schemes, with a range from brilliant reds, oranges and cerise-purples to soft lilac, apple blossom-pink and white. Not everyone likes the smell of geranium leaves but you only notice it when you tidy the plants.

How to grow You have to start off plants early if you want to grow them from seed, and seedlings require very good light to thrive. Propagation from cuttings in late summer is a better option, and is an easy way to overwinter plants if you don't have a frost-free greenhouse. Grow in full sun in free-draining, soil-based compost. Deadhead regularly, picking off brown petals and seedheads from within the flower cluster. Don't overfeed or overwater.

Height and spread 30–40 x 30–60cm/12–16 x 12–24in.

Hardiness ☀ Zone 9.

Other plants Upright bedding geraniums are usually zonal types, with rounded, hairy leaves with a darker banding. Ivy leaved pelargoniums such as the balcony or cascade types have a trailing habit with wiry stems and small, glossy lobed leaves. The flower clusters may be smaller but there is often more of them.

Petunia
Petunia

There are many types of petunia to choose from, and they come in a lots of colours, including ones with striped, edged or darkly veined flowers. Some have a lovely sweet fragrance after sundown. Bushy, compact forms are ideal where you don't have much space and the trailing kinds work well in baskets. Large, double flowers can suffer in rainy summers.

How to grow Protect from slugs and snails. Starting bedding types from seed is tricky as the seed is very fine and needs light to germinate. Try pricking out boxes of seedlings or using little plug plants instead. Plant in pots and baskets after all risk of frost has passed. Grow in a warm, sunny spot. Feed and water regularly and deadhead.

Height and spread 15–30 x 45–120cm/6–12 x 18–48in.

Hardiness ☀ Zone 7.

Other plants For baskets, choose trailing kinds such as Surfinia and Tumbelina Series or, for masses of small cascading blooms, grow the related *Calibrachoa*, such as Million Bells Series. Compact-growing multiflora petunias work well for pots.

▲ *Busy Lizzie*

▲ *French marigold*

▲ *Geranium*

▲ *Petunia*

▲ *Trailing verbena*

▲ *Tulip*

▲ *Tumbling tomato*

▲ *Twin spur*

Trailing verbena
Verbena cvs.

The newer, strong-growing varieties of these tender perennial trailing plants are smothered in blooms all summer. The small flowers are clustered into dome-shaped heads that are very attractive to butterflies and hoverflies and many have a sweet scent. They are now available in most shades, apart from yellow, and plants have neat, toothed-edged or sometimes ferny leaves and wiry spreading or trailing stems.

How to grow Buy trailers as rooted cuttings or young plants in spring and plant up in pots and baskets when all risk of frost has passed. Use any compost recommended for containers and feed and water regularly. Drought and overhead watering can promote powdery mildew disease. Deadhead before flower-heads have completely faded as it can be difficult to tell seed-heads from flower-buds! Take cuttings in late summer and overwinter in a frost-free location.

Height and spread 20–25 x 20–45cm/8–10 x 8–18in.
Hardiness ✳ Zone 7.
Other plants
Tapien, Temari and Babylon Series are all excellent for hanging baskets. Quartz Series plants are bushy and upright, ideal for pots.

Tulip
Tulipa cvs.

Some tulips flower early in spring, but most bloom a bit later and are perfect for bringing colour on to the patio. Tulips come in all colours and some have striped or streaked petals, frills and flounces.

How to grow Plant bulbs in mid to late autumn in crocked pots using well-draining potting compost. Stand the pots in a sheltered spot outdoors. Don't let the compost dry out. Move to a sunny spot when the shoots appear. To help build up the bulb, deadhead, feed with tomato food and allow leaves to die down naturally.

Height and spread 20–60 x 15cm/8–24 x 6in.
Hardiness ✳✳✳ Zone 3.
Other plants 'Greigii' and 'Kaufmanniana' types are dwarf and early flowering. Some, such as 'Red Riding Hood', have striped leaves. The early double 'Angelique' has full blooms of pale pink, white and green. Later tall, lily flowered tulips such as 'China Pink' make a striking display in a container.

Tumbler tomatoes
Lycopersicon esculentum

Some plants seem made for pots and baskets and this variety is patio perfect.

How to grow These tender plants need warm weather to thrive, so you'll need to keep them in a sheltered spot until the risk of frost has passed or move under cover on any chilly nights. Choose a moisture-retentive potting compost or add water-retaining gel crystals, especially to hanging baskets. Feed and water regularly, changing to a high-potassium food once the flowers appear.

Height and spread 30–60cm/12–24in.
Hardiness ✳ Zone N/A.
Other plants As well as 'Tumbler' you could grow 'Gartenperle', 'Hundreds and Thousands' and red or yellow 'Tumbling Tom' varieties. For larger tomatoes, try 'Totem'.

Twin spur
Diascia

This tender perennial produces a froth of shell-shaped blooms in shades of pink, orange, purple or white. The spreading or cascading habit suits hanging baskets and window boxes well.

How to grow Diascias like well-drained compost, especially in winter, but plentiful moisture in the summer growing period. Add water-retaining gel crystals to hanging baskets. Trim spent flower stems and feed to encourage new flushes. Plants often overwinter in sheltered gardens. Trim away the old flower stems at the beginning of the new season.

Height and spread 25–45 x 45–60cm/10–18 x 18–24in.
Hardiness ✳✳✳ Zone 5.
Other plants There are many new cultivars but 'Ruby Field', is hardy and flowers through summer and autumn. Also try the aptly named 'Coral Belle' and 'Lilac Belle' and the related *Nemesia* cultivars, which include more blue-purple shades.

Other plants for pots & containers

✳ **Black-eyed Susan**
Thunbergia alata
✳ **Double daisy**
Bellis perennis
✳ **Dwarf daffodils**
Narcissus cyclamineus types
✳ **Dwarf pincushion flower**
Scabiosa 'Butterfly Blue' or 'Pink Mist'
✳ **Fuchsia (bush and trailing)**
Fuchsia cvs.
✳ **Lily**
Lilium American hybrids
✳ **Mini cyclamen**
Cyclamen cvs.
✳ **Nemesia**
Nemesia Maritana Series
✳ **Swan River daisy**
Brachyscome mulitifida and others
✳ **Winter flowering violas**
Viola Sorbet Series

Planting to attract wildlife

Poached egg plant
Limnanthes douglasii

Nestled close to the ground, this hardy annual makes a big impact with its yellow and white blooms, which attract hoverflies and bees. Plant with other hardy annuals among fruits, vegetables and roses to encourage natural predators and help control aphids and other pests.

How to grow This plant self-seeds freely. In spring, sow directly into well-drained, raked soil in full sun. Make repeat sowings later in spring and summer for continuity of flowers. There's no need to deadhead or feed plants.

Height and spread 15 x 15cm/ 6 x 6in.

Hardiness ✳✳✳ Zone 5.

Other plants The species is the best for wildlife.

Cotoneaster
Cotoneaster spp. and cvs.

Members of this genus range from large, sprawling shrubs and small trees to low, dense bushes. Masses of tiny white or sometimes pink-tinged flowers open in spring and early summer and are usually followed by red berries, though some cultivars have yellow, orange-red or pink fruits.

Cotoneasters provide cover and nesting sites for birds, nectar and pollen for insects and fruits for birds and mammals to eat.

How to grow In general, they are very tolerant and will grow on quite heavy clay soils and in cold, exposed positions. They prefer sun but tolerate partial shade. Prune lightly in spring – last year's branches and older wood bear the flowers. Dig up unwanted seedlings.

Height and spread 30–300 x 180–300cm/12–120 x 70–120in.

Hardiness ✳✳✳ Zone 4.

Other plants Larger plants include *C. franchetii* and *C. frigidus* 'Cornubia'. For ground cover try *C. salicifolius* 'Gnome' or *C.* x *suecicus* 'Coral Beauty'. Medium bushy shrubs include *C. conspicuus* 'Decorus' and *C. horizontalis* when not wall-trained.

Purple top verbena
Verbena bonariensis

This slightly tender perennial from South America has an exceptionally long flowering period and often continues from midsummer through to late autumn given shelter from frost. It's a magnet for bees and butterflies. The flat or slightly domed heads of tiny purple blooms are held at the ends of stiff, wiry branches and the whole plant has an upright feel.

How to grow Full sun, well drained soil and a warm sheltered spot can help plants through the winter, but even if they die, you'll often find the little square-stemmed, slightly bristly seedlings coming up in spring and early summer. They rarely need support, though some twiggy sticks pushed into the ground early on will help in windier spots. Easy to grow from seed raised on a windowsill in spring. Pot on and harden off plants before they go into borders.

Height and spread 180 x 60cm/70 x 24in.

Hardiness ✳✳ Zone 7.

Other plants Verbenas are varied and many half-hardy upright and trailing kinds, such as Temari and Tapien Series, are used in containers, and these attract small hoverflies. The upright tender perennial *V. rigida* has violet blooms. It too is popular with bees and butterflies.

Ice plant
Sedum spectabile

This perennial comes into its own in autumn when lots of butterflies and bees zoom in to its domed heads of tiny flowers. The pink-darkening-to-brownish-red of many cultivars, including 'Indian Chief', works well with other butterfly flowers, such as butterfly bush. The fleshy blue-green leaves and broccoli-like appearance of the flower-buds make this a lovely front-of-border plant.

How to grow It tolerates most soils, including clay ones. It likes full sun but also light shade. Leave the dead heads as these are ornamental well into winter. Tidy old stalks in spring and divide plants every two or three years as otherwise they have a tendency to flop when in bloom.

Height and spread 45 x 45cm/ 18 x 18in.

Hardiness ✳✳✳ Zone 3.

Other plants As well as the pink or white *S. spectabile* cultivars, try the brick pink *S.* 'Herbstfreude' (Autumn Joy) and dark-stemmed *S. telephium* 'Matrona'. Lower-growing sedums, usually called stonecrops, include many excellent insect plants such as the creeping *S. acre*, which has yellow flowers, and pink-flowered 'Vera Jameson' and 'Ruby Glow'.

▲ Poached egg plant

▲ Cotoneaster

▲ Purple top verbena

▲ Ice plant

▲ *Butterfly bush*

▲ *Grape hyacinth*

▲ *Sunflower*

▲ *Geranium*

Butterfly bush
Buddleja davidii

In late summer, the tapering, cone-shaped blooms of these quick-growing shrubs are often covered with butterflies feeding on the nectar. Buddleja cultivars are numerous, but all seem to be attractive to insects. They come in shades varying from purples and purple-pinks to white, and look best in mixed borders with herbaceous perennials, roses and other flowering shrubs.

How to grow Grow in well-drained soil in full sun. Plants flower on the current season's growth, which means they can be cut hard back in spring to a low framework of branches. Pruning is a good idea as plants can otherwise get very tall and leggy and don't live as long. Dead flowers provide sanctuary for minibeasts in winter.

Height and spread 180 x 150cm/70 x 60in.

Hardiness ✳✳✳ Zone 5.

Other plants *B. davidii* 'Black Knight' has very deep purple blooms. 'Pink Perfection' has larger than normal rich pink flowers and 'Dartmoor' has purple blooms with many forks, producing an eye-catching display. 'Lochinch' has paler purple flowers, each with an orange 'eye', and silvery green leaves.

Grape hyacinth
Muscari armeniacum

For early butterflies and solitary bees, finding a clump of these rich blue bulbs in flower in spring is a bonus. Although there are numerous ornamental cultivars and species, this grape hyacinth is best for the wild garden, where it spreads to form colonies.

How to grow Plant the small white bulbs in large clusters at least 10 at a time, but don't plant them too close to one another as the bulbs will need space to expand. Any well-drained soil in sun will do. They also work well in shallow pots as a foil for yellow violas and dwarf red tulips.

Height and spread 20 x 30+cm/8 x 12+in.

Hardiness ✳✳✳ Zone 4.

Other plants 'Valerie Finnis' is an ice-blue variety. Avoid the double 'Blue Spike', which isn't useful to insects.

Sunflower
Helianthus annuus

This hardy annual can produce towering plants with giant sun-shaped blooms. Others are smaller, but the disc-shaped centres are still attractive to honey bees. The black seeds provide a feast for finches.

How to grow Start off in individual pots on a warm windowsill in spring or sow directly in the ground where they are to flower. They thrive in well-drained soil and full sun. Large forms may need staking with a bamboo cane. Grow medium or dwarf kinds in pots. Feed and water potted plants in summer.

Height and spread 90–300 x 45–60cm/35–120 x 18–24in.

Hardiness ✳✳✳ Zone 7.

Other plants Avoid doubles such as 'Teddy Bear', which are no good for wildlife. For towering blooms try 'Russian Giant'. 'Music Box' is a compact form with banded blooms in a range of colours.

Cranesbill
Geranium 'Johnson's Blue'

There are several blue cranesbills, but the dish-shaped blooms of 'Johnson's Blue' seem to glow, even in partial shade. Like most blue flowers, this perennial is a favourite with bees, which are attracted by the colour and the nectar guides. It flowers all summer and the foliage makes good ground cover.

How to grow Any fertile soil will do as long as it isn't very dry or waterlogged. Plant in spring or preferably autumn to give plants chance to establish. Tidy spent flower stems after the main show.

Height and spread 45 x 60cm/18 x 24in.

Hardiness ✳✳✳ Zone 4.

Other plants All the single hardy geraniums are good for bees and range from long-flowered alpines, such as *G. cinereum* 'Ballerina', to ground-cover plants, such as the *G.* x *oxonianum* 'Wargrave Pink'. *G. himalayense* have large, purplish-blue blooms and the late-flowered *G. wallichianum* 'Buxton's Variety' is light blue with a large white eye.

Other plants to attract wildlife

* **Aster/Michaelmas daisy**
  Aster spp. and cvs.
* **Aubrieta**
  Aubrieta
* **Balkan scabious**
  Knautia macedonica 'Melton Pastels'
* **Bee balm/bergamot**
  Monarda didyma cvs.
* **Bellflower**
  Campanula percisifolia
* **Bidens**
  Bidens ferulifolia
* **Black-eyed Susan**
  Rudbeckia fulgida
* **Californian poppy**
  Eschscholzia californica
* **Catmint/catnip**
  Nepeta x *faassenii*
* **Cornflower**
  Centaurea cyanus
* **Firethorn**
  Pyracantha
* **Tickseed**
  Coreopsis tinctoria

Planting for quick-growing veg and salads

Lettuce
Lactuca sativa
There are two main types of lettuce: ones that make a solid, crisp 'head', and loose-leaf kinds. Loose-leaf ones are better as leaves are picked individually, allowing you to crop over a longer period. Some varieties are suitable as cut-and-come-again baby leaf salads, where the root and base of the plant are left in the ground after cropping, allowing them to regrow for another harvest.

How to grow Start seed off in pots on the windowsill in early spring, ready for planting out after hardening off. When the weather warms up you can sow directly in the ground every couple of weeks to ensure continuous supplies. Cold-hardy varieties allow you to extend the season in cold frames or under cloches. Improve germination in hot weather by making a seed drill and watering it before sowing. Watch out for slugs. Improve soils by adding moisture-retentive compost and manure, and water plants in hot summers to prevent 'bolting' (producing flowers).
Height and spread 15–30 x 30–40cm/6–12 x 12–16in.

Hardiness ✷✷ Zone N/A.
Other plants For colour, sow 'Lollo Rossa' types with red frilly leaves, or other red-leaved types such as 'Red Salad Bowl'. Mixtures are also sold as cut-and-come-again lettuce. For small, quick heads try 'Little Gem' or 'Tom Thumb'.

Rocket
Eruca sativa
The spicy salad leaf, rocket, or to give it its Italian name, arugula, is perfect for livening up lettuce or tomato salads and for flavouring pasta dishes, risottos and omelettes. It is an incredibly easy summer crop to grow outdoors and, once it is in the garden, it tends to seed around.

How to grow Sow this hardy annual under cover in early spring or autumn, in a cold frame or under cloches. Sow directly outdoors as soon as you can prepare a well-raked seedbed in mid to late spring. Make repeat sowings every couple of weeks. Avoid sowing on ground previously used for brassicas, such as cabbage, as rocket is closely related and land needs to recover for two years to avoid disease build-up. Neutral to alkaline soils are best. Keep well watered to prevent it from bolting (producing flowers) in hot weather. Pick whole young plants (they will re-sprout from a basal stump) or young leaves. Protect against flea beetle using horticultural fleece.
Height and spread 30 x 30cm/ 12 x 12in.
Hardiness ✷ Zone N/A.
Other plants 'Apollo' and 'Skyrocket' are good varieties. Wild rocket has stronger-flavoured leaves.

Radicchio
Cichorium intybus
The deep red radicchio leaves, with their prominent white veins, make this one of the most attractive-looking vegetables to use for salad leaves. The flavour becomes more bitter with age, so pick sweeter baby leaves in early summer if you don't like the bitter taste, or mix just a few with salad leaves, such as lettuce, to add a sweet note. Try brushing leaves with olive oil and baking them in the oven for a side dish.

How to grow For early pickings of baby leaves, sow directly in the ground in mid spring in shallow, pre-watered drills. For a later autumn crop, which will survive light frosts, sow again in midsummer. Or, sow every three weeks for continuity.
Height and spread 30 x 30cm/ 12 x 12in.
Hardiness ✷✷ Zone N/A.
Other plants 'Treviso Precoce Mesola' and 'Palla Rossa' are attractive and yummy.

Cress
Lepidium sativum
One of the fastest salads to grow, tasty cress seedlings can even be raised on moist kitchen paper on a windowsill in winter, ready for cropping in a week!

How to grow Sprinkle seed on the surface of any moist growing surface, including seed or potting compost. Water and cover pots or trays with a plastic bag and stand in a warm place with some indirect light. Once the seed germinates, take off the bag and move to a spot with better light. Keep moist. Crop using scissors. Also sow directly in the soil outdoors between crops in summer
Height and spread 5–7.5 x 1cm/2–3 x ½in.
Hardiness ✷✷✷ Zone N/A.
Other plants Common, broad-leaf or curled cress (such as 'Extra Double Curled')

▲ Lollo Rossa lettuce

▲ Rocket

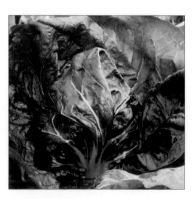
▲ Radicchio

▲ Cress

▲ *Salad onion*

▲ *Radish*

▲ *Carrot*

▲ *Sweetcorn seedlings*

has a peppery flavour. In supermarkets you usually find boxes of seedlings marked 'cress' that are mainly grown from the milder flavoured rape seed. Mustard seed can substitute for cress too.

Salad onion
Allium cepa
Salad onions (also called spring or bunching onions) are useful for sowing in gaps where slow-maturing crops have been harvested, as well as in patio containers filled with loam-based potting compost. They are ready for harvesting in around three months and you eat both the leaves and the swollen stem base.

How to grow Sow from early spring to midsummer in short rows 13mm/½in deep. Thinning out seedlings isn't really necessary. Repeat sowings every three weeks to keep you supplied with plants throughout the summer and into autumn. Late summer sowings using a hardy variety will produce a spring crop.
Height and spread 30–45 x 30cm/12–18 x 12in.
Hardiness ✳✳ Zone N/A.
Other plants *Allium cepa* 'North Holland Blood Red' is dual purpose – use thinnings for salad onions and leave the rest to mature as red maincrop onions. 'Lilia' is also dual purpose. 'Summer Isle'

and 'White Lisbon' are mild-tasting. 'Guardsman' is easy and reliable as it is resistant to frost and disease.

Radish
Raphanus sativus
This mustard family plant has crisp, juicy roots with a peppery tang. It is an annual and is quick and easy to grow. Crop the round- or cylinder-shaped roots when small and tender, as large, old radishes go woody and are more strong-tasting.
How to grow Sow every two or three weeks from mid spring. Keep well watered and shaded from strong sun. In containers, grow in a loam-based compost with added slow-release fertilizer granules. Watch out for cabbage caterpillars and flea beetles. Protect sowings with horticultural fleece.
Height and spread 6–7.5 x 5–7½cm/2½–3 x 2–3in.
Hardiness ✳ Zone N/A.
Other plants Grow 'Cherry Belle', 'French Breakfast' (cyclindrical) and 'Jolly' for a long growing season and mild flavour.

Carrot
Daucus carota
Growing your own mini carrots is easy and it is very satisfying to pull bunches from the ground with their leaves intact. Look out for round varieties and unusually coloured types.

How to grow For ease of growth, go for quick-maturing, short or round carrots for summer and early autumn cropping, as these don't mind less-than-perfect soil and can be grown in tubs. Sow thinly in short drills directly where they are to grow. To protect carrots in the ground from carrot root fly, use a barrier of horticultural fleece held up with canes.
Height and spread 18–25 x 20cm/7–10 x 8in.
Hardiness ✳✳✳ Zone N/A.
Other plants Try the quick-cropping round 'Parmex' or cyclindrical 'Amsterdam Forcing'. 'Ideal' is good for baby carrots. 'Purple Haze' is purple on the outside!

Sweetcorn
Zea mays
You can now grow sweet, juicy cobs reliably, even in poor summers. Supersweet varieties are bred for – you guessed it – extra sweetness. Pick, cook and eat cobs straight away for maximum flavour.
How to grow Start off seed in mid spring by sowing in peat or fibre pots (to avoid root disturbance) on a warm windowsill. Pot on and plant out when danger of frost has passed. Choose a sunny, sheltered spot. Prepare the soil well, digging in plenty of manure and applying slow-release fertilizer. Cover the soil

with black plastic or cloches for a couple of weeks to warm soil before planting out seedlings. Plants are pollinated by wind and produce better crops when grown in blocks rather than rows. Tap the male flowers or tassels in midsummer to encourage pollination. Feed plants with liquid fertilizer when cobs start to swell and keep well watered.
Height and spread 150–230 x 25cm/60–90 x 10in.
Hardiness ✳ Zone N/A.
Other plants 'Sweetie Pie' and 'Lark' are sweet and juicy with a soft texture.

Other quick veg and salads
* **Baby leeks**
  Allium ampeloprasum porrum
* **Lamb's lettuce/ corn salad**
  Valerianella locusta
* **Mizuna**
  Brassica rapa var. *nipposinica.*
* **Pak choi**
  Brassica rapa chinensis
* **Pea shoots**
  Pisum sativum
* **Spinach**
  Spinacea oleracea
* **Spinach beet**
  Beta vulgaris
* **Watercress**
  Nasturtium officinale

Planting for slower-growing veg

Sweet pepper
Capsicum annuum var. annuum

These tender members of the potato family, closely related to hot chilli peppers, need a long growing season to produce their fruits. Given the chance to ripen, peppers turn from more strongly flavoured green peppers to sweeter yellow, orange or red fruits.

How to grow Sow seed in individual pots in a heated propagator in early spring and pot on as they grow, providing warmth and plenty of light. Or, buy seedlings or young plants. Harden off and plant out after all risk of frost has passed and grow in grow bags or large pots on a sunny, sheltered patio. Support with small stakes and soft twine. Water regularly and feed with tomato fertilizer when fruits begin to form.

Height and spread 30–65 x 23–40cm/12–26 x 9–16in.
Hardiness ☀ Zone N/A.
Other plants The dwarf variety 'Redskin' is ideal for pots.

Tomato
Lycopersicon esculentum

No sunny patio should be without a few pots or grow bags of tomatoes and these productive plants provide sweet, juicy treats through from midsummer until autumn.

How to grow Sow in a warm, light place in early spring, covering with clear plastic, or use a propagator. Seedlings must have good light to grow strongly. Alternatively, buy sturdy plants with dark green leaves. Pot on and plant out after all risk of frost has passed in individual 25cm/10in pots or grow bags. Hanging, tumbling and dwarf bush varieties are ideal for baskets and troughs (*see* page 235). Feed with liquid tomato fertilizer when flowers appear and keep well watered. Pinch out side shoots of cordon varieties when they are about 2.5cm/1in long. When plants have produced four fruit clusters, pinch out the growing point a little way above the tomatoes so that fruits have a chance to ripen. Stake cordon varieties with canes and twine.

Height and spread 45–90 x 45cm/18–36 x 18in.
Hardiness ☀ Zone N/A.
Other plants Cherry fruited cordon types include the red coloured 'Sweet 100', 'Gardener's Delight' and the yellow 'Sungold'.

Squash
*Cucurbita pepo/
C. moschata/C. maxima*

The so-called winter squashes, including pear-shaped butternut squash and round pumpkin lookalikes, are harvested in autumn and the skin left to harden in the sun, allowing the fruits to be stored. Summer squashes are more like courgettes and include patty pan squashes, which look like mini flying saucers. These are cropped during the growing season when the skin is soft.

How to grow Sow one seed to a pot on the windowsill in late spring and cover with a plastic bag. Remove the bag when the seeds germinate and pot on as necessary. Harden off and set out after all risk of frost has passed. Some are bush types, which need no support, and others are trailers, which can be coaxed to climb up a sturdy frame – check the packet for instructions. Add manure to the ground and water well during the growing season. All make large sprawling plants so make sure you leave enough room.

Height and spread 45–90 x 90–400cm/18–36 x 36–160in.
Hardiness ☀ Zone N/A.
Other plants Try 'Sunburst' F1 (patty pan type) or the squash 'Baby Bear', which produces small orange pumpkins.

Cucumber
Cucumis sativus

This tender salad vegetable is most often grown as a climbing plant in a greenhouse or in large cold frames. Some compact, bushy varieties are ideal for grow bags or 25cm/10in pots on the patio. Choose a warm, sheltered, sunny spot. The fruits of these are quite small, sweet and juicy. Peel those with prickly skins.

How to grow Raise plants on a warm windowsill in spring, planting the large, flat seed on edge. Cover the pots with plastic bags. The young plants have large leaves and grow quickly but can't be put outdoors until warm nights (16–24°C/60–75°F) are guaranteed. Use loam-based potting compost with added granular fertilizer. Water with liquid tomato food when flowers form. Pick fruits regularly.

Height and spread 60–90 x 90cm/24–36 x 36in.
Hardiness ☀ Zone N/A.
Other plants Rocky F1 and Zeina F1.

▲ *Sweet pepper*

▲ *Cherry tomato*

▲ *Squash*

▲ *Cucumber*

▲ *Yellow courgette*

▲ *French bean*

▲ *Oregon sugar pod pea*

▲ *Beetroot*

Courgette
Cucurbita pepo

A tender but quick-growing summer vegetable, the courgette is productive and you should only need one or two of these large plants to keep you supplied with courgettes from midsummer through until autumn.

How to grow Young plants are readily available from garden centres in late spring and early summer, but you can also sow in pots on a warm windowsill throughout spring. Pot on and harden off gradually and don't plant out until all risk of frost has passed. Plants require humus-rich soil with plenty of manure to thrive. Water during dry spells.

Height and spread 30–60 x 120–160cm/12–24 x 45–62.5in.
Hardiness ✳ Zone N/A.
Other plants Grow green or yellow cylindrical- or ball-shaped varieties, such as 'One Ball F1' or 'Tristar'.

Runner and dwarf French beans
Phaseolus coccineus/ P. vulgaris

Unlike hardy broad beans, these tender climbers can't be planted out until all risk of frost has passed. The large, heart-shaped leaves and colourful pea flower blooms make runner beans attractive plants for large containers on the patio, growing up cane wigwams. Dwarf bushy French beans need minimal staking. Pollinated mainly by bumble-bees, bean pods are produced for a long period.

How to grow Start beans off in pots on a warm windowsill in early to mid spring. Plant out after plants are hardened off and all risk of frost has passed. Protect early sowings with cloches and pre-warm the soil with black plastic. You can also sow directly in the ground. Prepare soil thoroughly beforehand. Water plants well when in flower and fruiting. Pick regularly to encourage more beans to grow. Don't eat raw pods.

Height and spread 45–180 x 40–50cm/18–70 x 16–20in.
Hardiness ✳ Zone N/A.
Other plants The dwarf runner bean 'Hestia' is good in patio pots. The dwarf French bean 'Purple Teepee' has attractive purple pods.

Mangetout or snap peas
Pisum sativum

Unlike maincrop peas, mangetout and snap peas are relatively easy to grow. The sweet, crunchy pods of snap varieties are irresistible eaten raw or very lightly cooked. Mangetout types contain embryonic peas and are flatter than some snap peas, but are cooked in the same way.

How to grow They are best sown into soil that has been warmed up in early spring with black plastic. For early crops, sow in peat pots or modular trays on a windowsill. Plant out as soon as shoots appear and protect with horticultural fleece or cloches. Prepare the ground by digging in manure. Most varieties need support in the form of twiggy pea sticks or a frame of canes covered in pea and bean netting. Make a repeat sowing in late summer for an autumn crop.

Height and spread 45–90 x 45–180cm/16–35 x 16–70in.
Hardiness ✳ Zone N/A.
Other plants 'Sugar Ann' is a dwarf, podded snap pea that doesn't need staking. 'Oregon Sugar Pod' is a taller mangetout type.

Beetroot
Beta vulgaris

Very easy to grow, you can harvest sweet little baby beetroot in only seven weeks for use in a range of dishes. The dark, handsome leaves are red-veined and can be picked young for salads or steamed lightly.

How to grow Sow seeds directly in fertile soil using a bolt-resistant variety if you are sowing in early spring, under cloches. Add a granular fertilizer containing plenty of nitrogen. Keep the plants well watered. Make repeat sowings until midsummer for a steady supply of baby beetroot throughout the season.

Height and spread 30–40 x 25cm/12–16 x 10in.
Hardiness ✳✳✳ Zone N/A.
Other plants 'Boltardy' is ideal for early sowings. 'Pablo' is a good variety for patio pots.

Other long-cropping veg
* **Aubergine 'Baby Rosanna'** *Solanum melongena*
* **Broad bean** *Vicia faba*
* **Cabbage** *Brassica oleracea* form
* **Curly kale (borecole)** *Brassica oleracea* form
* **Onion/shallots** *Allium cepa/ A. ascalonicum*
* **Potato** *Solanum tuberosum*
* **Pumpkin 'Little October'** *Cucurbita pepo* form
* **Purple sprouting broccoli** *Brassica oleracea* form

Planting for easy-growing fruit

Strawberry
Fragaria X ananassa
You can buy strawberry varieties that fruit in early summer, as well as so-called 'perpetual' or 'ever-bearing' types that may flower at intervals through summer into autumn. Mixing varieties carefully gives a range of fruiting times and flavours. Early strawberries may need their blossoms protecting from spring frosts with cloches. Strawberries don't take up much room and you can even grow them in hanging baskets (see page 65).

How to grow Plant in late autumn into well-prepared free-draining soil that has had plenty of manure dug in. With summer-fruiting types, take off the flower stems in the first year to help plants build up a strong root system. When establishing perpetual types, take off the spring flowers but leave the summer ones to develop fruits. Feed with liquid tomato food as fruits start to develop. Avoid watering overhead. Raise fruits off the ground with straw to keep them clean and to deter the main pest – slugs! Take off dead foliage in autumn to minimize disease.

Height and spread 30 x 60cm/12 x 24in.
Hardiness ✳✳✳ Zone 5.
Other plants 'Malling Opal' and 'Aromel' are both 'ever-bearing' types.

Raspberry
Rubus idaeus
These soft, red summer fruits can be worked in to any corner of the garden, even lightly shaded areas. They grow best in the ground.

How to grow Plant bare-rooted summer- or autumn-fruiting raspberry canes in late autumn or winter in well-prepared ground with plenty of manure dug in. Fix canes to a support of horizontal wires. Mulch. Feed and water during flowering. Net to protect from birds. Cut fruited canes down to 5cm/2in from ground level, but tie in the paler green new canes to the supports, ready to flower and fruit next year. With autumn-fruiting types, cut all canes back after cropping.

Height and spread 150–200 x 120+cm/60–80 x 45+in.
Hardiness ✳✳✳ Zone 4.
Other plants Try non-bristly stemmed summer raspberries, such as 'Glen Ample' or 'Glen Rosa', or the autumn raspberry 'Autumn Bliss'.

Blackberry
Rubus fruticosus
The large, juicy black fruits of this rose relative are easy to grow and bumble-bees love to forage among the white, dish-shaped blooms. Choose thornless varieties and ones that aren't too vigorous so that you can grow them in large tubs (see pages 68–9) or control their spread by growing in the ground and tying the canes to support wires on a fence. Good varieties fruit from late summer well into autumn.

How to grow Plant bare-rooted canes in late autumn or winter (avoiding frosty periods). They tolerate a wide range of soils but best results come from a sunny spot and well-manured soil. Cut off fruited canes when they have finished cropping, about 5cm/2in above ground level. Allow the new growth (which hasn't fruited) room to expand. Tie these new canes in to supports, bending the stems diagonally or towards the horizontal to stimulate flowering.

Height and spread 90–180 x 120–180cm/35–70 x 45–70in.
Hardiness ✳✳✳ Zone 4.
Other plants 'Loch Ness' and 'Oregon Thornless' are excellent prickle-free varieties.

Blueberry
Vaccinium corymbosum
These ericaceous (acid-loving) shrubs not only have rich autumn leaf tints, but they also produce delicious blue-black berries.

How to grow Even if you don't have the right soil, you can grow blueberries in large pots using ericaceous compost with added loam. Plant several different cultivars to improve pollination and fruiting and keep plants well watered when in active growth. See page 67 for further care instructions.

Height and spread 120–180 x 60–120cm/48–70 x 24–48in.
Hardiness ✳✳✳ Zone 5.
Other plants Try 'Blue Crop' and 'Bluetta', but also check with local nurseries for their recommendations.

Gooseberry
Ribes uva-crispa
Though thorny, this delicious summer fruit has a unique flavour. Tart green gooseberries require cooking, but there are also sweet ones that can be eaten raw once fully ripened.

How to grow Plant bushes on well-prepared ground with good drainage, but avoid dry sites. Some shade is tolerated

▲ Strawberry

▲ Raspberry

▲ Blackberry

▲ Blueberry

▲ *Gooseberry*

▲ *Blackcurrant*

▲ *Cherry*

▲ *Dessert apple*

and even advised for some cultivars. Trained forms can be grown against a fence. Mulch in spring and water well in dry summer periods. Mildew is the most common problem so plant resistant varieties, and watch out for the little gooseberry sawfly caterpillars. Net to protect from birds, if necessary.
Height and spread 100–120 x 120cm/40–45 x 45in.
Hardiness ✳✳✳ Zone 3.
Other plants 'Invicta' is green-fruited with good mildew resistance. 'Pax' is a red-fruited dessert variety with good resistance.

Blackcurrant
Ribes nigrum
The tart summer fruits of blackcurrant add zest to pies and make wonderful jams. Some varieties have extra-large and sweet fruits.
How to grow Plant bushes in well-prepared ground in late autumn/early winter if possible. Plant 5cm/2in below the original planting level to encourage new shoots to form underground. Firm in well with your foot. Next, cut down all the shoots to just above ground level. This again will encourage more shoots to appear but you won't get any fruits. When plants are established, prune lightly in winter, removing

some of the oldest stems to near ground level and thinning out bush centres to allow in more light and air. Mulch in spring and net to protect against birds.
Height and spread 120 x 120cm/45 x 45in.
Hardiness ✳✳✳ Zone 3.
Other plants 'Ben Sarek' is a compact form that is ideal for small gardens.

Cherry
Prunus avium
Sweet cherries on a dwarfing rootstock, such as Gisela 5, are not hard to grow even in a patio container if they are in a warm place. Sour or acid cherries such as 'Morello' will even grow and ripen against a cool wall.
How to grow Cherries need deep, fertile soil with plenty of manure to thrive. Drape fleece over early blossom if frost is forecast but remove it during the day for pollinating insects. Plant two or more cherries for cross-pollination or, if you don't have room, plant self-fertile cultivars. Pick the summer fruits before the birds move in or net to protect the crop.
Height and spread 300 x 300cm/120 x 120in.
Hardiness ✳✳✳ Zone 5.
Other plants Self-fertile sweet cherries include 'Stella', 'Lapins' or 'Sunburst'. 'Morello' is also self-fertile.

Apple (dessert)
Malus domestica
Grown on semi-dwarfing rootstock, apples (dessert or cooking varieties) are easy to look after and you can fit several different types into a garden, even making use of patio tubs (*see* pages 68–9). There are scores of cultivars and it is best to talk to your local nursery or garden centre to work out which will do best in your garden. Most apples need another apple or crab apple to pollinate the flowers, so you need ones that bloom at roughly the same time (perhaps your neighbours' gardens have suitable trees?). Apples should belong to the same pollination group (listed in books and catalogues) or be self-fertile.
How to grow Plant bare-rooted or container-grown trees in early spring. Protect blossom if late frosts are forecast using fleece at night, but uncover by day to allow bees access. Trees can be free-standing or trained against a wall or fence or on a system of horizontal wires to save space. Avoid hot, dry wall situations. Prune in summer to reduce the amount of new growth. Water plants in tubs freely in summer and mulch with manure to help conserve moisture. Feed as young fruits develop using tomato fertilizer.

Height and spread 160–180 x 90–120cm/65 x 70 x 35–45in.
Hardiness ✳✳✳ Zone 5.
Other plants 'Queen Cox' is a self-fertile cultivar if you only have room for one plant in the garden or on a patio.

Other fruit
* ✳ **Apple** (cooking)
  Malus domestica
* ✳ **Cape gooseberry**
  Physalis peruviana
* ✳ **Cobnut/hazel nut**
  Corylus avellana
* ✳ **Crab apple**
  Malus cultivars
* ✳ **Fig**
  Ficus carica
* ✳ **Grape**
  Vitis vinifera
* ✳ **Kiwi fruit**
  Actinidia chinensis
* ✳ **Lemon** (hardier kinds)
  Citrus X *meyeri*
  'Meyer'
* ✳ **Nectarine**
  Prunus persica var.
  nectarina
* ✳ **Peach**
  Prunus persica
* ✳ **Pear**
  Pyrus communis
* ✳ **Plum**
  Prunus domestica
* ✳ **Redcurrant**
  Ribes rubrum
* ✳ **Wild/woodland strawberry**
  Fragaria vesca

Planting for herbs and edible flowers

Basil
Ocimum basilicum
Sweet basil is a half-hardy annual that can be grown in patio pots and grow bags. It makes a great team with tomatoes or in the summer vegetable garden. Pick the leafy shoots, strip off individual leaves and use in a wide range of hot and cold dishes.

How to grow
Buy a pot of supermarket basil, carefully separate out the seedlings and pot up individually. Keep these in a warm, light spot out of direct sunlight until they are established. Pinch out shoot tips to promote bushiness. Alternatively, grow from seed on a warm windowsill in spring, prick out and pot on indoors until it is warm enough outdoors to start hardening them off.

Height and spread 30–45 x 25cm/12–16 x 10in.

Hardiness ☀ Zone N/A.

Other plants There are many different basils and you could end up with quite a collection. 'Genovese' is well-flavoured but also try the pretty purple *O. b. purpurascens* varieties, such as 'Dark Opal' and the frilly 'Purple Ruffles'.

Chives
Allium schoenoprasum
This versatile hardy perennial herb is one of the easiest to grow and will even thrive on heavier soils. Use it to edge beds and borders, allowing the drumstick mauve-pink flowers to come in flushes, or try in pots and window boxes along with other herbs. Cut the leaves with scissors. The flowers are edible and useful for garnishes.

How to grow
Though you can raise plants from seed, the easiest method is to start with a pot of chives or lift a clump from a friend's garden, pull apart small clumps with roots attached, and plant. Avoid dry soils. Clip frequently to encourage new young leaves but leave some plants to flower. Cut back to ground level to rejuvenate plants afterwards. Lift and divide, planting in different parts of the garden to reduce rust disease.

Height and spread 15–25 x 25–30cm/6–10 x 10–12in.

Hardiness ☀☀☀ Zone 3.

Other plants Chinese or garlic chives (*Allium tuberosum*) are larger with white flowers and a more intense onion/garlic flavour.

Parsley
Petroselinum crispum
This versatile, vitamin-packed herb can be added to any number of dishes, used as a garnish, or mixed with other herbs and spices to blend and soften flavours.

How to grow Sow on a windowsill in late winter/early spring. Plant out after hardening off, or sow directly in rows 1.25cm/½in deep in the vegetable plot in early spring and again in early summer (for a winter crop). For ornamental edging, use one of the pretty Moss Curled types. Cut off flower stems and cut leaves frequently. Plants often overwinter.

Height and spread 30–60 x 30–60cm/12–24 x 12–24in.

Hardiness ☀☀☀ Zone 5.

Other plants Flat or plain leaf types, sometimes called French parsley, have more flavour and include 'Gigante d'Italia'. For a frilly Moss Curled type try 'Lissette' or 'Rosette'.

Sage
Salvia officinalis
The strongly flavoured grey-green leaves of sage are used in cooking and are usually combined with other common herbs for general flavouring or for herb stuffings. The blue-purple flowers in early summer are very attractive to bees. Ornamental varieties look great in patio pots and decorative herb/flower baskets, or as border edging.

How to grow Plant in any well-drained soil, including those containing lime, in full sun. Cut old, leggy plants hard back in spring to rejuvenate. Pick young leaves and shoot tips and remove old flower spikes.

Height and spread 45–60 x 90cm/18–24 x 36in.

Hardiness ☀ Zone N/A.

Other plants The yellow variegated *S. o.* 'Icterina' is strong growing and very ornamental. The pink-and-white-splashed 'Tricolor' is pretty but not vigorous. Purple sage *S. o.* 'Purpurascens' has dusty purple foliage.

Coriander
Coriandrum sativum
The parsley-like leaves of this pungent herb are sometimes called cilantro. The seed is even more strongly 'curry' flavoured. It is invaluable for Indian and Thai cooking.

How to grow This hardy annual is best raised directly in a well-prepared seed bed

▲ *Basil*

▲ *Chives*

▲ *Moss-leaved parsley*

▲ *Tricolour sage*

▲ *Coriander*

▲ *Oregano*

▲ *Rosemary*

▲ *Nasturtium*

outdoors or in a greenhouse border. Wait until late spring to sow for best results and repeat sowings every few weeks to give continuity of supply. Any well-drained soil will do, but choose a warm, sheltered spot. Cold snaps can cause plants to flower (known as bolting) and die.
Height and spread 30–90 x 30–60cm/12–36 x 24–36in.
Hardiness ✳ Zone N/A.
Other plants For a feathery alternative grown as a cut-and-come-again salad, try 'Confetti'.

Oregano
Origanum vulgare
This important culinary herb, sometimes called wild marjoram, makes low bushy hummocks, topped later in summer with purple flowers that are attractive to bees and butterflies. The small, pungent leaves are invaluable for Mediterranean dishes, such as pizza and pasta, herb butters, breads and omelettes. It is good in patio pots or can be grown as edging in herb and cottage borders.
How to grow Oregano grows in any well-drained soil in full sun. Add grit to compost to improve drainage in patio pots. Creeping/carpeting forms can be divided to increase numbers. Shear off old stems in spring to reveal basal growth of leaves.

Height and spread 30 x 30cm/12 x 12in.
Hardiness ✳✳✳ Zone 5.
Other plants 'Aureum' has ornamental golden-yellow leaves and there are also numerous cream or yellow variegated forms of this mint relative. Sweet marjoram (*O. marjorana*) is grown as a half-hardy annual and has a spicy, pungent flavour.

Rosemary
Rosmarinus officinalis
Brushing past the branches of a rosemary bush releases a pungent aroma from the needle-like leaves. In spring, plants are smothered in small grey-blue flowers – a powerful lure for bees. It is valuable finely chopped or use sprigs to flavour roast potatoes, meats, chicken or barbecued fish.
How to grow This shrubby evergreen herb needs a hot, sunny spot with well-drained soil. It will grow happily even in quite poor or stony ground containing lime. Plants grow quickly and can be trained into short standards for pots or clipped into a loose hedge. Don't prune plants hard back as they may not recover.
Height and spread 150 x 150cm/60 x 60in.
Hardiness ✳✳✳ Zone 6.
Other plants 'Miss Jessopp's Upright' is a popular cultivar with blue-grey flowers, suitable

for hedges or wall training. Other forms may not be as hardy, but are grown for their more vividly blue flowers or trailing habit.

Nasturtium
Tropaeolum majus
The bright orange blooms of traditional hardy annual nasturtiums are peppery tasting and great for livening up a green salad. You can also eat the young, almost circular leaves. Weave in plants between herbs and vegetables or plant to tumble out of hanging baskets. Single, old-fashioned nasturtiums are best for bumble-bees as they have the most nectar.
How to grow Simply push the large seed into planters filled with a well-drained potting compost in spring. The seedlings will come up between plants in hanging baskets and window boxes for a surprise burst of colour. Overfeeding or planting seed on rich, manured soils causes plants to produce all leaf and few flowers and encourages black aphids. Watch out for cabbage caterpillars. Provide pea and bean netting for vigorous climbing nasturtiums.
Height and spread 30–38 x 60+cm/12–15 x 24+in.
Hardiness ✳✳✳ Zone N/A.

Other plants 'Empress of India' has red flowers and dark tinted leaves. 'Alaska' has white marbled leaves and tastes good in green salads. 'Climbing Mixed' grows to 2.4m/8ft.

Other herbs and edible flowers
✳ **Angelica**
Angelica archangelica
✳ **Bay**
Laurus nobilis
✳ **Borage**
Borago officinalis
✳ **Bronze fennel**
Foeniculum vulgare 'Purpureum'
✳ **Cotton lavender**
Santolina chamaecyparissus
✳ **Dill**
Anethum graveolens
✳ **French tarragon**
Artemisia dracunculus French
✳ **Heartsease**
Viola tricolor
✳ **Hyssop**
Hyssopus officinalis
✳ **Lavender**
Lavandula spp.
✳ **Lovage**
Levisticum officinale
✳ **Mint**
Mentha spp.
✳ **Pot marigold**
Calendula officinalis
✳ **Thyme**
Thymus spp.

What to do in spring

This is just about the busiest time of year for gardeners. The borders need tidying in preparation for the season ahead, seeds are sown and patio pots planted up. You'll also notice how active insects and birds are.

▶ You can start to grow new plants in the garden in spring.

Early spring

- Start tuberous begonias and dahlia tubers into growth in a warm, light place and pot up lily bulbs.
- Prick out ready-grown seedlings purchased from the garden centre and pot up plug plants and flower 'tots'. Keep on a warm, light windowsill.
- Start sowing half-hardy bedding in pots, trays and windowsill propagators.
- Divide and also plant new herbaceous perennial flowers.
- Lift, divide and replant snowdrops.
- Tidy borders, removing dead stems and leaves that have been left to protect plants from cold and provide cover for wildlife. Weed.
- Cut back penstemons, blue spiraea (*Caryopteris* x *clandonensis*) and butterfly bush to just above the new sprouting shoots.
- Begin sowing hardy annual flowers outdoors. Sow in short rows so that you can spot weeds.
- Chit early seed potatoes in egg boxes on a cool windowsill.
- Start sowing hardy vegetables, such as broad beans, spinach and spinach beet and leeks, directly into the ground outdoors and in patio containers.

Mid spring

- Deadhead spring bulbs and feed with a high-potassium (potash) feed.
- Sow quick-maturing half-hardy annuals, such as French marigolds, on the windowsill, as well as hardy annuals such as sunflowers, pot marigolds and sweet alyssum.
- Prick out seedlings sown earlier and pot on young plantlets. Give liquid fertilizer to plants being raised indoors.
- Plant summer-flowering bulbs and tubers such as gladioli and lilies in beds and borders.
- Plant out early sown sweet peas.
- Plant evergreen shrubs and herbs.
- Begin feeding houseplants that are starting into growth.
- Sow herbs, such as parsley, salad vegetables, carrots, brassicas, leeks and spinach, and start off peas and French beans in pots.
- Pot on tomato, pepper and aubergine seedlings sown earlier in spring.
- Plant sprouted potatoes in patio containers. Also plant onion sets.
- Cut back woody based herbs, such as sage, curry plant and cotton lavender.
- Plant new strawberry beds, planters and hanging baskets.

Late spring

- Start hardening off half-hardy annuals raised indoors by standing them outside for a few hours a day during fine weather. (*See* page 13.)
- Begin planting up flowering patio pots and hanging baskets. Keep planters in a protected spot and bring under cover at night.
- Deadhead any remaining spring bulbs and bedding plants.
- Thin hardy annual seedlings sown earlier in beds outdoors to give them room to grow. Weed at the same time.
- Sow tender vegetables in individual pots on windowsills, such as cucumber, courgette, pumpkin and squash, runner beans and French beans.
- Sow most salads and vegetables directly in pots or beds. 'Float' horticultural fleece over sowings to protect them from wind and cold nights and to reduce pest problems. Tuck the edges under the soil or weigh down with bricks.
- Start to harden off tender vegetables sown earlier to prepare them for planting out in patio pots and grow bags.
- Earth up potatoes as they grow. (*See* page 62.)

▲ *Chit seed potatoes on a cool windowsill.*

▲ *Plant strawberries in baskets and beds.*

▲ *Deadhead bedding plants and bulbs.*

What to do in summer

The main tasks during the summer months are watering, weeding and deadheading faded flowers. You'll also need to do some pest control to make sure creepy-crawlies don't get out of hand. Harvest your salads and vegetables!

▶ Plant up colourful flowerpots and tubs for the patio in summer.

Early summer

- Plant patio and bedding plants in pots and borders.
- Provide staking and support for early summer-flowering perennials. Deadhead to encourage more blooms. Weed borders.
- Begin regular feeding of plants in pots and baskets with liquid fertilizer or use slow-release granules. Water as needed.
- Feed roses and other flowering shrubs with granular rose fertilizer unless you are using manure.
- Sow biennials for flowering next spring, such as sweet Williams and double daisies.
- Increase humidity for houseplants by standing them on a gravel tray (see page 210) or misting. Start bringing succulents, citrus plants etc. outdoors. Harden off carefully.
- Plant out tender vegetables that have been hardened off and continue sowing hardy vegetables. Re-sow quick-maturing salads.
- Water leafy salad vegetables in dry spells.
- Net cabbages against birds and to prevent butterfly caterpillars. Also erect a carrot root fly barrier around patches of carrots using horticultural fleece. Hunt slugs and snails (see page 31).

Midsummer

- Remove faded flowers on patio and border plants. Save time deadheading by clipping or shearing over plants with lots of blooms that have gone over together (e.g. catmint, geranium) or which have flowered earlier in the year (such as arabis, yellow alyssum and aubrieta). Clipping and cutting hard back also promotes bushiness and rejuvenates flagging clumps. Feed and water the plants afterwards.
- Deadhead roses and control aphids by rubbing off colonies or blasting with a jet of water.
- Ask an adult to help you prune early summer-flowering shrubs such as mock orange (*Philadelphus*) and weigela. Rake in granular fertilizer.
- Take cuttings of woody herbs, such as rosemary, sage and thyme.
- Keep picking sweet peas for the house to encourage more to flower.
- Start summer pruning trained fruit trees as well as plums and cherries.
- Regularly pick beans, mangetout peas, baby courgettes and so on.
- Feed tomatoes, peppers and aubergines in patio pots and grow bags every two weeks using liquid tomato fertilizer.

Late summer

- Pick over patio plants, bedding and border perennials. Cut back leggy or threadbare stems. Feed with tomato food and water well.
- Supplement rainwater collected in butts with water recycled from the kitchen. Only water leafy vegetables, developing fruits and container plantings.
- Thin out and transplant biennial plants sown earlier.
- Shear over lavenders after flowering to promote bushiness.
- Plant daffodils and other hardy bulbs.
- Plant 'prepared' bulbs ready for forcing, such as scented daffodils, hyacinths, and giant flowered *Hippeastrum* (amaryllis).
- Start moving houseplants back indoors. Check for bugs.
- Continue regular feeding and watering of tomatoes, aubergines and peppers in pots and grow bags and pick ripe fruits.
- Crop runner and French beans regularly and pick courgettes even if you aren't able to use them.
- Continue removing pests by hand.
- Net soft fruits and berries to protect from hungry birds.
- Sow quick-maturing crops and winter salads in gaps, and harvest onions.

▲ Plant containers and beds.

▲ Pick beans, peas and other vegetables.

▲ Recycle kitchen water.

What to do in autumn

The gardening year is winding down but there are still lots of jobs to do. You can plant bulbs, perennials and shrubs, take cuttings and harvest fruits and vegetables, as well as preparing wildlife for the coming cold weather.

▶ *It's great fun picking autumn apples and other fruit, but leave a few for the birds!*

Early autumn
- Continue planting spring bulbs as well as ornamental alliums in borders, but leave tulips until mid or late autumn.
- Pot up dwarf and low-growing bulbs in patio containers and add colourful evergreen shrubs and trailers as well as autumn/winter bedding.
- Plant new herbaceous perennials and lift and divide overcrowded perennials.
- Take cuttings of tender perennial patio plants as a safety precaution against losses in winter. Cover potted cuttings with a plastic bag supported on canes to encourage rooting.
- Sow a few hardy annuals for some early border colour next year.
- Sow quick-maturing salads in sheltered spots outdoors, in cold frames and under cloches for extra protection. Use cold-hardy varieties.
- Harvest shallots, chard, cabbage, French and runner beans. Lift pumpkins and squashes off the ground to prevent rotting while they finish ripening.
- Harvest autumn fruit as it ripens, including apples, blackberries and autumn raspberries.
- Check harvested onions for signs of rot and discard any that are bad.

Mid autumn
- Finish planting spring-flowering bulbs in pots, borders, lawns and wild corners.
- Start planting tulip bulbs directly in borders or plant in plastic mesh pots designed for pond plants and sink into the border. It makes lifting them after flowering easier.
- Plant container-grown deciduous shrubs, roses, clematis, ornamental and fruit trees.
- Take hardwood cuttings of bush roses.
- Apply a deep, dry mulch over the crowns of dahlias to be left in the ground. Move cannas, tender fuchsias and pot geraniums to a frost-free place.
- Feed and water garden birds.
- Create hibernation sites and shelters for animals. Leave herbaceous perennials intact for extra cover.
- Collect seed.
- Harvest figs and any other remaining fruits. Pick green tomatoes for chutney or ripen in sealed bags with a ripe banana. Cut squashes and pumpkins for storage.
- Lift potatoes planted in the ground before hard frosts come.
- Prune back fruited blackberry stems and autumn raspberry canes.

Late autumn
- Reduce houseplant watering. Avoid splashing hairy leaved plants. Move sun-lovers to brighter windowsills. Mist glossy leaved foliage plants.
- Check forced bulbs to make sure they haven't dried out.
- Finish planting tulips and hyacinths.
- Start planting bare-rooted deciduous shrubs, roses, ornamental trees and fruit bushes/trees.
- Continue to take hardwood cuttings.
- In colder regions, lift remaining dahlia tubers when frost has blackened foliage and wrap tender shrubs and climbers with horticultural fleece and other materials.
- Tie in the shoots of climbers and wall shrubs to protect them from damage.
- Continue planting bare-root ornamentals and hedging. Finish planting evergreen hedging.
- Tie new raspberry canes into supports to prevent wind damage.
- Continue planting bare-root cane and bush fruits/trees.
- Remove old foliage on strawberry plants to reduce risk of disease.
- Tidy and clear vegetable plots and cover empty beds with black plastic to keep down weeds.

▲ *Pick and eat autumn fruits.*

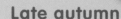

▲ *Collect seed from plants such as lavender.*

▲ *Take hardwood cuttings.*

What to do in winter

This is a time for planning ahead and working out what you want to grow in the next season. There's planting and soil preparation to do and, in late winter, pruning. Birds will need help to survive the cold winter months.

▶ *Keep bird feeders topped up in winter, and don't forget to check water baths.*

Early winter

- Continue planting bare-root and container-grown deciduous shrubs, trees and hedging. Avoid frosty periods.
- On mild days cut willow and dogwood stems for weaving projects or for making living willow structures (see pages 154–7).
- Deadhead and remove yellowing leaves from autumn and winter bedding plants, such as pansies and violas, to reduce fungal diseases.
- Continue to feed garden birds, providing a range of foodstuffs and feeding methods. Give high-energy foods such as the fat snack on page 170 during cold snaps, especially in the morning and late afternoon when they need to warm up. Provide clean drinking and bathing water.
- Continue to tidy up vegetable beds. Empty spent vegetable planter compost on to borders or add to the compost heap.
- Pot up some hardy herbs, including mint, parsley, marjoram and chives, for the kitchen windowsill.
- Make indoor windowsill sowings of leafy salads.
- Bring hyacinths and potted 'forced' bulbs into the light once the shoots start to show.

Midwinter

- During mild periods, spread a mulch or fork in well-rotted animal manure, spent mushroom compost or home-made garden compost over soil around plants. This will seal in moisture, feed tired or poor soils (especially important on fruit and vegetable beds), and improve the texture and drainage of clay soils.
- In mild areas, and avoiding frosty periods, ask an adult to help you begin pruning hardy foliage or late summer flowering deciduous shrubs (excluding *Hydrangea macrophylla* cultivars). Also prune late-flowering clematis, such as Viticella types, to around 30cm/12in above ground level.
- Shake snow from branches of shrubs and conifers to prevent the weight causing breakages and damaging the shrubs and trees.
- Firm-in any newly planted shrubs that have been lifted by frost or wind. Use your foot.
- Keep birds well fed and thaw birdbaths after frosts. Hang roosting pockets if you have not already done so.
- Pick winter crops, such as leeks, cabbage and curly kale.

Late winter

- Sow pot geraniums on a sunny windowsill. Also sow snapdragons and summer-flowering pansies.
- Sow sweet peas. (*See* page 92.)
- Finish planting bare-root trees, shrubs, hedging and fruit bushes.
- Use ready potted spring bulbs to add spots of colour to borders or patio pots and planters.
- Prune bush and modern climbing roses with secateurs. Ask an adult to help you. Wear thick gloves to protect you from sharp thorns.
- Continue pruning deciduous shrubs (with an adult's help). Don't prune spring- and early summer-flowering shrubs or climbers.
- Remove dead heads from forced indoor bulbs and feed the plants with tomato fertilizer.
- Sow tomato, sweet pepper and aubergine seed on a warm windowsill using a propagator (mild regions and sheltered city gardens only).
- Carry out soil pH tests in the vegetable garden to see if areas need added lime.
- Sow early broad beans, such as the dwarf 'The Sutton', on the windowsill or outdoors under cloches.

▲ *Sow salad seed on the windowsill.*

▲ *Fork manure or compost into beds.*

▲ *Check the pH of your soil.*

Some suppliers

Many garden centres and websites sell children's tools, so check out your local store or have a look on-line. Here are some websites to get you started.

United Kingdom

Anthony Peters's Young Gardener
www.younggardener.com
Sell a range of children's tools.

Briers
www.monrobrands.com/briers/
A range of gloves and footwear for adults and children.

Bulldog Tools
www.bulldogtools.co.uk
Sell a range of tools, including ones for children.

Haemmerlin
www.haemmerlin.ltd.uk
Wheelbarrows, including ones for children.

Joseph Bentley Horticultural Products
www.josephbentley.co.uk
Sell a range of tools, including ones for children.

Sand Edge
www.younggardener.com
On-line garden centre stocking children's tools and accessories.

Suttons
www.suttons.co.uk
Sell a range of seeds and plants, including the 'Fun to Grow!' seed range.

Thompson & Morgan
www.thompson-morgan.com
Sell a range of seeds and plants, including 'RHS Garden Explorers' seed range.

Unwins
www.unwins.co.uk
Sell a range of seeds and plants, including 'Seeds4kids'.

Wilkinson Sword Garden Buddies
Sold at various outlets
A range of children's tools and accessories.

Yeomini's Garden Tools
Sold at various outlets
A range of children's tools and accessories.

United States

Garden Time Online
www.gardentimeonline.com
On-line garden centre stocking children's tools and accessories.

Quality Garden Tools
www.qualitygardentools.com
On-line garden centre stocking children's tools and accessories.

Shovel and Hoe
www.shovelandhoe.com
On-line garden centre stocking children's tools and accessories.

The Garden Décor Store
www.thegardendecorstore.com
On-line garden centre stocking children's tools and accessories.

The Gardener's Warehouse
www.thegardenerswarehouse.com
On-line garden centre stocking children's tools and accessories.

Seed and bulb suppliers directory
www.gardenguides.com/supplies/retailers/
On-line directory of seed and bulb suppliers.

Canada

Garden Works
www.gardenworks.ca
Garden centre stocking children's tools and accessories.

Sunnyside Greenhouses Ltd.
www.sunnysidehomeandgarden.com
Home and garden centre.

Australia

Garden Express
www.gardenexpress.com.au
On-line garden centre.

on-line directory of nurseries
www.nurseriesonline.com.au

New Zealand

Out To Play
www.outtoplay.co.nz
Sell a range of children's products, including gardening tools.

Yum Yum Kids
www.yumyumkids.co.nz
Sell a range of children's products, including gardening tools.

South Africa

Garden Pavilion
www.gardenpavilion.co.za
National garden centre.

Plant hardiness

Hardiness descriptions
Plant entries in the Plant Profiles section of this book have been given hardiness descriptions, which tell you the minimum temperature different plants can cope with. It is important to know this because if the weather is too cold then the plants may die – ruining all your hard work!

As well as temperature, lots of other things play a part in how a plant will survive. These include altitude, wind exposure, how close to water it is, soil type, the presence of snow or shade, night temperature, and the amount of water received by a plant. So, it is important to check all a plant's requirements before buying it.

Frost tender – may be damaged by temperatures below 5°C/41°F;

✳ **Half hardy** – can withstand temperatures down to 0°C/32°F;

✳✳ **Frost hardy** – can withstand temperatures down to -5°C/23°F;

✳✳✳ **Fully hardy** – can withstand temperatures down to -15°C/5°F.

United States hardiness zones
In the United States the hardiness of plants is given in a different way. The country is divided into zones, shown on the map, and these show the average annual temperature in that area.

As a general rule, if a plant is said to be, say, Zone 4, it will be able to survive in any zone that has higher temperatures, but not in ones that have colder ones. When a range of zones is given for a plant, the smaller number tells you what the coldest temperature the plant can take is, and the higher number tells you how hot it can get before it starts to struggle. These are general guides, however, so do have a look at what plants grow well locally and do some research.

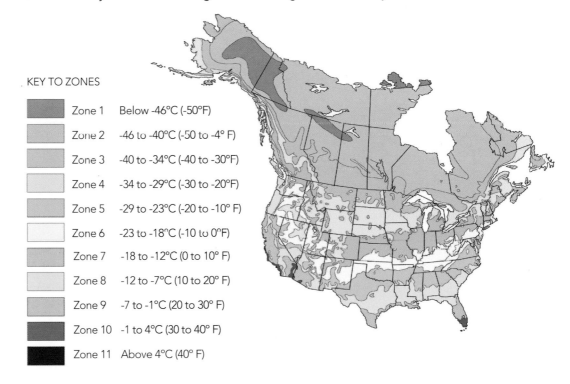

KEY TO ZONES

	Zone 1	Below -46°C (-50°F)
	Zone 2	-46 to -40°C (-50 to -4° F)
	Zone 3	-40 to -34°C (-40 to -30°F)
	Zone 4	-34 to -29°C (-30 to -20°F)
	Zone 5	-29 to -23°C (-20 to -10° F)
	Zone 6	-23 to -18°C (-10 to 0°F)
	Zone 7	-18 to -12°C (0 to 10° F)
	Zone 8	-12 to -7°C (10 to 20° F)
	Zone 9	-7 to -1°C (20 to 30° F)
	Zone 10	-1 to 4°C (30 to 40° F)
	Zone 11	Above 4°C (40° F)

Acknowledgements

Author's acknowledgements
I'd like to thank all the wonderful children who took part in the photography as well as the parents, who were most helpful and patient. Special mention goes to Leslie Ingram and Viv Palmer for finding so many willing models and for allowing us to take over their homes and gardens. I'm also grateful to the other garden owners for generously providing access. So much of the visual success of the book is down to the marvellous photographs of Howard Rice and Viv Palmer's artistic flair is evident throughout.

Index